MW00988795

THE UNSAVVY TRAVELER

WOMEN'S COMIC TALES OF CATASTROPHE

EDITED BY ROSEMARY CAPERTON,
ANNE MATHEWS
AND LUCIE OCENAS

INTRODUCTION BY PAM HOUSTON

SEAL PRESS

Published by
Seal Press
An Imprint of Avalon Publishing Group Incorporated
161 William Street, 16th Floor
New York, NY 10038

Cover design by Trina Stahl
Text design by Anne Mathews
Cover photograph by Theo Westenberger, courtesy of Tony Stone

An earlier version of "On Being at Sea" by Lucy Jane Bledsoe appeared in *Women on the Verge* (St. Martin's, 1999). Used by permission of the author.

"Mussels" is reprinted from *Singing the Mozart Requiem* (Breitenbush Books, 1987). © 1987 by Ingrid Wendt. Reprinted by permission of the author.

An earlier version of "Nowhere to Hide" by Ginu Kamani was published under the title "Riding the Rails in India Becomes a Ceremonial Journey" in the *San Francisco Examiner*, November 27, 2000, C4. Used by permission of the author.

An earlier version of "Saving the Guaymi" by Lea Aschkenas appeared in *Passionfruit* magazine. Used by permission of the author.

Library of Congress Cataloging-in-Publication Data
The unsavvy traveler : women's comic tales of catastrophe / edited by Rosemary Caperton, Anne Mathews, and Lucie Ocenas ; introduction by Pam Houston.
    p.cm.
    ISBN: 1-58005-058-1 (alk. paper)
1. Women travelers—Anecdotes. 2. Voyages and travels—Anecdotes. 3. Women travelers —Humor. 4. Voyages and travels—Humor. I. Caperton, Rosemary. II. Mathews, Anne. III. Ocenas, Lucie.

G465 .U52 2001
910'.82—dc21

                                           2001049732
Printed in Canada
First printing, November 2001

10 9 8 7 6 5 4 3 2

Distributed to the trade by Publishers Group West
In Canada: Publishers Group West Canada, Toronto, Ontario
In the United Kingdom, Europe and South Africa: Hi Marketing, London
In Asia and the Middle East: Michelle Morrow Curreri, Beverly, MA

CONTENTS

Introduction:
Mathilda, the Original Savvy Traveler

Pam Houston

THE FIRST time I went to Alaska, I went with a man I was dating, largely because of all the wilderness to which he had easy access. In the winter he was a backcountry ski instructor in Utah's High Unita Mountains. In the spring he ran his own whitewater rafting company on the rivers of the Colorado Plateau, and in the summer and fall he was a dall sheep hunting guide in Alaska, which took him to the remotest corners of the Alaska and Brooks Ranges for weeks at a time. The year we started dating, he agreed to take me along for the whole ten-week hunting season.

I would be expected to cook meals for the hunters, and carry an extra heavy pack to alleviate their loads. I was to stay in camp when I was told, scout for sheep when I was told, keep a stiff upper lip about the rain and cold that we would inevitably encounter and always make myself either useful or invisible, whichever seemed most appropriate at any given time. In exchange for these services, I would simply be allowed to be there, and since Alaska was at the time on the top of my wish list, spending ten weeks in her various wildlands would be more than payment enough.

Our first hunt was to be in the Brooks Range, arguably one of America's wildest and most remote regions. We would drive north from Fairbanks on the gravelly pipeline haul road for—if we were lucky—eight hours. Just before we reached Atigun Pass, the gateway to the North Slope, we would park our vehicle off the road and hike into the mountains for two days and make base camp, from which we'd day hunt for the next two weeks. We'd be accompanied by four hunters, a second guide, a mule handler and a mule, who would help carry in some of the larger gear.

The road to Atigun Pass was in far worse shape than we expected. The Alaskans call the Brooks Range part of the "dry interior," which must be their idea of a little joke. When we stopped in the haul road's only little town of Cold Foot—really more of a truck stop than a town, where a bowl of split pea soup costs $7.95 and a chef salad made with iceberg lettuce and Kraft American slices will run you twenty dollars—we were told it had rained every day for the last fourteen, and there was no break in the forecast.

We donned our packs and ponchos and set off down the trail into a heavy sky and constant drizzle. Still, I was in Alaska, and it was true, the mountains looked bigger, the scree fields looked steeper, the snowy cornices looked whiter than anything I had seen before.

By the time we got to our first night's camp, we were pretty well soaked through, but I had promised a good attitude, so I went about setting up a kitchen tarp and the North Face tent that my boyfriend and I would share with our hunter. In fifteen minutes I had a big old pot of mashed potato flakes and another of freeze-dried chicken stew on the stove.

The other three hunters and their guide, I noticed, had brought two tents that were clearly K-Mart $39.99 specials. If there had been any change in the weather since we left the trucks, it was only that a stiff wind started blowing up and the precipitation had increased from what you could still get away with calling a drizzle to what you would definitely be forced to call rain. I already had plastic bags inserted between my socks and my hiking boots. I had serious doubts about that K-Mart tent keeping those hunters dry for two hours, let alone two weeks.

The individual days of that Brooks Range trip have blended in my memory into a very uncomfortable but very beautiful patina of gray clouds sitting on gray mountains at endlessly changing heights in a gray, gray sky. Cumulus clouds hung near the stately, treeless peaks; ground fog made it impossible to see a tent that was standing less than ten yards away. I remember that in the ten days we actually stayed in the mountains it never quite stopped raining. I remember getting up every morning and putting my feet into new plastic bags, and my feet growing rings of green and black fungus anyway. I remember running the little backpacking stove inside the tent (against all manufacturers' warnings) to try to dry the nylon inside. I remember seeing the poles of the K-Mart tents first bent and then broken, seeing a river of water running right out of the tent door, seeing the faces of the men who had to sleep in that wet ball of nylon each night get grimmer each day. I remember that neither of the guides could find hide nor hair of any sheep anywhere, and I remember thinking that no sheep in his right mind would be out wandering around in that weather. I remember the mule most of all, whose name was Mathilda—how unfazed she seemed by the constant rain that beat down on her, how her handler, Joe, had brought no food for her and how she would stand near the rising riverbank with her front legs hobbled and pull tiny willow shoots out of the ground, eating them all the way down to their roots. There, I thought, was a savvy wilderness survivor.

It was the tenth day of all rain and no sheep. The weather had made everybody perpetually hungry and in spite of my frugality, in the absence of fresh sheep meat we were down to Minute Rice and Jell-O Instant Vanilla Pudding. I had abandoned the kitchen tent (it was now actually wetter to stand under the tarp than beside it) and I was cooking all meals in the North Face, the only tent left standing of the three.

The men were out hunting; it was just me and Joe, huddled in the soggy VE-24, and I was trying to do with freeze-dried spices in the rice pot what normally would be done with meat. Joe was telling me stories about Mathilda, how she had bailed many an exhausted and hypothermic hunter out of trouble by carrying all his gear, and sometimes even the hunter himself, back to the safety of cabin or car.

The little stove was making a happy humming sound in the tent, drying a little circle in the oversaturated ceiling. We were both wearing thick, damp long johns, our boots and ponchos too soaked through to warrant bringing inside, and I don't need to tell you what it smelled like in that tent.

I thought the rumble of the stove was getting gradually louder and I checked the fuel intake valve a few times before deciding it was my imagination. But then the rumble turned into a roar and I could tell by the look on Joe's face that he was hearing it too.

Our waterlogged brains kicked into gear simultaneously and we leapt for the tent door just in time to see a huge wall of mud descending upon us. It was more than a football field wide and three feet deep at its tongue, maybe deeper higher up. It was roughly the consistency of cookie batter, carrying rocks as big as Volkswagens in its flow.

"Holy shit," Joe yelled. "Grab your boots and make a run for it." And we did, stumbling with our laces untied along the leading edge of the mud toward the moraine at the head of our little valley, a glacially laid bed of rocks that stretched from the base of the mountains into the river, and rose, in some places, over a hundred feet high. We reached the moraine out of breath but just ahead of the mud, having managed to grab only our ponchos and boots. We turned to watch as the mud engulfed our tent, our packs, what was left of our kitchen supplies and three spare rifles, watched as it carried them, with a kind of authority, to the river. It was there our eyes fell upon Mathilda, hobbled, now almost belly-deep in mud, but with the same Zen expression she always wore on her face.

"I gotta get my mule!" Joe said, and that was all, before he leapt down into the thick mud that hit him at hip level and started to drag his legs, one at a time, back across the valley toward Mathilda. But the mud was getting deeper, and, it seemed, moving faster toward the river. It hit Joe mid-chest a couple of times and was throwing Mathilda off her balance; she started braying, softly but plaintively, from the river's edge.

I wondered briefly if I should have tried to stop Joe, or at least said something rational that might have made him hesitate. But after ten days that rainy Alaskan valley had become the whole world to me, and if Joe thought he should get swept into the Atigun River trying to cut his mule free of her hobbles, it didn't seem right not to let the story reach its inevitable end.

Time slowed down the way it always does when death is lurking behind the next bad decision, and I watched Joe take what seemed like forever to climb up on one of the Volkswagen-sized rocks, and then jump from it to another, and another after that. Rock hopping through the moving boulder field increased his progress significantly, but had its downside, too: Every so often he'd either misjudge the movement of the rock and miss entirely, slip off right after he landed or stand there helplessly while the rock he had chosen sank into the mud underneath him, leaving him sputtering and spitting up from the muck, his form barely discernible as human.

What seemed like ten years later, Joe reached Mathilda, who had by now all but fallen on her side. The mud was still flowing, though the clouds had lifted a little off the mountain the slide had come from, and I could see the slump block it had left behind and thought that before too long the flow would have to slow.

Joe wrapped one arm around Mathilda's lowered neck, brandished his hunting knife and dove like a frogman down between her front legs. He emerged ten seconds later with severed hobbles, took an instant to grin at me through the rain and then threw himself onto Mathilda's back and spoke into her ear for a moment. There was another moment when the whole mud sculpture, man and horse, leaned dangerously over the river. In the next moment Mathilda had righted herself and was walking slowly, one sure hoof at a time, through the slowing but still-deep mud.

When the hunters returned from yet another unsuccessful day, they found us deep in happy-to-be-alive euphoria. We lay in the rain in our ponchos and soggy long johns, telling and retelling the story to each other, slapping Mathilda repeatedly on the neck and reaching down into the thin spaces between the rocks to pull up for her some of the sweet shoots of grass that grew there.

The hunters were, needless to say, a little more alarmed than we were by all the lost gear, the guns in particular, and the prospect of the two-day hike back to the road with no food or means to heat water.

"It's no problem," we said, punch-drunk by then on the rain and the cold and the power of all things wild and once wild. "Mathilda will get us out of here." And of course, as it turned out, she did.

The pages of this anthology are filled with stories of slightly less savvy travelers than Mathilda. Toni Landis, for instance, gets peed on in Paradise, and Julie Gerk gets stalked by a turkey whose manhood she apparently threatens. Christine Schick goes on a really bad date in the Czech Republic, and Marilyn Abildskov's toilet commits a serious indiscretion in Japan. Kristin Beck finds out everything she doesn't know about changing flats on the I-5 Grapevine, and Sarah Weppner finds herself eating sea penis, much to her great dismay.

Still, the cumulative reaction when reading these essays is not disdain toward the unsavvy travelers, or even amusement, as much as a kind of wonder at all the crazy places and situations in which these women find themselves, nearly all of them by their own choice and at their own hands.

With only a few exceptions, the women in this book are intrepid, and while their lack of savvy might land them in dangerous, embarrassing or life-threatening situations, their will and fortitude (along with a healthy dose of rage) always get them out. Like Sharon Grimberg, who finds herself way over her head on the Kokoda Trail, abandoned by her much stronger companions, having to bully her way back out of the jungle, lost, alone and eventually at the mercy of a truckload of men. Or Tanmeet Sethi, who nearly gets publicly stoned after trying to steal her own jacket back from a waitress in the suburbs of Beijing. In one of the anthology's most memorable essays, Ayun Halliday finds herself malarial in Rwanda at the hands of a slipshod touring company that boasts of their record of one tourist death for each year they've been in business. What I love best about this essay is the relief Ayun feels when a squinting doctor behind a flashlight finally declares her malarial. "In my fog I was half-happy to hear it," she writes. "What an exotic souvenir to take back to the States, far more interesting than a bamboo comb." It is those moments of complete surrender to our circumstances, almost all of these essays agree, and the happy occasions on which we live through them, that become the very best things about travel, over and over again.

What's endlessly charming about the essays in this book is the way each woman starts out with an entirely unrealistic fantasy about how paradisical each destination and her experience of it will be—even the most seasoned travelers among them. When Patrice Melnick tosses her sister's cat onto the map of Africa to see which country they will visit, she can't imagine the life-threatening sandstorms that await them. When Lucy Jane Bledsoe agrees to accompany her partner as crew on a Caribbean cruise on a nineteenth-century-replica schooner, all she pictures are white beaches lined with palm trees—not the half-ruined, cockroach-infested, puke-inducing disaster of what used to be a sailing vessel they actually embark upon, or the drenched and frightening all-night bilge watches they will be forced to endure.

A traveler's misguided expectations—especially a woman traveler, I think—are less about ignorance, and more about hope; a way to find the motivation to leave the comforts of home for the great unknown in the first place. These women's fantasies are shattered, one by one. But they are replaced, in every case, with that unexpected turn of events that winds up being the right thing, the healing thing, the funny thing, the retrospective reason they set out in the first place. Whether that thing is good, bad or indifferent is almost beside the point. These women left home with something as ephemeral as a fantasy, and came back with something as solid and lasting as a story.

Pam Houston
September 2001

THE UNSAVVY
TRAVELER

MOB MENTALITY

TANMEET SETHI

A THRONG of men and women run after me on a suburban Beijing street. I am out of breath, running frantically to escape. They yell and shriek in a continuous stream, but the sounds blur, along with the street before me. Bystanders move aside for our parade; some join the mob's frenzy. I hear the stampede of feet behind me and clutch my jacket for dear life.

I wonder, is this really happening? Or am I acting out a surreal scene from an Indian movie? I had seen it many times, growing up in the States, in the mass of films that came through my house. Bollywood, as the Indian film industry is affectionately called, has a knack for producing movies that, while melodramatic, reflect certain truths of life in overpopulated India. Mob mentality runs strong there, and God have mercy on the individual who riles someone up in a public place. It is not unheard of for a small group to grow large, and although many of the crowd members may not know the original subject of strife, they are more than happy to solve a social injustice in their idle time. A car accident or a simple confrontation between a stall vendor and customer can become everyone's business in India.

Maybe it is the lack of private space, or the sheer number of people standing around looking for an exciting way to pass the day. Whatever the reason, one must be careful not to provoke the masses.

I thought I was familiar with the concept of mob mentality. But I suppose you never truly understand something until you experience it yourself. I had been in China only one month, a fraction of the year I planned to stay to teach English. It was 1992, and I had just graduated from college. I wanted to immerse myself in an environment different from the American and Indian cultures with which I was so comfortable, so I chose China as my destination. Fortuitously, my friend Dawn and I were placed at the same institute in Chaoyang, China, a suburb about forty-five minutes from Beijing (on a good traffic day). It was comforting to have a friendly face in this region of the world where I knew no one and spoke not a word of the language.

Ironically, I learned most of my Mandarin that first month because the Chinese were obsessed with my ethnic origin. Their fascination with Indian culture is a direct result of Bollywood's influence. India's film industry produces the largest number of movies in the world, and the lure of its cinematic productions extends deep into the Middle Kingdom. The Chinese are enamored with the movies' musical fanfare, as well as the actresses' physical attributes. They frequently asked me to sing popular movie songs or stopped to comment on my "beautiful eyebrows." I learned the Mandarin word for eyebrows on my first day in Beijing. I was on a crowded bus, lost, of course. Next to me sat an elderly gentleman with a traditional navy blue Mao suit, a calm disposition and a wrinkled face, staring directly and unapologetically at me. Before getting off the bus, after at least twenty minutes of uninterrupted silent staring, he made a gesture outlining his own eyebrows and then pointed to mine. With his thumb up in the universal gesture of approval, he uttered his first words to me, *"Méimao, hěn hǎo kàn."* ("Your eyebrows are beautiful.") I had never been complimented on this particular body part by a complete stranger, but it was to become a common occurrence; my body hair was a constant source of interest for my students and passersby.

My hair was not the only thing that distinguished me from others. I struggled daily with the language. One particular day, Dawn and I were walking home from the market after another embarrassing round of feeble attempts at this foreign tongue. I was sure I had asked a vendor for a concubine instead of an eggplant by mispronouncing one tone in a word. I was unaccustomed to a tonal language, and at this point, in order to sound out words correctly I bobbed my head in the intended direction of the tone. The market vendors probably thought I had some strange neurological problem as I contorted my body in rhythm with my speech. But I wanted to be sure I pronounced the tones correctly, and the head movement was my only recourse—after all, one wrong inflection could translate into calling someone's mother a horse. I hoped that this melodious language would come more naturally to me one day.

Dawn and I stopped for a snack in a restaurant on the way back to our school. We wanted to find a place to have dinner, outside of the cafeteria or our apartment—a neighborhood hangout of sorts. We needed a social outlet other than our nights of watching Chinese opera on a static-filled TV. We entered the restaurant to find a large, barren room with old tables, rusty chairs and little semblance of the inviting, cozy décor we had imagined. At two other tables were people, mostly men, who stared at us inquisitively as we entered with our market wares still in our hands. On the tables, wooden chopsticks stood in dirty glasses. We were convinced they harbored bacteria in search of an intestinal hideaway. We sat down, hesitantly, but after a couple of minutes we began to feel more comfortable and decided this place could be not only our hangout, but a setting for a "true" China experience. After all, we were not part of an organized tour that shuttled us to acrobatic shows and sterile restaurants serving Kung Pao chicken. We thought of ourselves as travelers, not tourists, and wanted to live as anyone in our neighborhood would.

By the time our waitress reached our table, we had become tentative again. The gentlemen at the table next to us had started their meal, and the main dish consisted of a live fish that still moved as they picked at it with their chopsticks. We had heard this was a local delicacy, but the thought of a fish watching us as we ate its insides terrified us. We grew more nervous, realizing one tonal slip-up might lead to a meal we could not stomach. Our waitress's sweet disposition calmed us, however. She couldn't have been older than seventeen and seemed genuinely excited to try to understand our broken Mandarin. She was extremely patient, although she couldn't comprehend that we didn't want any meat in our dishes (vegetarianism was difficult to explain during my stay in China). We enjoyed a small meal of mushrooms, broccoli and rice, and were quite pleased with ourselves: We had managed to order an entire meal, and our small triumph gave us confidence that we might eventually blend into our surroundings.

We returned to school, a short walk from our recent culinary discovery. Our "compound," as we referred to the school, was surrounded by a tall brick wall topped with shards of broken glass and guarded by the most stoic military official imaginable. He stood stiffly in a drab, khaki-green uniform with red trim. He acted as if someone would punish him if he spoke to us, never smiling or showing even the slightest hint of interest despite our attempts to interact with him. Similar security guards watched over all the area's university campuses, as if the students needed protection from the outside world. This at first seemed an amusing contrast to our lakefront college campus at home, where we roamed as we wished and answered to no one. But we became slightly uncomfortable when we realized they locked the gate at night and kept our actions under surveillance.

We were sure our *láobăn* wanted it that way. When we'd been told that láobăn meant "leader," everything made perverse sense. Upon our arrival, he had taken us to his office for a long talk about his role as our leader and our "duties" as teachers at the school. These obligations included upholding the school's good name in the community—so, he'd said, we should watch where we went and what we did during our time in China. He had insinuated that there were ways for him to find out about our free-time activities. With the recent events at Tiananmen Square lurking in my memory, his threats had not appeared groundless.

I was attempting my usual facial antics, trying to get the guard to react and show some sign of life, when I realized I had left my jacket at the restaurant. I did not have a vast wardrobe with me in China, so you can imagine my dismay at leaving behind my weather-resistant travel companion. I was sure there was no REI or North Face in China to replace it.

Dawn and I retraced what seemed an endless route to our new hangout. When we entered and did not see the jacket draped on my chair, my heart sank. It would be impossible to track the jacket in this enormous city; I couldn't even communicate my plight to the restaurant staff. The fish-eating men at the table next to us were gone, and I was certain that they were the perpetrators. I wondered what they thought of the Colorado ski passes still dangling from it. Annoyed that someone had taken one of my few possessions in this unfamiliar land, I asked our waitress (actually, I mostly gestured) if she had seen the men take the coat, but she had no answer for my charades. It seemed hopeless. This time, as we walked back home, I was less excited about our adventure. I did not bother trying to engage the guard, and he, of course, was undisturbed by my change in demeanor. Over the next few days, I failed in my attempts to adopt a new Zen attitude about material goods. I was too disappointed in my carelessness.

Walking back from the market the next week, I stopped in the restaurant to see if the jacket had turned up. I knew Dawn would have warned me that I was setting myself up for more disappointment, but I was optimistic that lost-and-found was a universal phenomenon. I was unprepared for what I saw when I walked in: There was our sweet, gentle waitress serving food in my jacket, lift tickets and all. She had blatantly lied to us.

When she looked up and saw me, I am not sure whose face showed more disbelief. The naiveté in her face vanished, and we stared at each other for what seemed like forever. Then, the stillness of that moment erupted into pandemonium. She took off, running back through the kitchen, making no attempt to explain herself. Reacting with pure adrenaline, I shot after her. I was in such shock that I didn't even notice if anyone was in the kitchen, or if they were upset by my intrusion. I followed her through the back door into a scenic alley. Cement walls with small colored metal doors lined our raceway. Children played in our path while mothers, some with bags in their hands, braced themselves against the walls to avoid our mad dash. I finally caught up with her, grabbing my jacket as we both fell to the ground. I shouted at her in a mixture of English profanities and whatever Mandarin words I could remember (I think I even called her an eyebrow). I wrestled the jacket off her and, without looking back to see if she was chasing me, raced toward the main street, my heart still exploding in my chest. I slowed down as I reached the street and tried to catch my breath. I could not believe what had just happened. But my reflection did not last long.

Something, a sound or vibration, made me look back. There they were, what seemed like dozens of men and women running down the street. I didn't think they were coming for me, but then I caught a glimpse of the "sweet" waitress, leading the mob as she yelled and waved her arms in my direction. I turned around and sprinted ahead. The crowd's screams accosted me, their rant seeming more torturous because I could not understand a word of it. I had some near-collisions with bicyclists and pedestrians, but had no time to stop and apologize. As my pursuers grew closer, I started to cry and laugh at the same time, not knowing what emotion to feel—terror that I would be trampled; astonishment that I, the theft victim, was being chased like a criminal; or sheer amusement, since no one at home was going to believe this. I could see it now: my parents getting a call that their daughter was trampled to death in China over a jacket.

I feared that the horde behind me would grow even larger as curious pedestrians joined our insane parade. It crossed my mind to stop and inform them that *I* was not the one they should be chasing. But not only would my Mandarin fail me in that discussion, all that flashed before me were those damn Bollywood scenes of out-of-control mobs, catching their victims and attacking them insensibly. Melodramatic or not, I had to trust my Indian-movie reality and keep running.

When I finally reached the school gate, there he was. The guard who had previously unnerved me morphed into the most comforting figure I could have imagined. "Let me in that gate and do some military thing to scare them off," I thought. "Don't you have some backup somewhere—tanks or something?!?" I suppose this was the kind of excitement necessary for him to show some interaction with the world, because I actually saw his eyebrows furrow as I ran up, panting and disheveled. He opened the gate and shielded me from the rowdy crowd of people with his body.

Now that I could take a calmer look at this throng of frantic faces, I was able to see the woman in front who'd been shouting so loud I thought I would hear her voice all night. She looked about sixty years old, and could not have stood much higher than my waist. Embarrassed, I started to think I was part of some weird *Candid Camera* joke. The mob was shouting at the guard, and for the first time I was glad I could not understand what they were saying.

The next time I looked up from my panting, my láobǎn was trying to mediate the chaos. After somehow dispersing the crowd, he turned to me with a disappointed look on his face. I had escaped the insanity of the street mob, but I now had to incur my boss's wrath.

Once in his office, he explained the crowd's rendition of the events. Apparently, the waitress had told them that I stole the jacket from her, and they were chasing me to avenge the insult. Thankfully, it did not take long to convince him of my innocence. It would have been difficult for the waitress to prove that she had skied in Breckenridge, Colorado, the previous April. (I knew there was a good reason to leave those tickets dangling from the jacket!) He apologized for my experience, and in his stern, unnerving manner assured me he would address the issue. I was uncertain what he meant, just wanting to get back to the safety of my room. That night, I actually felt thankful that broken glass and a locked gate protected me from the outside world.

A couple of days later, our láobǎn informed Dawn and me that he had met with the owner of the restaurant, who was deeply embarrassed by the entire situation and had sentenced the waitress to six months of kitchen duty. I felt guilty about her punishment—by now, her kleptomania had become great fodder for letters home. Moreover, this experience had distinguished me as a traveler—the unstated goal of all ambitious wanderers. He then told us that the owner had invited us for a complimentary dinner as her apology. I felt uncomfortable, not only because I had no desire to reenter the restaurant, but also because frankly, I was still scared to walk down that street. But the last thing I wanted to do was spark another controversy by refusing her request.

The owner turned out to be a very sweet woman who insisted we call her *dàjiě* (older sister). Ironically, Dawn and I did spend a good deal of time at that restaurant during our year in China and grew very close to her. She treated us like old friends and became our culinary interpreter, helping us decipher the menu's maze of puzzling Chinese characters. That uninviting restaurant became one of our comfort zones in Beijing's busy surroundings, and over time, the jacket escapade became an amusing and surreal memory. It wasn't exactly how I thought our cultural immersion would begin, but I did find it reassuring that my melodramatic Indian movie scene in Beijing had a happy ending—just like the ones in Bollywood.

"BORN AGAIN" IN PARADISE ☠

TONI LANDIS

"PUT ON your shoes, you'll get a cold." "Warsh your hands, the dog is dirty." I sneeze. "You're getting a cold!" my father declares.

Paved streets, meticulous lawns, squeaky beach sand and showers, showers, showers. This was my childhood universe. But for a while I led a double life, daring disaster to strike. Could my father have known? I cleaned corrals, played in the barn barefoot and cuddled pet rats, hamsters, rabbits and guinea pigs—with no hand "warshing." Not one cold, no dreaded tetanus, not one spiteful rodent germ entered my system; even so, I embraced my father's religion of germs and consequence long into my adult life.

My husband Tom was raised as a Christian Scientist. He received his first shot at age twenty-two for foreign travel. Colds, the flu, goiter or ear infections were minor inconveniences, given little or no prime time. Treatment for a bad cold was a few good hours in the surf—the colder the water, the better. Germs did not exist. Flies in the kitchen, Thanksgiving turkey in the sink—no notice. Baby eating bugs and crawling in the dirt of the forest floor—not a thought of catastrophe. One suburban Saturday, as I retched my guts out kneeling on the bathroom floor, Tom attempted to sway my beliefs with the observation that it was all in my head. Well, anyone could see that "it" was in the toilet! If the twenty-four-hour flu was a figment of one's imagination, if puking was all in one's head, I would have been hollow-headed by age eight (I had a nervous stomach).

This marriage of Christian Science pragmatism and Protestant hypochondria created a novel approach to our children's health care. I tried to adopt a mind-over-dirt attitude when the kids were young, but Tom's out-of-bodyment approach was often no match for my father's well-ingrained early warning system. So the child who cleaned corrals barefoot and ate sandwiches directly after rodent handling became the mother who alternated between denial and meltdown. I never could get it quite right. I denied symptoms existed while green snotty noses bubbled at each breath, or I overreacted to the slightest cough. We either raced to the pediatrician's office or went to the beach.

Thanks to a sabbatical, Tom and I spent 1974 traveling in the Southern Hemisphere with our children. Brooke was seven; Hayden, five. We purchased four round-trip tickets to Sydney, Australia, rented out our house and left. While traveling, our mode of transportation depended on the size of the continent or the expanse of sea between island groups we were exploring. Large jetliners moved us from hemisphere to hemisphere and continent to continent. Small planes took us from country to country. Boats took us from island to island. Once on land, we walked, biked and hitchhiked, carrying our clothes, kitchen, bedroom and dwelling in three duffel bags and two red Kelty backpacks.

Our first stop was Tahiti. A fellow teacher of Tom's in the States had relatives on the south shore, outside Papeete, who offered to let us camp in their yard. More than just a yard, it was a gorgeous home with a waterfront dock, sunset views and lovely green grass for our mosquito-net tent. That first evening, as the sun glided to meet the water, we walked on the dock and decided to let the kids go for a swim. Holding on to little hands, we lowered them into the two feet of warm, blue Pacific and were immediately met with screams of pain, the children clawing frantically as we hauled them back up. Sea urchins, spiny thorns filled with itchy venom, were coming out from under the dock for their evening stroll, and we plopped those four tender little feet right onto them. We later learned from our concerned and apologetic hosts that urine will immediately relieve the stinging pain. I didn't remember urination mentioned as an option in my first-aid training. But if Tom and I had gathered up those crying babies and peed on their wounds with the nonchalance characteristic of Band-Aid application, Brooke and Hayden probably would have taken it in stride. Mom and Dad did approach illness and injury in slightly unpredictable, not to mention contradictory, ways. But this time, we comforted our sweet victims as we humbly walked back to our tent, bent by guilt, chagrined at our naiveté, bladders full.

For two weeks we hitchhiked our way around Tahiti and nearby Moorea, I in a dress, Tom clean-shaven, the kids blond and smiling. We were beginning to despair that sea urchins and sunsets would be the limit of our South Seas memories, and decided to move explorations to Raitea. While in Papeete, we had noticed that the interisland boats transporting piles of pungent copra (dried coconut meat) also carried passengers and freight. So we left for Raitea on a rolling remnant of a boat, the two-hour trip not a long enough voyage to contemplate alternatives.

For some reason, lost to me now, we decided to leave Raitea for Huahine—an overnight cruise—on the same local copra boat. Rusty, bulbous, low in the water, small and definitely suspect in the clean-and-sanitary department, it was a boat to avoid even if wedged in sand in Kansas. But the lure of local culture and cheap transportation overcame sanitary requirements and my nervous stomach. We boarded this water equivalent of the village bus, staking out our territory on the deck along with some two hundred Tahitians, their boxes, crates, chickens, pigs and cows. Blankets spread out, children sufficiently fed and watered, we sat and watched Raitea retreat as the sun left for other places and the boat swayed in a large, slow hula. We were campers. We were travelers—self-contained and savvy. We slept.

The boat sails into Huahine's bay at first light. I'm up early to be sure I have everyone and everything ready on time. I turn over, my hand landing on Brooke's blankie, green, crocheted and wet. "Funny, Brooke doesn't wet her bed," I think. "Poor kid must be really tired." It's time to get organized, wake the kids and stuff the packs. I reach for Hayden's Snoopy, casually flipping it to my side of the space. Drops of liquid land on my face, my shirt and my blanket. Snoopy hangs between thumb and forefinger, *drip, drip, drip*. Water? It didn't rain. Pee? My kids don't wet their beds. I look toward the foot of my blanket. Sloshing slowly, side to side, water rolls in and out of the scuppers.

As I sit on my Ensolite pad, rolling with the boat, watching the liquid ebb and flow, a thought crosses my mind. The next few moments hang suspended, dripping with disbelief. Aaargh! It's urine! People and pig and cow and chicken urine! Deposited during the night in the scuppers, basting our belongings as the boat rocked and we slept! Death by germs—human waste, recycled beer, poi, rice, hay and whatever else. I can't touch anything, can't move.

Tom is up. "Urine," I hiss. "On Snoopy, on our things!" I have forgotten what Tom said to register his irritation and disgust, but I do remember that it did not contain the visceral panic, the epidermal loathing I wanted, needed to hear. "Time to pack up," says Tom, "we're almost there."

The island rises before our little deck domicile like some creature out of the sea. All around us are people preparing to disembark, which means a lot more peeing. I wring out the soggy blanket ends and smash them into stuff sacks. The kids are up, curious, excited. "Don't touch anything!" I growl under my breath, but too late. Hayden reaches for Snoopy. His fingers rub the white ear, then move to his mouth, sucking up all of that urine, all of those scupper germs. Snoopy's coveralls and engineer's cap, crafted from old jeans and adorned with stitched insignia, are dark with moisture. No, they are glistening, dripping, soaked to capacity with the effluence splattered, dripped, sprayed, streamed into the scuppers of this rolling boat. I grab the white dripping bit of fuzz and wring it out.

We are assembled, packed, organized and standing near the little section of railing that will swing open to reveal my escape ramp. My Kelty pack is buckled tightly around my waist; I try to ignore the drips descending from knee to calf to foot to deck. Snoopy is firmly grasped in my left hand, Hayden to the far right. The sky begins to color and we lean forward, anticipating the bump of the dock. Tom, grinning and sniffing with excitement, looks toward the rising sun and exclaims, "Ahhh! Paradise!"

Brooke and Hayden, armed with backpack and blankies, jabber and jostle to descend. Snoopy and I stand together, staring to the left of Tom's head at the glowing sun, sullen, soaked, subdued.

Yes, I remember that very day, that hour, the animal, sweat smell of the moment I gave in, gave up, accepted and acknowledged the presence of a higher power. I was granted immunity. There are no germs, there are no colds waiting for those without shoes. Bile and vomit are a figment of the imagination. We are all living in a big pot of vegetable soup, and Snoopy has soaked up a bit of broth. Not to worry, we can warsh in the surf. We are invincible. We are in Paradise!

Hoofed Ham and a Pair of Boots

L. A. Miller

Fat Tuesday it's called, though not in Barcelona. I stopped my-self before inquiring as to whether *el martes gordo* was the rea-son more small children than usual were throwing firecrackers on my feet, the butane deliverymen were tossing water balloons and candy and the hard-assed Spanish matrons were showing even more edge, elbowing and tripping passersby on their way to buy tomorrow's *bacalao* and fava beans. Just bacalao—no crusty black blood sausage for little Javi and Montserrat. To-morrow was Ash Wednesday, the beginning of Lent, all absten-tion and an extra helping of godly guilt to go along with the beans. But *today* was Fat Tuesday, and by any name that meant an entire country throwing Catholic caution to the wind to drink and dance and fornicate its way toward the requisite cinematic processions of gaunt, stapled Jesi and flaming Marys. Spanish Catholicism always came with flame. And ex-Lutheran though I was, I meant to be included.

It had been a long winter.

I'd tried my damnedest to be a Good American, because that's what Jerry and Sylvia had asked of me when I interviewed for my year abroad back in L.A. And I'd succeeded, I thought, though that didn't extend to eating the local *butifarra* (the aforementioned and wrongly colored meat-treat) and did extend to smoking the local *chocolate*. What I hadn't realized as I sat with Jerry and Sylvia, so full of extant wisdom and flush with glossy photos of sangria pitchers and gothic churches, was that the other side hadn't agreed to the deal. Sure, they'd mentioned I might get some "extra attention" for my coloring, and had gone so far as to suggest I dye my hair, just if I wanted to blend. At the time I had resented the very idea of going to Spain in costume just to avoid a look or two. But Jerry and Sylvia had understated the situation; while my visit thus far had been as "complexly enriching" as promised, it had also been hell. Blond American Girls released into Spanish cities like so many bulls into the ring had to use their horns aplenty, and I found myself eyeing black hair dye in the windows of the *farmacias*.

Don't misunderstand, I had no complaints regarding my environs: Barcelona was majestic. The salt air, the brilliant, broken-tile mosaics, the contorted balconies and grillwork on Gaudí townhouses—the city was warped art, a melting box of Crayolas left out in the hot Mediterranean sun. In Gracia—one of the more bohemian neighborhoods—I found a room in an apartment with soaring ceilings, marble floors and a lush *terraza*. María, the owner, answered the door wearing a T-shirt that read *"Lee poesía"* (Read poetry), and as we spoke, I caught strains of Maria Callas in the background. I was in heaven—until I moved in.

I was frequently late to bed, being a run-of-the-mill insomniac and enthusiastic sampler of night culture, often turning out the light just as the first rays of sun broke through the wooden shutters. The first morning, I lay frozen in disbelief as hundreds of children arrived at the school across the street and ran, screamed and foamed, for all I knew, like rabid dogs, in the fenced play yard. The implications of the hopscotch chalk hadn't occurred to me before taking the room—I'd simply admired the bright, neat urban school tucked so peacefully among apartments and bakeries and cheese shops. Only then, thin blanket pulled over my head, did I realize I had first seen my prospective abode late in the afternoon, after all the precious bundles had already been carted home. It got so that I would wake, shuddering, at seven o'clock every morning in anticipation of *the children,* who conspired to drive me Poe-mad with lack of sleep.

As the stress took its toll, my insomnia worsened, and so did María's bizarre behavior. Though I hacked my way through a wet Barcelona winter with bronchitis, María rarely bothered to buy butane for the hot water heater or the portable radiators that provided the only warmth in the marble sarcophagus (my room) that I'd once admired for its eleven-foot ceilings. As I politely spit chunks of lung into a teacup, she lectured me on my "lifestyle," for not acting *"como un adulto"* and not taking care of myself. Meanwhile, María—the big faker—read no poetry, nor chatted with me, answered the phone, socialized. I would never hear her play music again; instead she moaned—loudly, constantly—locking herself in her bedroom with a tray and her television for company. I was left to feel my way along the walls of the narrow apartment in the dark—she crowed every time I switched on the light, a vampire burning. I would stumble about in the kitchen making my own tray, more than once accidentally grabbing the hoof on the *jamón serrano* that swung from a nail on the door. The prized Spanish ham was sold in quarters—hindquarters, that is, and the *thump thump thump* of the swinging haunch reminded me daily that I was a vegetarian in the wrong country, that I did not belong here. And there were other reminders: el jamón and *los niños* were not the only sounds that plagued me.

"*Tss tss tss.*"

The first time I heard it I swiveled my head, trying to locate the origin of the sound. I thought it was a bicycle tire, a slow leak, or maybe the warning of some urban Spanish snake.

"Tss tss tss, ay rubia!" Ah, it was a snake: a sixty-year-old man, older than my father, issuing forth what I came to know as the Spanish version of the construction worker's whistle. But a whistle is melodic, harassment with a little light-hearted whimsy added in. This sound wasn't a whistle; it was a hiss—menacing, rimmed with saliva, vulgar. And I would hear it every time I exited my apartment, in every café I entered. On the way to the university, on the way to buy my own bacalao and fava beans. I became fluent in survival *castellano,* in delivering with authority my colloquial screw-you's and dream-on-grandpa's. And then came a day when I heard the hiss no less than twenty times. Beleaguered, I was almost home, walking along the west edge of the *Plaça de Gracia,* when a nice man rolled up next to me in his car, perhaps to ask if I was okay, to defend me from the boorish behavior of his compatriots. I turned and smiled. The nice man was wearing no pants.

That was back in February, Black February as I came to call it, when I holed up in my apartment for a week with another Blond American Girl, and we smoked more hashish and talked about how, sometimes, it was okay not to be a Good American. We claimed self-defense and talked Spanish trash that would have made Franco blush.

But spring had sprung all over the city, ending my self-imposed exile. I couldn't hear the hisses over the sound of the firecrackers, and if the nice man wasn't wearing pants, well, hey, it was Carnaval. Even María's cat, Panta, had celebrated by having kittens in my coat on top of my bed. I had only one class that afternoon, Early Spanish Poetry, and then I would be free to milk Fat Tuesday for all it was worth. I smiled as I walked, ready to renew my love for Barcelona by buying the whole city a drink.

I reached the university somewhat deaf but intact, passing through an imposing gothic archway into my literature class. *La profesora* walked in and slammed down her briefcase—despite, or perhaps because of, the celebration around her, about as mirthful as Sor Juana Inés de la Cruz. Squinting her eyes at the class, she lit up, then exhaled dramatically against the blackboard, every bit a butch, Spanish Joan Crawford. When the students saw her light her cigarette each dove for her own pack of *Ducados,* and soon a high-school-bathroom haze kissed the gothic rafters.

"Somos pocos, no?" Her throat crushed each word like tin, the growl of a longtime smoker. We chose to treat her question rhetorically because yes, less than half the students were in class that day and, more important, she was scary as hell.

"Pssshh." She made a sound like so many sounds that Spaniards make that aren't words but are much more meaningful in a lush, Latin sort of way. Class dismissed. Thrilled, I wended my way through bodies already packed in pre-Lenten fever, and found my friends sitting in a courtyard. We went to have a beer, killing time before the departure of the train that would take us to Sitges, a small resort town twenty miles south of the city renowned for its Carnaval celebrations.

In Sitges one can find French fries in paper cones with herbed mayonnaise on the side, miles of white sand beaches lapped by a Mediterranean so warm it feels like bathwater, and many, many gay men. As the biggest fiesta of the year raged throughout Spain, it seemed like a solid strategy to seek out the largest concentration of gay men in Catalonia; gay men knew how to party. The drinking began on the train, every passenger passing a bottle freely around the car. Soon the smells of *sidra* and San Miguel beer overpowered the musk of sweat and cigarettes. The flashing illumination of the car by tunnels and external lights revealed faces thick with makeup, feathers and sequins, leather chaps and yes, even an odd cowboy hat. When we arrived and the train poured out her semiliquid cargo, I saw wall-to-wall bodies, some human, some something else for a night: dragons, mice, cats and enormous, gothic papier-mâché heads and flamenco drag to die for. Though not in costume I was intoxicated enough—part Spanish cider, part atmosphere—to believe I was. The costumes and the colors and the concentration of gay men combined to make me feel safe, big, more powerful than I had felt in months. *Viva la Carnaval!*

I don't remember who suggested it—probably one of the skinnier American Girls—but soon enough we were walking along the beach, stripping off our clothes to the winking moon and swishing in the tepid waves of the Mediterranean. I stripped, too—and splashed and swam, doing the breast stroke when I wanted to stay modest, my fish-white hiney bouncing on the surface like a crabbing buoy. Girls kissed boys, girls kissed girls and we swam, writhing our bodies together like a shoal of Lenten herring. After a good half-hour, our bodies started to prune up and, more importantly, to sober up. We trundled out of the water, dripping but warm; there was the slightest breeze. And that nice fat moon to help us find our clothes, strewn over a good twenty yards of beach for various reasons: haste, lust, modesty, avoidance of the odd deposit of sea-goo. One by one, piles were discovered and then donned, until the whole group stood talking idly, waiting for the last person to get dressed.

But it's hard to dress if you can't find your clothes, and mine simply weren't there. And if I'd hesitated for a scant minute before tearing off my underwear five feet from the water, doing the catwalk—nude—in front of ten fully clothed and now-sober friends and acquaintances was a true test of chutzpah. I called to them to help look for my clothes and was met with howls of laughter as they realized I was an accidental exhibitionist. I desperately paced the ten square yards where I was *certain* I'd left my clothes, alternately covering breasts and booty with my wizened little hands. My girl-friends all joined in the search; the boys did not.

"I found them!" I raced over to where Erica stood, pointing to my boots. *Only* my boots. No pants, no shirt, no skivvies, no sweater. They'd even taken my watch. A pair of black suede Doc Martens was all that stood between my familiars and the biggest party of the year. I sank onto the sand, moaning. It was too bold a costume.

I huddled, arms wrapped around my now knocking knees. "I'm not going anywhere," I said.

"Leslie's not coming!" Erica yelled.

"Why not?" they chorused.

"She's . . . " She couldn't finish the sentence, laughing so hard her tears fell on my bare shoulders.

"What?" The group wandered over, some giggling when they saw me, and some—girls visualizing my fate—gasping little *ooh*s of horror.

"Someone stole her clothes. She's naked," Erica finished. I defiantly slipped on a boot. Not entirely, anyway.

"We've got to help her."

"No one will notice."

"Wouldn't *you* notice?"

"We could buy her some clothes?"

"Nothing's open, you idiot, it's one o'clock in the morning. And it's Carnaval." I listened to them discuss me in third person, sand wedged in my ass. My wrist felt naked without my watch. My hair wasn't long enough to cover a nipple; a Lady Godiva was out of the question. Who had taken my clothing? Were they common thieves, out to sell my Levi's on the black market for the sixty or seventy dollars they could fetch? An extension of the hissing brigade holed up somewhere on the dark beach, watching the event with lascivious pleasure? I mused on hurting them.

I was still caught up in my superhero fantasy when something dropped on my head. A pair of men's underwear. An undershirt followed. One of the men in the group had sacrificed—family jewels hanging loose, chest bare—so that I might be clothed. I'm sure it's what Jesus would have done. I put on the underwear, then the shirt, which hung loosely on my shaking shoulders. And my boots. With my stringy wet hair and smudged mascara, I looked like an odd baby-punk, but I wasn't sure the Spaniards would understand that; that year Barcelona's most oft-heard club song came from the *Grease* soundtrack.

I had little choice, however, and did the only thing I could given the circumstances. I drank, heavily. If people stared, I didn't notice (at least after a while) but felt instead very warm in the throng of painted faces with melting makeup wilder than mine and tanned Sitges hardbodies shaking tight Latin booty in naught but a thong. God love gay men. We lasted the evening, boarding a train only when the sunlight came over the beach like daylight into a dance club, accentuating every scrap of ugliness—the spilled drinks, the cups and trash, the condoms and cigarette butts. It was Lent, and it was time to go home. Transferring from the commuter train to the Metro, I said goodbye to my friends and shuffled onto a car packed with businessmen in impeccable suits. I had felt nearly normal surrounded by all the drunks and drag queens, but the flared nostrils and shaking heads of the pinstriped crowd implied that the hookers gracing the Rambla de Catalunya at night looked ten times better than I did now. I tapped my squishy boot as we lurched toward home. As I blew one blatant gawker a kiss, I felt eyes boring into the side of my face. I slowly turned to meet my neighbor's gaze. At that point my hold on decorum was tenuous at best, but when he fixed his thick hair and straightened his gorgeous tie, I smoothed my boxers like petticoats and squared my shoulders under the thin white T-shirt. Then I stared him straight in the eye, and I issued my warning: *"Tss tss tss!"*

(CARRY ME) OUT OF AFRICA

AYUN HALLIDAY

THE MOSQUITO must have bitten me the first night. Lots of mosquitoes bit me that first night in Tanzania, but this one was special. This one had a snoutful of malaria, or some jungle crud that caused me to stagger across our campsite two weeks later like a lion-felled gazelle, erupting at both ends.

When I planned the trip, I was looking for any excuse to get away from a live-in boyfriend who'd become as irritating as a sinkful of dirty dishes. Attracted by an advertisement prominently featuring a baby gorilla, I signed on to travel through East Africa for two months with an adventure trucking company. It turns out that I needn't have spent thousands of dollars and traveled thousands of miles to be free of him. By the time I left Chicago, headed for Dar es Salaam, I'd replaced the old boyfriend with a new one. The hefty deposit for the trip was nonrefundable, though, so I went. Unlike Karen Blixen, I had no desire to penetrate deepest Africa, but I am a member of the clean plate club. Having based my choice on little more than the sex appeal of a newborn ape, I had picked Tanzania, Rwanda and Kenya from a wide menu of travel options. Now the time had come to get my money's worth by licking the platter clean.

The first night, I was full of hope. There were eighteen of us, from seven countries. We sat in a circle near the truck, introducing ourselves by name and nationality, sizing up potential tentmates. Later, one of the frat boys from Wisconsin told me that I'd had food all over my teeth.

Elsie, a stout, capable Swiss girl, asked to tent with me. I was delighted to reject her, having already hooked up with Deborah, who bore a passing resemblance to Ally Sheedy. Having just come from kibbutz, she seemed to know what was what. I'd learned a thing or two Eurailing after college: I had learned to sleep on the floor of a train station, and belatedly figured out not to brag that you're starving to death when really you're gaining twenty pounds from eating nothing but bread. Even so, I feared I wouldn't know how to set up a tent. Deborah seemed like she'd be able to get the job done. Elsie did, too, but she was so formal. I wanted to share my tent with a booty-shaking funmaker. Experience had not yet taught me that the booty-shaking funmakers are inevitably Australian.

At bedtime, Deborah told me that she and Arnold had decided to splurge on a hotel room. Arnold, the last of our group to arrive, had swaggered in from Zimbabwe, full of himself in a tank top and Panama hat. He was prematurely balding, but he had eyes like a jungle cat. Arnold wanted a break from the bush and Deborah wanted a hot shower, so just for that night they had rented a room at the hotel adjoining our campsite. They extended no invitation to join them. I stood around uncertainly. The rest of the group was busy unfolding tents and fitting metal legs into canvas cots. Elsie expertly whacked iron pegs through the rings of her fly sheet as her wan Canadian tentmate watched.

"Maybe I'll just sleep in the truck," I announced, stretching and scratching as if I, too, had been roughing it for the last few months. "Why deal with the hassle of setting up a tent?"

The truck had two long rows of dusty velour seats that looked more comfortable than any train station floor. In lieu of glass windows were sheets of plastic that could be untied and dropped down in case of rain. I correctly figured that the truck would be cooler than a two-man tent with a black fly sheet. I lay on top of my sleeping bag, telling myself that mosquitoes prefer the open air to semienclosed spaces.

The next day we rolled out, headed across the horrible pitted roads of Tanzania toward Rwanda. The civil war that resulted in the slaughter of hundreds of thousands was a couple of years away, and *Gorillas in the Mist* had just been released. Few Americans had heard of Rwanda. I hadn't either until I was leafing through the adventure trucking company's brochure. I hoped to become part of a crew, a wild, piratey lot, rumbling around Africa having adventures only dreamed of by our friends back home. I found out that everybody else on the truck signed up because they liked gorillas.

We had a few hours to kill in Dar es Salaam as we waited for the Rwandan embassy to issue our visas. I watched in awe as Elsie haggled for vegetables in the market. She looked prepared to shiv the guy who tried to charge her four dollars for a bushel of carrots. I wanted to seem tough, too, so I volunteered to join the black-market money-changing expedition. The black market turned out to be a Muslim housewife's spotless kitchen table.

Our first full day on the road was not unlike every other day in the weeks ahead, except that manners were still cordial, no one had malaria and the storage containers under the velour bench seats had not yet begun to stink of decayed mango. The rutted dirt roads made for a bumpy, irritating ride with lots of red dust flying in the windows. We passed settlements of small thatched huts, but did not stop. When it was time to make a pit stop, we pulled over so the men could pee on the side of the truck and the women could walk far across the savannah in search of a modesty bush. Our taciturn English driver confirmed the horrifying rumor about another group traveling with the same adventure trucking company: While stopped on the shoulder of a narrow mountain road so that the men could pee, the dirt under the wheels had given way and the truck rolled over, squashing them all. There was one death for every year the company had been in business, he told us, including a mass execution and one decapitation by hippo.

Lunch was a constant drag: white bread sent over from England, along with dehydrated curry and some stale Weetabix. And Blue Boy margarine, which was murder on a butter snob like me. It tasted like petroleum, but I loved the bright blue can with its wide-mouthed schoolboy rendered in mid-chomp. (I am still kicking myself for passing up a small ladle made from a can of Blue Boy—an actual household implement for sale in a hardscrabble middle-of-nowhere market. I was so green that I bypassed that truly worthy souvenir, amassing instead countless Masai necklaces, thumb pianos and salad forks carved to resemble giraffes, none of which have Blue Boy's Proustian ability to recall my Africa.) We had bananas. The Australians on the trip had jars of Vegemite, an oily black substance that they claimed was their national peanut butter. Basically, we had shit, and we fought over who had to prepare it and who had to pack it away.

Every time we stopped for lunch, a crowd of locals gathered. They stood at a slight distance, watchful as we choked down the unappetizing grub. The villagers who came closest were the children, and they were never shy. My long hair went over particularly big with the little girls, most of whose heads were shaved as lice prevention. They handled my locks like antique silk and admired the very stinky pink T-shirt I'd been wearing all week.

My hair was nothing compared to Pete's Polaroid camera. He was smart to bring it. Pete was just smart in general. A research scientist for Miller Brewing Company, he confided that they'd had the formula for dry beer for four years before unleashing it on the public. They could have started selling it right away, but they waited until the zeitgeist was ready for dry beer. No wonder he'd thought to bring a Polaroid camera. What overjoyed astonishment when he handed a small gaggle of children their photograph and gestured for them to keep it! These children had never seen themselves in a photograph. They lived alongside a red clay canyon too remote to attract busloads of day-trippers on photo safaris. Unlike their Masai countrymen, they had no exotic necklaces or stretched earlobes or ceremonial face paint. They wore rags the approximate color of the canyon. No one was going to seek them out any time soon, and here was Pete, passing out Polaroids as if Polaroid film grew on trees. For those kids, we were about as exotic as it gets. I hope they're still alive. I hope that all of the children in my photographs are alive.

Rwanda came as a great relief. For one thing, it had paved roads. Our driver explained that this was because the Rwandan government used foreign aid for its intended purposes, whereas the Tanzanian government used it to throw lavish parties. Rwanda was green and hilly. Elsie confirmed that it looked something like Switzerland. After the dusty brown monotony of Tanzania, photogenic Rwanda's tightly packed vegetable gardens seemed the very model of wholesomeness and industry. It even had sweater weather in the evenings. The land was farmed in terraces and the cash crop, pyrethrum—a common ingredient in most insecticides—smelled like pot. In the early morning, we passed women in bright head scarves with babies slung across their backs, harvesting the daisy-shaped pyrethrum in misty fields reeking of doobie. I imagined myself capable of painting this pastoral scene, and told the others that I would render it in oils. I jabbered about stretching canvas and attending gallery openings as if I knew what I was talking about.

We spent Christmas Eve in an Episcopal church in Kigali. The church had a washtub and enough hot water for all of us to bathe, as long as we went two by two. I had my bath with Agnes, a prim-looking Canadian who shouted, "Whoo, time to wash the old snatcheroo!" Her high spirits set the tone for the holiday. Cleaner than we'd been in weeks, we hit the market, where I scored a handful of "hash" from a nervous man in a madras shirt. We bought a plastic bag of popcorn as a Christmas gift for Bradford, the frat boy who had stayed behind, running a fever. We bought rake-shaped bamboo combs and bananas to give to each other. We used paper money printed with gorillas to buy postage stamps printed with gorillas. I stepped on an eyeball in the meat section. It was a wild hedonistic spending spree. Whacking each other with giant banana leaves, we marched back uphill with our purchases. We burst into the church's spartan dormitory shouting, "Ho! Ho! Ho!" and shaking the bag of corn in our fevered friend's face.

"Jesus Christ, what the fuck is that?" he screamed, scuttling to one end of his bunk.

"Popcorn," we crowed, pleased at our own magnanimity and resourcefulness. By this point, food had assumed totemic status on the truck, and we were well versed in who would order what, should a genie appear in our culinary wasteland. Our frat boy's first choice was a twice-baked potato. Given the circumstances, we figured popcorn was almost the same thing.

"No, I mean what the fuck is *that*," he groaned, pointing to a black exoskeleton disappearing between the kernels. We held the bag up to the bare bulb. Dozens of hard-bodied bugs were marching purposefully in the corn.

That evening, after the little bald girls who'd been invited in to admire my hair finally dispersed, the Old Snatcheroo and I broke out the hashish. We invited Elsie to join us and to my surprise, she immediately rolled a cigar-sized joint with typical Swiss precision. Before we could light up, the rector of the church poked his head in the door, determined to pad his Christmas Eve service with as many cleaned-up travelers as he could hunt down. Episcopal Mass proved no more exciting in Africa than in Indianapolis, Indiana, where I was once awarded a lime-green polyester prayer pillow for being the child with the best command of Bible verse.

The next day we drove up a volcano to the Mountain Gorilla Project. By this time, I was tenting with Madge, a forty-year-old Australian nurse. She'd noticed my solo fumbling at each new campsite and delicately suggested that we'd both save time if we threw in together. So Madge set up our tent by herself while I rushed to the equipment box to score us as many of the dwindling cot legs as I could. She was a classic good egg. Efficient and cheerful, Madge never complained about the toxic, silent farting I unleashed in our tent every night. My bowels grew more rebellious with every passing day, but childhood conditioning is a stern master. Rather than ask Madge, a nurse, if she cared to speculate on the medical nature of my agonized intestines, I remained ashamed and silent. After all, the one who smelt it dealt it. One night it got so bad, I burst out of the tent and planted a caramel-colored loam behind the frat boys' tent next door. There was no way I could make it to the campsite's toilets a quarter of a mile down the road, especially in the dark. When the frat boys put up an understandable squall early the next morning, I held my tongue. They quickly blamed Deborah and Arnold, who were roundly despised for making camp as far from the rest of us as possible.

We spent nearly a week at the base of the volcanoes where the Mountain Gorilla Project was headquartered. I enjoyed the respite from the daily grind of making and breaking camp. I hung around the fire for hours, writing postcards to my new boyfriend, reading *One Hundred Years of Solitude* and chewing the fat with anybody who happened to draw up one of the mildewed campstools.

We were taken to see the gorillas in shifts. They were awesome, well deserving of the A-ticket status. They behaved just as they did in *Gorillas in the Mist,* so I tried to act like Sigourney Weaver—an attempt spoiled by a wealthy American tourist who would not stop talking about California real estate. Actually, as cool as the gorillas were, I preferred the bamboo along the walk to the gorilla nesting area. To me, reared among maple and oak, bamboo was more exotic than the great apes I'd been primed to see.

Things really went to hell back in Tanzania. Bradford had never fully recovered, and now the other frat boy fell ill, too, both of them shivering under the African sun even when they pulled on all the gear they'd brought to climb Kilimanjaro. Bradford started hallucinating under the jacked-up truck as our driver struggled to jury-rig it for the third time that day. This slapstick routine was sheer delight to the gaggle of children watching every move. It seemed possible that Bradford might die while the rest of us perished of boredom waiting for a mechanical miracle. I pretended to be Sigourney Weaver tending a sick gorilla.

With the truck finally fixed, we rolled on, down to rotting mangoes, Cremora and some dehydrated curry. When Deborah and Arnold dumped an inedible amount of Tabasco into the communal curry pot on their turn to cook, it almost came to blows. As we passed great herds of gazelle and zebras, I barely glanced up from my book. My friend, the Old Snatcheroo, was eager to swap for *Interview with a Vampire,* which she'd found wedged under a seat. It was only missing the first forty pages or so.

The only break in the monotony came courtesy of my intestines. Whenever the driver successfully got the truck going, he was loath to stop it for any reason, even a bathroom break. Clenching every muscle in my body against the impulses of my ravaged bowels gave me something important to do. My thoughts were evenly divided between my boyfriend at home and the clean porcelain toilet bowls of my youth. How I longed to rest my cheeks against their alabaster coolness!

The road seemed to stretch on forever.

We heard the chosen ones before we saw them. With "Born to Be Wild" blasting from big speakers, they exploded from a cloud of dust, tan as hell. Most of them lounged on the roof of their truck, sarongs wrapped around their heads like guerilla commandoes. Our trucks were owned by the same company, but they'd been traveling on theirs for almost a year, driving through Europe and the Middle East before hooking down into East Africa. I could see they were a lean, groovy unit. These campers didn't wander off to photograph the sunset or fight over cot legs when they stopped for the night. They didn't throw their forks in the bushes to avoid washing them. They loved each other; they finished each other's sentences and sprang about like monkeys. One of the group had died a few months back, but otherwise the trip was great! Endless summer, mate. If they considered us flabby wieners, irritable and weak, they didn't show it. We socialized for fifteen minutes, while the drivers gossiped and exchanged crucial driver-type information, and then they bombed away, like the commandoes they were. That was the trip I thought I was signing up for. My wild piratey lot. We lumbered away in the opposite direction, soiled and surly, past endless, identical lines of wildebeest.

Finally, my incubation period ended and I got sick, too. The mosquito that nipped me on that first night got me good. At last, justification for my terrible bowels, even if it did come with a high fever and vomiting. On New Year's Eve, our driver left the rest of the group squabbling around a fire that wouldn't catch and drove me and the frat boys to a fancy hotel on the edge of a game preserve. Leaving us sprawled on the seats, he told the desk clerk he had three "very sick people" in his truck. The clerk took one look at his filthy shorts and his tire-tread sandals and told him there was no doctor on staff. Bless the English-speaking maid who overheard the conversation and fetched the doctor before the truck could turn around in the driveway. She held a flashlight while the doctor examined us. "Malaria," he pronounced.

In my fog I was half-happy to hear it. What an exotic souvenir to take back to the States, far more interesting than a bamboo comb. Then the doctor produced an enormous hypodermic full of procaine penicillin and asked us to lower our pants. Bradford went first. "It feels like somebody's shooting peanut butter into my ass!" he howled. I blacked out.

I woke in a relatively posh hotel room. Madge had sprung for a room with two twin beds. The frat boys occupied a room on one side of us; Arnold and Deborah were on the other. The walls were so thick I couldn't even hear their coupling, if they were still coupling. They seemed to like each other only slightly better than we liked them. Several group members availed themselves of the hotel's helipad to buy their way out of this mess. The others camped on the grounds. In the mornings, they ventured into the preserve on the truck, returning to the cocktail lounge at night. The frat boys and I slept, the hotel's clean sheets and firm mattresses a pleasant hallucination.

Madge made me take three tablets of Fanzidar to carpet-bomb the malaria. A doctor back in Chicago had prescribed them for me, along with chloraquine, but he warned me not to take them unless I was dying because they caused blindness and kidney failure. When I protested to Madge, she scoffed, "That's why you Americans are the only ones getting sick. That chloraquine they gave you is worthless. These mosquitoes are old hands. Chloraquine means nothing to them. I take my Fanzidar every day and I'm a nurse!"

I swallowed the Fanzidar and wrote my boyfriend a postcard saying that I had malaria and I'd taken a dangerous drug but not to worry—I was sharing my tent with an Australian nurse.

On the morning the frat boys and I felt well enough to venture into the hotel dining room, a baboon stole our toast rack. That big old monkey bounded through the huge glass doors and snatched it off the table before anyone could get a slice. I remember him far better than any gorilla. We'd waited forty-five minutes for that toast.

There were no tearful goodbyes. When "good" people like Madge or the Old Snatcheroo left, I made pleasant noise about staying in touch. When Deborah and Arnold took their leave, I made myself scarce. Elsie and I met a yacht captain in the bar, and he invited us to join his crew. She would be the scuba instructor. I would be the cook. I went home, like an idiot, because I had a boyfriend. Elsie, sensible, stolid Elsie, sailed to the Seychelles on a yacht. For a year, I received postcards extolling the islands' indescribable beauty and describing her swims alongside whales and shark. I slipped Elsie's postcards in the back of my African photo album. Elsie's adventures sounded genuinely exotic, not to mention glamorous. I can't imagine she had to fight it out for cot legs on a yacht. Still, there's something about my blurry, faded photos that make the mundane, uncomfortable details of our unexceptional trip seem kind of fun, in their own way. Reliving a Kodak moment of Madge muscling our tent poles into position, it seems kind of fun, camping outdoors, cooking our communal meals over an open fire, buying mangos and bananas in bulk in little flyblown markets. When I look at that group photo from one of our last nights together, all of us perched on the roof of our orange-and-blue truck, I can almost convince myself we had a pretty good time. I remember how Deborah and Arnold had refused to pose for that photograph and how the rest of us had laughed, feeling united in our hatred of them and their hatred of us. That wasn't so bad. I wonder what Deborah thinks when she looks at her pictures of Arnold. Surely they aren't still in touch.

I have pictures of people carrying things on their heads and of raggedy children, clumped together in fascination. I have pictures of a skinny bendable Santa wrapped around a bottle of Johnnie Walker Black Label from our post-Mass celebration in Kigali. I have pictures of distant wildebeest and one real standout, a lucky shot of a silverback gorilla roaring, his fangs glinting in a wide open mouth. If I didn't know better, I'd say he was yawning.

On and Off the Kokoda Trail

Sharon Grimberg

THERE IS really only one sensible way to get from the south to the north coast of Papua New Guinea, and that's in the comfort and safety of an airplane. Don't let anyone persuade you otherwise. A densely forested, precipitous mountain range rises out of the interior, and fast-flowing rivers that become deadly, raging torrents in the rainy season crisscross the region. The roads only stretch halfway across the country, so driving is impossible, and there are no railways. Some people still do the traditional thing and walk. This is unwise. It's hot and hazardous and you could get lost. I know, because I did.

To be fair, my getting lost did have something to do with the planning, which was, on reflection, not extensive. The adventure began in a bustling youth hostel kitchen in Cairns, Australia, where I had been passing most of my time, mesmerized by a Japanese traveler's way with very large knives. But on an evening when the Japanese cook had gone out to dinner, I struck up a conversation with a serious-looking woman called Penny. She was, she said, planning to hike across Papua New Guinea. I impetuously offered to accompany her. It might seem like a remarkable decision: I had never climbed anything higher than the stairs to my mother's attic. I barely knew where Papua New Guinea was. And Penny, innocuous though she seemed, was a total stranger. For all I knew, I could be heading into the wilderness with the sort of unlikeable person who talks loudly in movie theaters, forgets to bring booze to BYOB parties and (the worst sin ever) borrows books and never returns them. At the time, however, the idea didn't seem ludicrous. I was lured by the romance of traveling across one of the last places on Earth explored by Westerners.

Until the late 1920s, much of the world believed that the forested highlands of what is now Papua New Guinea were uninhabited. A gold rush changed everything. In 1926, the precious metal was discovered on a tributary of the Bulolo River in the north of the island. Michael Leahy, a Queensland timber cutter, was among the hordes of Australians who rushed to New Guinea in search of a fortune. What he found first was one of the last sizeable populations of people unknown to the outside world.

It's not surprising that so little was known about New Guinea's interior; the island is so impenetrable that even the indigenous people had little contact with each other. They lived in small communities in isolated pockets of the jungle. Some of these groups believed they were the only people on Earth. They developed languages totally unrelated to those of their closest neighbors, who often lived just a few miles away. Approximately eight hundred languages are spoken in Papua New Guinea, about half the world's total.

Leahy's first unexpected encounter with the people of the interior took place in May 1930. The gold prospector and his party had set out over the Bismarck range. One night, he was appalled to see pinpoints of light in the distance: The countryside surrounding him was obviously inhabited. Leahy spent a sleepless night fashioning a homemade bomb from gelignite. Fortunately, he didn't have to use it; the highlanders were just as petrified of him as he was of them.

In some of Leahy's first encounters with bow-and-arrow toting tribesmen, the warriors simply turned on their heels and ran. Others were thunderstruck by the first Caucasians they'd ever encountered. Questioned fifty years later by two Australian filmmakers, some villagers remembered thinking that white men must have enormous penises because their pants were so long. Others confessed to spending many hours wondering whether Caucasians defecated: "We think they have no wastes in them," one puzzled villager reported. "How could they when they were wrapped up [in clothes] so neatly and completely?"

The route Penny and I planned to take across Papua New Guinea was along the Kokoda Trail, a tortuous path that climbs over some of the country's most rugged terrain. Along its fifty-five-mile course, it repeatedly rises steeply before suddenly plummeting almost perpendicularly into narrow valleys. Should I have walked from one end to the other, I'd have gone up and down almost twenty thousand feet.

I prepared for the rigors of climbing some of the steepest jungle mountainsides in Southeast Asia by occasionally jogging around a park in Sydney. My running partner was a plump, blond English nanny who claimed she was about to be a key prosecution witness in a large drug bust. She fretted over the prospect of spending the rest of her life in a witness protection program. I wondered whether it would be rude to interrupt and ask whether we could pick up the pace a bit. Penny's preparation for the trip was simpler. She found Thomas, a bald, stocky German student nurse. He was, as Penny pointed out, indispensable: He owned a stove.

Just three short months after the youth-hostel conversation, Penny, Thomas and I arrived in Port Moresby. Everyone had warned us that Papua

New Guinea's capital could be a scary place. Ever since independence in 1975, crime has been one of the city's most pervasive problems. An American security company recently rated Port Moresby among the ten most dangerous cities in the world for visitors. Its population has tripled in the last quarter century, and the unemployment rate is very high. Frustrated young men are drawn into notorious "raskol" gangs that terrorize the city. The government's draconian law-and-order measures, which include periodic curfews and tattooing the foreheads of convicted criminals, have had little effect.

It was obvious even to us that violence haunted many Port Moresby inhabitants. The wealthier residents had barricaded themselves behind security guards and monolithic walls topped with broken glass and barbed wire, and kind locals on the buses warned us frequently to watch our backpacks carefully. It was not, however, fear of assault that drove us from Port Moresby in less than twenty-four hours. It was stinginess: It's really quite hard to find somewhere cheap to stay.

At dawn, the morning after our arrival, we sat squashed on wooden planks in the back of a truck between baskets of produce and women nursing infants. The vehicle strained and jolted and wound its way along an unpaved road up into the mountains. It deposited us a short walk from the trailhead. As the rest of the passengers headed home, we plunged into the steamy jungle.

Most people hike the Kokoda Trial simply because it's spectacularly beautiful. But since it's also an old route that links forest communities, some trekkers spend a night or two in one of the villages along the way. Others find the trail's World War II history appealing.

The Japanese decision to use the Kokoda Trail to take Port Moresby by land was perhaps the biggest mistake of the Japanese New Guinea campaign. At the end of August 1942, several thousand Japanese men began the march from Kokoda. But they couldn't turn the trail into a road for vehicles as they had planned; it was simply too steep. With U.S. and Australian air forces pounding the Japanese supply lines, shortages at the front became desperate.

By September 16, five thousand Japanese troops had come within thirty miles of Port Moresby, but they were on the verge of starving to death. There were reports that some soldiers had resorted to cannibalism. And so on September 24, with their goal almost in sight, the Japanese gave the order to retreat.

I knew this story before I set out. When I realized that Japanese soldiers—whose physical training I suspect was somewhat more vigorous than a biweekly jog around a perfectly flat park—failed to conquer the Kokoda Trail, I briefly considered heading to the British seaside resort of Brighton for my vacation. But a constant light drizzle, pebbly beaches, greasy fish and chips and the annoying synthesized noises that emerge from amusement arcades didn't quite capture my imagination.

The Japanese hiked along the trail in the dry season. In our wisdom, we arrived at the beginning of the wet season. The normally muddy path was treacherously slippery. I soon established what was to become my main form of locomotion: enthusiastic bounding steps forward, some screeching as I slipped and an inelegant plunge down a slope that left me bruised and embracing the undergrowth. Somehow the mud made little difference to Thomas and Penny. They both tore off at an alarming rate. (I suspected Thomas was going to be difficult to keep up with when I discovered he was carrying two huge nursing textbooks in his backpack.) By the end of the day my mile-per-hour average was causing universal consternation. I vowed to do better on day two.

But things only got worse. Within the first ten minutes, I'd fallen over, ripped my trousers along the inside seam and grazed my thighs. In my anxiety to keep up, I didn't stop to change. As the ripped clothing rubbed against my legs, my sores become more and more painful. After several hours I realized I had bleeding, pus-oozing, red raw gashes about the size of my hands on the inside of each thigh.

By nightfall I hadn't seen Penny and Thomas in hours. I munched pathetically on a bag of trail mix and set up camp. This, since Thomas owned the tent, consisted of spreading my sleeping bag on the ground under a mosquito net—an arrangement that, I convinced myself, presented an insurmountable obstacle to any of Papua New Guinea's many varieties of venomous snakes that might want to invade my personal space. I can now advise against sleeping on a rain forest floor, unless you enjoy intimacy with insects and like to be lulled to sleep by the sounds of unknown predators rustling through the undergrowth just inches from your head.

By sunrise on morning three, I knew I would turn back. My sores were septic, and I was beginning to entertain more than just an intellectual curiosity about the causes and consequences of gangrene. As I was packing up, Penny emerged from the path above me. "I think I should go back," I said. "Well, if you must, you must," she replied, and having refilled her water bottle from one of mine, she headed back toward Thomas. Penny, I realized, was not the movie-interrupting, non-book-returning variety of annoying person; she was merely the sort of hiking partner who had things to do, places to go.

Between them, Penny and Thomas had the compass, the map, the stove and the tent. I had a bunch of dry food I couldn't cook and two rather nasty-smelling sores. Having so succinctly taken stock of the situation, it took me less than an hour to get completely lost.

I can't really describe how it happened, except to say that at a certain point I had to face facts—I was not on anything remotely resembling a trail. There were several clues: Huge fallen trees blocked my path where none had been the day before, and I began to get the distinct impression that the thickly entangled undergrowth was forcing me to wander around in circles.

The people of the region are expert at communicating with each other across vast tracts of jungle. Some use conch shells; others, drums, gongs and smoke signals. Many communities yodel. Having neglected to pack a musical instrument, I tried yodeling. It went something like this: "Yoo-hoo. I'm lost. Can anyone give me directions to Port Moresby?"

I soon began fantasizing about finding a group of vacationing Australians clutching their sides and gasping for breath just beyond the next soaring, flange-buttressed canopy tree. At one point, I heard the engine of a light aircraft just above the trees. I caught a glimpse of its wing. I was invisible under the dense foliage. The plane flew on. I felt like I was playing the lead in an action movie—the sort where the semidelirious, half-starved yet still incredibly sexy (well, she would have been in the film) heroine falls to the ground, her diaphanous shirt clinging to her sweat-drenched breast, her body racked with sobs, as the hum of the aircraft fades and she is surrounded once more by the raucous sounds of the jungle. The good news was that if I were, in fact, in a movie, I would soon be rescued by Harrison Ford.

But before an aging movie star charged triumphantly onto the set, things really took a turn for the worse: One of my two water bottles had sprung a leak. I was almost out of water. I now faced the ultimate humiliation of dying of dehydration in a rain forest.

After many hours, I finally found water. I'm not sure of the official terminology, but I think I can accurately describe it as a dribble—a tiny, muddy puddle of water that bubbled up from the ground and trickled over a rock. I sat down and slowly filled up my water bottle. My one hope of finding the trail again, I realized, lay with this pathetic tributary. The day before, the trail had crossed a creek. If I were lucky, this dribble would trickle down toward that creek.

Trudging slowly downhill, picking my way from one slippery rock to another as the spring grew larger, I promised myself that if I ever escaped this jungle, I would return to my hometown and never venture farther than Woolworths or the pub on the corner. I would work at the checkout of the local supermarket, if that's what it took to always know where I was.

I had plenty of time to muse over the details of my uneventful future—it's remarkable how long it can take for a dribble to turn into something resembling a creek. But eventually it did. Then, miraculously, the little creek dead-ended into a wider creek. I waded across the larger stream in search of those paint marks on the rocks, those telltale signs that you're actually on a trail. By this time daylight was fast disappearing. From a distance, and in the dim light, many a rock appeared to be paint-splattered when it was instead moss-covered. I had finally given up, put my backpack down and started thinking about where to roll out my sleeping bag when I saw the daubs of red that meant I had found the route home.

I had two more nights alone in the jungle, but now that I was on the trail, I began to believe I might make it. Little signs that I was definitely retracing my tracks—like finding rice grains in the bed of the creek where we had washed our pots two nights earlier—made me deliriously happy, jumping-up-and-down, whooping-and-hollering happy.

Along the way I did face challenges for which my upbringing in the suburbs of north London had left me unprepared. It rained both nights, a tremendous tropical deluge both times. As little rivulets of water ran down the path where I had planned to sleep, I envisioned dying of exposure. (I blame the Lonely Planet guidebook for my hysteria—it claims that a Canadian woman hiker met that nasty end after losing her way on the Kokoda Trail in the late 1960s.) Fortunately, I had come armed with a needle and some black elastic. I sewed up the head hole in my poncho, creating a makeshift tent, which I strung between two trees.

By day, the trip was strangely peaceful and exhilarating. I had developed an inelegant, lurching gait that worked reasonably well. Each time I clawed my way to the top of a ridge and stood above the tree line, looking across waist-high grasses at jungle-covered peaks stretching one after another into the distance, I felt a tremendous sense of achievement. My satisfaction was uniquely enhanced by two putrid-smelling sores and a pair of trousers caked in blood and pus.

Only once during those two days did I see anyone. I was sitting on a large rock watching two palm-sized, brightly colored butterflies land on my hands and then take off again, when a man wearing flip-flops and carrying a bottle of water and a dilapidated sports bag came bounding downhill toward me as if the terrain were no more challenging than a path through New York's Central Park. He nodded hello and jogged on past. I no longer needed rescuing—I was probably only a couple of hours from the end of the trail and proud of my newly acquired wilderness skills—so I nodded back and watched him disappear into the undergrowth.

Almost as soon as I emerged from the rain forest at the end of the trail, I was spotted by a band of inquisitive little boys. All alone, splattered with mud from head to toe, staggering and lurching, I'm surprised the children didn't either run into the bush wailing or tether me to a tree as an exhibit of a newly discovered curiosity. Instead, they followed me along the deserted mountain road, chattering noisily in Tok Pisin, bombarding me with questions, most of which I couldn't understand. They asked me where my husband was. Though unmarried at the time, I began wondering the same thing. They suggested I spend the night at a Christian mission, which wasn't far—just a four-hour walk, they insisted. They might as well have said: "Don't worry; if we leave now, we'll get there before you turn fifty." The most talkative of the bunch, a serious kid wearing nothing but a maroon-and-pink-striped T-shirt, took the lead. The others followed.

I fell in line. As the children jabbered, I felt sorry for myself. We had made very little progress when a pickup truck drove up and stopped. Three men inside offered to take me to Port Moresby. The children begged me not to go. One shy little boy tugged on my pants, looked up at me anxiously and asked if I had a knife. I knew they were right to be concerned, but I didn't have the energy to say no to a lift. I bounced around in the back of the truck the whole way down the mountain, clinging to the tailgate and planning my escape should the men emerge from the cab with evil intentions. They did stop the truck twice, but both times they simply offered me a seat up front where I'd be more comfortable.

As daylight faded, they pulled over once more. We had reached the dusty outskirts of the city, and the men wanted to know where I'd like to be taken. I had no idea. Back in the jungle, I had fantasized about staying in Port Moresby's most luxurious hotel, but that seemed ridiculously decadent now. I asked the men if they had any suggestions. Slightly bemused, they dropped me in front of a guarded complex surrounded by huge concrete walls. It turned out to be a boarding house for unmarried, working women.

The residents were kind, concerned and a little baffled by my story. They gave me a room and fed me dinner. At first they thought I had boils; it was the way I walked, they said. They took me to an Australian doctor, who took one look at my legs and said, "Crikey, what did you do to yourself, girl?" One older woman at the hostel scolded me. She had apparently been traveling down from the mountains and had seen me in the pickup truck. "You know," she said, "you are so lucky nothing happened to you. I saw you in the truck with the men, and I thought, that girl doesn't know what trouble she is in."

I didn't see Penny and Thomas again. I imagine they emerged from the rain forest looking cheerful, relaxed, spotlessly clean, well-pressed and ready to climb Everest. As for me, I never returned to Papua New Guinea. But I've come to realize I must be the only person to have spent five long days on and off the Kokoda Trail without so much as glimpsing a single piece of abandoned military equipment or spending a night in a village. It occurs to me from time to time that I really ought to return and do the whole thing over again properly. But my husband refuses to accompany me on what he calls the "death march," and my mother never fails to remind me how nice Brighton is at almost any time of year.

THE MONGRELS

NOVELLA CARPENTER

AFTER A bike accident, a cigarette helps. Even if you don't smoke. This I learned in Portland, Oregon. I smoked and laughed with the drunk driver who had just clipped my back tire and sent me sailing through the night air. I had run a red light, so we were both at fault. Standing there on the curb, my left foot dangled off to the side like a smelly panhandler neither of us wanted to acknowledge. "Oh, I'll be fine," I said, stubbing out the cigarette. I limped home, dragging my mangled bike behind me. The accident happened the night before I was to embark on a cross-country road trip with a couple and their three dogs.

That night, lying with my foot propped high over my head, I closed my eyes and envisioned the fabulous adventures awaiting Kate and Dave and me. I conjured the image of us driving into a small town in Ohio, the town's children circling our van, brandishing flowers. Maybe we would be invited into front-porch rocking chairs to share our pithy observations. Before I drifted off to sleep, I pledged to take up jogging as soon as the foot healed, picturing the wispy trail of dust I would kick up on Kansas roads nestled between cornfields.

I climbed into Kate and Dave's Vanagon in the morning, my left foot contorted in pain. I handed Dave all the money I had in the world—eighty dollars—which went toward gas and other expenses such as AM/PM hot dogs. Promising I would be able to help drive in a few days, after the swelling went down, I flopped on the back couch. After much sniffing, the dogs—Akira, Haus and Fern—draped themselves over me. I was one of the pack!

About two hours into the trip, Kate announced she needed to pee. I lounged in back, placing my leg in various positions to alleviate the throbbing pain. A light summer breeze whipped the van's curtains to and fro. When a sudden splash of yellow hit the side window and a spray of liquid misted me and the dogs, I sat up and yelled. My eyes scoured the skies for an enormous bird. Not finding the culprit in the heavens, I turned to Kate, who grinned and clutched an empty sixty-four-ounce Big Gulp container with a yellow film near its bottom. What had I gotten into? Later, my fears darkened when I saw them drinking from the same container.

Kate and Dave were a certain brand of hippie. Not the Grateful Dead and patchouli kind—this I would've recognized immediately, and eschewed. They were . . . earthy. Willing to share dinner bowls with the dogs, really at home when farting loudly in a truck stop and perfectly comfortable performing oral sex while driving. Sure, I had been living with them for a few months, so I had an inkling of what they were capable of. But back home, as long as I could retreat to my room, listen to Devo and peck away at my electric typewriter, I found their eccentricities harmless and amusing. What, Kate's scoring Ritalin from a twelve-year-old? Great! Dave's making an omelet out of food he found in the dumpster? Excellent, save me some! They had a certain spontaneity that was infectious. When I'd mentioned that I might want to hitch a ride with them as far as New York City, Kate had smiled and said, "You gonna start a rock 'n' roll band?"

"Of course," I answered, though I had never considered that possibility.

But now, in a van hurtling east, and with no means of escape—not even a wheelchair to roll down the side of the highway—well, it was a situation.

And we weren't even heading east. I realized this when I heard in the distance the crashing of the ocean's waves, just over the sound of the Nasty Boyz tape in the car stereo. Interrupting Kate and Dave's discussion about the virtues of not neutering pets, I pummeled the back of Dave's seat.

"Dave, you said we were going to New York," I pleaded, convinced I would be forced to join a commune where once yearly we would slowly swallow and digest a piece of twine and then weave it into a plant holder. Dave turned around, his crazy, frizzy hair bobbing in the wind, and said we were going to the Oregon coast first to visit Kate's sister, a doctor of Chinese medicine. Apparently, Kate had a scorching case of eczema.

Examining her collection of long needles, I reclined on Kate's sister's hemp beanbag and watched a pirate flag wave over her oceanside chicken coop. After the plates of quinoa were cleared and the marijuana smoke had settled, Kate's sister retrieved a bottle of grain alcohol from a drawer and sprinkled some seeds into it. "Take a shot of this tincture every three hours," she instructed. Kate nodded, clutching the bottle in red, scaly hands. Figuring I had nothing to lose, I unwrapped my foot and submitted it to her expertise.

She shook her dreadlocked head when she saw it. She blinked and prodded. The foot had turned the color of split pea soup, and my toes were little pieces of ham. "You should have gone to the hospital," she said. She had nothing to offer. No herbs? Couldn't we do some sort of ritualistic dance? Sensing my weak grasp on reality, she held my shoulder, looked me in the eye and explained, "You . . . will . . . *never* be able to do the Lotus position again." That emotional bomb dropped, she shuffled into her macrobiotic kitchen to fix me some tea.

Many hours later, I found myself on a craggy beach, clinging to the dogs and sobbing against their fur. I held a half-empty mug of mushroom tea, compliments of Kate's sister. While Kate and Dave had traipsed off in a fungal haze to "get busy in a tide pool," I began to believe that I could communicate with whales. They were telling me to join them. In the sea, we all have gimpy, useless legs, the chubby mammals were saying. I ignored their summons and limped around in circles to amuse the dogs.

Akira, being an Australian shepherd, had devoted herself to moving every grain of sand from one side of the beach to the other. After she grew bored with this, she mounted Haus from behind and began rhythmically pumping her hips. Akira had been mounting Haus since the day they first met—it was a sign of dominance. The dogs got together when Kate was still married to a guy named Tony. Before he knew Kate, Dave would walk by her house with Haus trotting alongside him. Akira would whine and bark at Haus while Kate watched Dave, his luscious, curly head of hair and his young body bobbing up and down, up and down, and she'd think, "God, Tony is so bald and old." Before long, Akira was pregnant.

With her bottle of grain alcohol in one hand and the other down the front of Dave's pants, Kate pointed the van east the next morning.

"Where'd you guys get this van, anyway?" I yelled from the back.

Dave began a long story about his special Volkswagen mechanic, Bob. After he finished recounting it—it involved a bag of weed and a guy named Toto—Dave swiveled around in his seat and said, "You know how Bob's mom died? She was driving her bus around in the desert in Mexico, and she just checked out."

"They found her body out there, in the middle of the desert in her bus." Kate clarified, looking into the rearview mirror.

"Man, that's exactly how I'd want to die," Dave said and smacked the dashboard to emphasize "exactly." The assorted flowers, rocks and driftwood living on the dash danced.

I noticed a clamshell nestled in his thick hair.

"Hell yeah, baby," Kate said and pitched her cigarette out the window.

I stared at the passing scenery. "No," I thought. "No. That wouldn't be the way to go." But then Kate began telling a story about the first time she ever did crystal meth, and I soon forgot my worries.

Though it was a romantic idea to camp next to the train tracks in Montana, it didn't ensure a restful night's sleep.

Instead of fighting it, Kate and I sat up by the campfire and talked over the roar of the hourly train. Drunk from her eczema-curing regimen, Kate brought out her guitar and played a few Johnny Cash songs before deciding she should smash the guitar against a tree. I agreed that this seemed like a good plan. We spent the better part of the night repeatedly pummeling the guitar against a cottonwood. Kate would be out of breath when she handed off to me, saying, "It looks easier than it is." I'd whirl the thing around from a semi-seated position as the train lights whooshed by.

By the looks of the van the next morning, it hadn't been a restful night for Akira, either, as she had shredded most of our clothing into tiny, tiny bits.

"Why you such a bad dog, 'Kira?" Kate asked rhetorically. Akira mounted Haus and dominated him for a few minutes, a faraway look in her eyes.

Because it was summer, Akira's placement of rips and tears afforded increased levels of ventilation for us. These rips also added a new punk sensibility to our pack. We began calling ourselves "The Mongrels." We held impromptu rock sessions at rest stops. Having liberated herself from the guitar, Kate sang, Dave beat the van's spare tire and I danced with the dogs. People took pity on us and showered us with money.

Soon it became obvious that there was a seventh member of the band. His name was Footy, and he wasn't getting better. Sweat streaming off their faces from a marathon morning of outdoor sex in Iowa, Dave and Kate would wake me and inquire, "How's Footy?" I'd stick him out and we'd *ohh* and *ahhh* about the new colors or the loss of yet another toenail before I'd carefully wrap him up again.

Before we reached our pit stop in Chicago, we positively reeked of canine. AM/PM workers, a hardy breed, doubled over in agony the moment we walked in for a corn dog. Gas station attendants covered in grease resorted to concentrated mouth breathing when we rolled down the window to pay for gas.

Lucky for us, Dave's friend Pete in Chicago didn't mind our dogginess and invited us to stay at his place for as long as we wanted. When Dave and Kate disappeared into the other room to get busy, Pete gave me a tour of his neat, clean brownstone. He had a huge book and record collection and a large, airy kitchen filled with fruits and vegetables, a change of pace from my previous diet of hot dogs and chunky peanut butter eaten with a beef jerky "spoon." Soon it became obvious that despite my limp—perhaps even because of it—Pete had developed a profound crush. A doting servant, when I complained about my foot, he scored pot to take away the pain. My shredded jeans were replaced with new pants, and my one "good" T-shirt—it only exposed half of my left breast—was whisked away and exchanged for some handsome frocks. One day Pete came home with the ultimate gift of love: a black lacquered cane with a mother-of-pearl handle.

Besides showering me with baubles and favors, Pete also got me on the path to wellness. He chauffeured me to the nearby swimming pool for what we called my water therapy. Therapy involved two hours of floating, two hours of napping and two ears of corn on the cob rubbed with mayonnaise and sprinkled with parmesan and chili powder sold at a nearby shack.

Two weeks into my rehabilitation, I was floating on a pink inflatable raft in the middle of the pool when Kate and Dave came to collect me. Thick, stinky smoke emanated from my lips as I dipped Footy in and out of the cool water.

I smelled them first.

They rushed into the pool area, like freaky mummies, tattered clothing blowing in the wind. Ignoring the No Pets Allowed sign and another that warned against swimming in clothing other than bathing suits, Kate and Dave stripped down to their ripped-up underwear and cannonballed off the high dive together. The accumulated power of their bodies created an enormous wave that engulfed several small children. I, too, was affected by their wake, and my simple craft overturned. The dogs jumped in to save me, but only succeeded in popping the raft with their long, unkempt nails.

As I flailed about in the water, Kate hopped out of the pool, recruited a small boy to find her some matches, and had a post-swim cigarette.

"It's still a long way to New York," Kate yelled in the direction of my struggling form.

I searched for Pete, who had gone to fetch the corn on the cob. Not seeing him, I grabbed Haus's tail with my left hand.

"We've gotta get back on the road," Dave commented loudly.

In my right hand, I grabbed Akira's tail.

"Yeah, it's about that time," Kate said, and made motions of getting up to leave.

My mouth clamped down on Fern's little tail. Thus buoyed by my canine friends, I paddled toward Kate and Dave. This aquatic Iditarod created quite a stir at the swimming pool. Children gathered and cheered along with Kate, Dave and Pete—who held steaming ears of corn in his hands. I gurgled muffled encouragement to my pack as we neared the edge. With my last bit of strength, I heaved my body onto dry land and then helped the dogs out. I panted. The dogs panted. Dave smiled and patted me on the back. Kate's eyes bugged out of her head. Pete handed me the corn and I munched away.

The reunited Mongrels sat in the sun for a while before packing up the van. I left the cane in Chicago. I told Pete I wouldn't need it, and I didn't— my feet didn't touch the earth for many more months.

EL JOLOTE LOCO

JULIE GERK

NESTLED IN the rolling green blur of hills in rural El Salvador, I could be spotted from miles away. A tall, big-boned, pale pink creature covered in freckles and habitually donning a big straw sun hat, I was no ordinary woman.

I arrived at the remote village of Perquín by way of a rickety pickup truck. I spent the journey sandwiched between about fifteen other people, overstuffed sacks of dried corn and beans and a slightly moving bag containing what appeared to be a sedated rooster. As we followed the road's twists and turns, the truck felt like a leaf adrift on the sea of mountains and valleys that spread out before us, outlined by the sky. The countryside was endlessly green, speckled with bursts of color in the papaya trees, wildflowers and huge, bright bowls perfectly balanced on women's heads.

A year working full-time in a windowless office in San Francisco had funded this volunteer trip to El Salvador. Right before I left the States, I'd had the good fortune to meet a Salvadoran woman who was coordinating several grassroots education and health projects in the countryside. A community of *campesinos* * in the rural north-east had started one of the projects, and I was to stay with a few families, learn about their history and see how the project was going.

My first self-assigned task was to record the story of the agriculture co-operative from its inception at the end of the Salvadoran Civil War in 1992 to the present. Besides being good for my Spanish, I expected it to be a great way to get to know people on a personal level and, at the same time, implement the "reverse mission" approach: I would send reports back home to educate fellow North Americans on Salvadoran campesino history and politics.

The U.S.–based groups I worked with wanted to create a tangible expression of solidarity with marginalized communities in El Salvador; volunteers were encouraged to develop relationships within communities and exchange information, ideas and resources. So as I settled into my first week in the village, I made it a priority to get to know people. I was invited to and attended all community events and celebrations, as well as meetings, meetings and more meetings: meetings for the agricultural cooperative, meetings for the health and education committee, meetings for the water project, pastoral team, women's group, couples' group (in which my presence caused endless joking)—the list went on and on. The community was organized on every level imaginable, a vestige of the revolutionary war effort.

And slowly but surely, as I followed people around, my month-long visit turned into a few months with no definite time limit. The longer I stayed, the more I became involved with various projects, programs, events and educational workshops. The community was overwhelmingly generous and open. My days were filled with colorful visits and rich conversations about culture, history, politics and life. Time slipped by so quickly in the countryside—life, governed by the rise and fall of the sun, possessed an almost hypnotic rhythm.

---

* *Campesino/a* can be directly translated as a countryman or countrywoman, a peasant farmer who works and survives off the land. It is also a political, socioeconomic and cultural identity.

I stayed with several different families at the beginning of my visit, but I was grateful when one family with whom I had a special rapport invited me to stay on a more permanent basis. The woman of the household, Seledonia, lived with her life partner, or *compañero,* and three children. Their house inhabited a far corner of the community and was renowned for two things: having one of the most beautiful flower gardens in Perquín, and housing the dental clinic equipment. I enjoyed the constant flow of visitors, the sustained hum of activity. Everyone treated me as part of the family, especially Seledonia, who became a surrogate mother to me.

Despite my comfort with my host family, I had difficulty getting used to everyday life. Of course, I had known that rural El Salvador would be radically different from Northern California, but I hadn't realized that I would need instruction in the basic tasks of existence on a daily basis. I learned that if I wanted to bathe, I should dress in a slip and stand in the front yard, pouring buckets of water over my head. Thank goodness I noticed how my next-door neighbor Lola did it before I attempted my first bath—I would've caused quite a scandal.

There was a distinct way a woman washed her clothes by hand (the campesina's technique would make a washing machine run away with its cord between its legs) or started her kitchen fire or shaped her corn tortillas. In an attempt to assist in the kitchen, I dragged myself from bed at the crack of dawn, but I couldn't help noticing that my incessant questions made me more of a nuisance than an aid.

My domestic skills (or lack thereof) were a constant source of humor for those around me. Seledonia's daughters shook with laughter and hid their faces when my tortillas came out oval-shaped, or as irregular squares. I could not make a round tortilla to save my life, nor could I transport a hundred pounds of water on my head, nor wash an entire barrel of mud-caked clothes by hand in half an hour's time. And the fact that I was trying to learn and simply failing was all the more bewildering. Weren't all women, even gringas, born with certain muscles in their hands perfect for shaping tortillas and washing clothes? Further setting me apart from my female companions, I remained without child and unmarried at the old-maid age of twenty-two, with no plans to marry in the near future. I was an anomaly, a freak of nature, a category unto myself.

Far surpassing the domestic sphere, however, was an even more difficult part of country life to which I needed to adapt: the multitude of animals milling around. There were hens and roosters, cats and dogs, horses and cows, turkeys and other unsightly birds, ignoring fences and doors—animals, animals everywhere. I had always lived in a city, so when I found a hen trying to lay an egg in my backpack, or when I was rudely awakened in the middle of the night by a rooster (whose vocal cords seemed to be hooked up to a megaphone underneath my cot), or when a cow broke into Seledonia's garden to eat all of her exquisite fruit and flowers, I couldn't help feeling disgruntled. It bothered me considerably that I was so averse to these creatures. I would never have thought that I, a long-standing animal rights activist and staunch vegetarian, would have a tough time showing solidarity with my animal brothers and sisters. The contradiction plagued me during many nights of insomnia. And the situation became even harder to reconcile when, out of the faceless but disturbing multitude, a particular predator arose.

I had seen him from afar, roaming our next-door neighbor Lola's yard: an unusually large, black-and-white-feathered turkey. The closest I had ever come to a whole turkey was on Thanksgiving. Having no comprehension of the bird's natural disposition, I first considered him as I considered all the other yard birds—innocent, docile, harmless.

The turkey made his presence known to me a week after I had settled in with Seledonia's family. I was walking home along the dusty path, feeling proud of myself for independently navigating around the community. As I waved to Lola right before she disappeared into her cement-block house, I noticed her big turkey trot out from under a mango tree and veer toward me in a potentially menacing manner. Deciding it would behoove me not to engage in activity that would further reinforce my image as the village foreign idiot, I tried to ignore his close presence. "Surely, I am imagining a turkey is following me," I assured myself.

I continued on a little faster and glanced behind me to monitor his whereabouts. After the third hurried glance, it was clear that this turkey was indeed following me and he seemed to be very, very angry. His countenance had radically changed in the span of seconds; his array of feathers had suddenly spread out around him, making him appear twice as big as usual and rather awkward because his wrinkly head remained the same scrawny size. As he flipped his hanging sac of facial skin back and forth over his beak, it grew redder by the second. Even more disconcerting was how he focused one eye (whichever was unobstructed by the facial sac) directly on my moving person.

Praying no one was watching, I dropped my handwoven bag in the mud and began to run, dodging a few of the turkey's jabs and sliding through the gate just in the nick of time. The irate bird stood on the other side of the wooden gate and gobbled so hard that I thought his feathers would eject.

Now, it is never fun to have someone out to get you. But it is a whole new ballgame when this someone is an animal with whom you cannot simply schedule a date and ask why. For the next several months, I had to shout out to Lola to hold her turkey as I ran by every morning. Every evening as I returned home, I would cautiously peek around the corner to judge whether I could pass by unscathed. My fleeting presence never failed to elicit an extreme reaction: The turkey would stop whatever he was doing, locate my position in the yard and sprint violently toward me. Even after I slammed the gate in his face, he would search for a way to break through the fence, gobbling mean-spiritedly.

The situation escalated. The more fearful I grew, the more he hated me. And nobody seemed able to articulate a reason, any reason, why innocent, pacifist, pathetic me had become the target of his intense animosity, let alone offer a strategy to appease him. It was no use trying to act casual about the situation, either. Everyone knew that the turkey tormented me, and that I would go so far as to schedule meetings at home in an effort to avoid the humiliating escapade of evasion. To add to my mounting concern, my host family revealed to me that the turkey's menacing behavior wasn't just an intimidating show: If he caught me, he would draw blood.

One day I noticed the turkey walking back and forth along the perimeter of Seledonia's wooden fence staring at me, as if keeping vigil. His complex squabbling call rose and fell in an eerie cadence while he shook his feathers in threatening display. I sprung from the shade, leaving my hammock swaying, to get a better look.

"Doña Seledonia, would you look at Lola's turkey!" I said in disbelief. "He is staring right at me and circling the house. How can he see me from so far away? And why in the world does he care? I am not even bothering him from here."

Seledonia covered her mouth politely and laughed, a reaction to which I was becoming accustomed. She finally wiped her eyes with her apron and said, "Aaaah, Julia, he is like that with everyone. *Es un jolote muy loco.* (He is a very crazy turkey.)"

"But he is not like that with everyone! He obeys you and Lola and Doña Petrona and all the kids. As a matter of fact, he likes all the women in the village."

And suddenly, it dawned on me. I had seen El Jolote Loco chase male visitors as they walked by. I had even chuckled to myself when I saw them stumble in macho embarrassment and brandish their machetes. Now it made absolute sense. I always wore pants instead of a skirt, and had huge boots instead of dainty sandals. To top it off, I was the tallest person in the village. The turkey thought I was a man.

Even though I had discovered an answer, some questions still remained. El Jolote Loco's intent was far more personal and intense with me than it was with the other men. Did he view me as the weakest male? Or did my ambiguous gender simply confuse and frustrate him? Could I be emitting a particularly antagonizing type of pheromone? Of all the possible barriers to assimilation in rural El Salvador, I had never imagined poultry would be one of them.

One glorious afternoon, hiking home from a trip to Honduras with the women's group, I was feeling particularly happy and at home. Feeling adventurous, I decided to take a new way back to the house. I followed the winding path in a state of sun-kissed bliss, and as I summited the final hill, I realized that the path led into Lola's yard, not Seledonia's. I continued along the towering fence that separated the two yards, heading directly for the gate, when suddenly, who should burst through the scene of my reverie but El Jolote Loco, like a maniacal Woody Woodpecker.

From across the yard he hurtled over sticks and stones, his scrawny pink legs so deftly maneuvering his gargantuan body that they seemed to defy gravity. I had never traveled the back route before, and he knew it; he had known this day would come. His hanging facial sac swelled with wicked, red delight.

I searched the yard frantically for my nearest exit and quickly realized that I could neither make it to the gate in time nor hop the too-high fence. I was completely trapped, with no weapon to defend myself with save the thick coat wrapped around my waist.

El Jolote Loco charged toward me, his black and white feathers erect in combat mode. Panicking, I whipped his disturbingly tiny head with my coat. I hit him so hard I expected he would back off, but instead he became enraged; he charged again and again, flapping his wings and flying up to eye level.

Realizing that the interaction was escalating out of control and that injury was imminent, I lost my cool entirely and screamed like terrified prey. My desperate cries drew the neighbors out of their houses, and they came running to the fence. Lola, however, didn't hear my screams at first. A few seconds passed when all I could see was a furious flurry of feathers and one beady evil eye locked on mine.

Finally, hearing my cry for help, Lola appeared like a savior in the doorway. With a heavy stick, she tiptoed behind El Jolote Loco and whacked him clear to the other side of the yard. The turkey, noticing who his assailant was, flew behind the house in a state of terror.

All the neighbors watched through the branches of the fence as Lola apologized profusely. I feigned a polite smile when she finished; waving my hand as if to brush the whole situation into the dusty shelves of history, I marched home with what little dignity I had left. I resolved never to venture outside Seledonia's house again without an escort.

A few days later, Lola stopped by to visit right before suppertime. As Seledonia served her a cup of *café de maíz,* Lola casually mentioned that she had killed the turkey that afternoon and wanted to invite us over for some turkey soup.

I could not believe my ears. El Jolote Loco? Soup? He who had been stalking me for half a year, who had made my life so stressful and humiliating, was now soup! I felt such a sudden surge of freedom that I wanted to climb the pine-covered mountain peak overlooking the village and announce this day as a holiday, a great human triumph over fowl.

The entire family filed out of Seledonia's house and walked across the yard to Lola's kitchen. As we situated ourselves around the bamboo hut in anticipation of the long-awaited delicacy, I glanced at the pot boiling over the fire and sure enough, I saw the remains of what was once El Jolote Loco. My excitement was so great I felt slightly ashamed. In a way, I had viewed the turkey as my last major cultural hurdle. His reaction to me had been a poignant symbol of cultural rejection. And now that I was about to partake victoriously in this feast, I felt an animalistic revenge possess me.

Lola circled the room, dishing out steaming soup for everyone until she came to me. Instead of ladling from El Jolote Loco's cauldron, she brought out a smaller clay pot and scooped up what I thought was an extra-special serving. But when she handed me my bowl, I realized it was just plain black bean stew.

"We would offer you some soup, Julia, but we know that you don't eat meat," Lola smiled. Aghast, I tried to suppress any sign of disappointment and smiled back as widely as possible while settling in the corner of the kitchen to mope.

"Incredible!" I muttered to myself, with a mouthful of beans. "The first time anyone here has acknowledged that I am a vegetarian, and it has to be today."

Unable to share in the feast, my sense of victory deflated like a party balloon. I could just hear El Jolote Loco's gobble echo from the boiling pot in a vengeful fit of laughter. But then the realization struck me: I was interpreting Lola's acknowledgment of my vegetarianism as yet another form of rejection, but by serving me beans instead of turkey soup, Lola had actually graciously accepted my idiosyncratic ways. I patted my belly full of legumes, suddenly feeling a great sense of peace. I would face many more hurdles adjusting to life in the Salvadoran countryside, but I had just surmounted two of them in one day.

As I left the celebration that night and walked across the "forbidden" turf of my now-deceased foe, I couldn't help but kick up my heels.

SEA PENIS

SARAH WEPPNER

I AM, like the rest of my family, an intrepid eater. A favorite meal of mine when I was living in an old avocado grove in Miami was frog-leg soup. When my family moved to Midwest dairy country, my tastes adapted to the regional fare. I can still vividly recall a meal of boiled cow tongue served intact bearing taste buds the size of quarters. As I ate, I had the eerie feeling that the disembodied tongue could somehow taste *me*. I felt with every bite that I was being licked by some slobbery bovine ghost, except that in my imagination, when the cow's tongue slopped across my lips, I tasted gravy.

As a kid, I was silently proud of the strange things I had eaten, proving to myself that I wasn't delicate or squeamish. If I got lost in the middle of nowhere or was one of the few survivors of a nuclear accident, I could stay alive by eating roasted grubs and fried grasshoppers. And if, after the bomb had dropped, I went to the grocery store and it had been raided of all the food on the shelves except for a ten-pound bag of Purina Chow, I could stomach it; I had already eaten a handful straight out of the dog's dish when I was seven.

When I moved to South Korea to teach English in the port city of Pusan, my students took me to all the best restaurants in town. Hell-bent on introducing me to Korean culture through its food, they taught me the proper way to hold chopsticks and that I must pass a dish or pour a drink for my elders with two hands instead of one to show respect.

I learned, a little too late, that it is considered rude to blow your nose in public, but it was perfectly fine to sniffle ceaselessly or spit. I learned that Korean meals are by no means languid; they are rushed and at times frantic, punctuated with healthy slurps and snorts and smacking of lips. My students explained that Korean meals center around communal dishes, and that everyone, old friends and new, eats from the same bowl. We bellied up to knee-high lacquered tables crowded with dozens of small dishes heaping with smoked fish, pickled vegetables, lotus root smothered in a sweet glaze, a dozen different types of seaweed, baked tofu, dried anchovies in spicy, sweet pepper sauce and rice, always rice, while our rumps warmed gently on the heated floor beneath us.

After I had been in Pusan for a couple of months and tried most of the popular dishes, my students tried to outdo one another by inviting me to taste stranger and stranger delicacies. I was even offered the opportunity to drink the blood of a nutria, a water-loving rodent similar to an opossum. This was supposedly "good for health," which seemed to be the only thing it had going for it. I refused, joking that I was hungry for a solid meal, not a beverage, but really I just didn't find the sight of an overgrown albino rat paddling around a tropical fish aquarium very appetizing.

I made a critical mistake one day when I mentioned to my class that I had not tried any raw seafood since I had arrived in Korea. My students immediately began talking amongst themselves in Korean and announced after a few minutes that they had planned a class trip to Chagalchi, a huge fish market alleged to be world-famous—more aptly, notorious—for its unrivaled assortment of fresh seafood. Like most coastal markets in Korea, Chagalchi sold sea animals that most Westerners had never seen, let alone eaten. I have to admit that the lumpy, spiny, warty, slimy, colorful creatures I saw for sale in the market were a curiosity. I always stopped to gawk at them; they were beautiful and strange. I often watched the vendors prepare them, scooping out their insides to be eaten or discarded, chopping them as they wiggled on the cutting board, skinning them while their gills and mouths slowly opened and closed, but I had never imagined actually eating them.

We agreed to meet for lunch later that day to try what my students said was a "Korean specialty." When I asked the class what we were going to eat, they replied that they had something particular in mind, but did not know the name for it in English.

An hour later, my students and I stood over several shallow buckets of seawater. Joung-il, one of the more eager students, pointed and called to a woman stooped over a large chopping block. She nodded her head and lifted what looked like a giant purple worm from the bucket in front of us. She held it at eye level a few inches from my face. It smelled like the ocean. Joung-il smiled at me and asked, "How do call this?" I shook my head, raised my eyebrows, shrugged my shoulders; I didn't know.

I had seen them in the market displayed in red plastic buckets. Bundles of dried seaweed lay on dishtowels around them, and clear plastic bags of skinned eels writhed behind them, resembling working lungs. Vendors wearing rubber cleaning gloves balanced on their haunches behind buckets of them, ready to grab the choicest specimen and slice and salt it on request. Metal buckets filled with a variety of snails and crustaceans lined the narrow market path, along with the ruddy-faced, middle-aged businessmen who sat perched on milk crates, eating strange raw seafood and gulping warming shots of *soju,* a Korean liquor. Several vendors boiled thin anchovy soup, and the bitter smell of steaming silkworm larvae lifted from bubbling iron cauldrons above them into the market air.

I had seen my would-be fare before when I walked through the market on my way to the school where I taught. I was fascinated by the way they moved, how they shriveled when touched and became engorged as they inched across the bottom of the buckets, sucking salt water in one end and spitting it out the other. They had soft purple skin, which changed color from chalky blue to pink and back to purple as it wrinkled and then stretched smooth. They looked like earthworms the size of cucumbers. Actually they looked more like uncircumcised penises—amputated genitals idly doing laps around a bucket of salt water.

And now, I stood over them as my good-natured students explained to me that they were "good for men's health" and "yes, very delicious" and "fine, fine, very good" for women, too. Until this moment, I had successfully avoided trying most of the things that seriously disgusted me, like raw beef or stewed dog, because more often than not they were touted as "good for men's health" and I was able to convince the offerer that I really was virile enough already. I was once offered *dok dung chib,* or chicken intestines, by the father of a good friend. When my friend translated the name for me, which literally means "chicken shit house," we laughed so hard that neither of us could eat any. Somehow though, I didn't think either of these approaches would work for me this time. My students were insistent. So, what could I do? At a certain point, considering all the kindness that I had been shown during my stay in Korea, I simply had to give in and try some of the bizarre delicacies offered me. At least I wouldn't have to chew this one, since the proper way to eat sea penis is to suck it down like an oyster on the half-shell.

After a nod from one of my students indicating that I was going to give it a taste, the vendor laughed heartily, grabbed the biggest, fattest slug of the bunch and chopped it, *whack whack whack,* in seconds. I asked her to put extra salt on it, hoping it might disguise its former life, and prayed it would be quick and painless. I was told to wash it down with some alcohol to kill any parasites that it might be harboring. So there I stood, poised, shot glass in hand, chopsticks raised above a slimy puddle of now unrecognizable bloody goo. I picked up a piece; it slid from my chopsticks, over my hand and down my arm into the sleeve of my sweater. I flicked my arm to rid myself of the offending slime, and the blob flew out of my sweater and landed with a splat at my feet. One of my students told me to be careful with my food, as this delicacy was especially spendy. The rest stared expectantly and a little anxiously at me. So I tried again. This time I lifted my chopsticks to my mouth, tilted back my head and dropped the goo in. I let it roll around on my tongue just long enough to get grossed out, and then I swallowed.

As I gained my composure (the nausea was subsiding) and began to savor the tangy aftertaste, my students pestered me with friendly questions: "Did you enjoy?" "Is it good?" and "Sarah, how's taste?" I thought for a minute about what to say, about how to describe the experience, as this had possibly been the defining moment in my history of trying interesting new delicacies. Had I finally reached the point at which I was willing to relinquish my pride and be labeled a wimp, squeamish or—god forbid—a "picky eater"? I felt like I had just swallowed whale snot. Spicy, salty snot. "It was delicious," I smiled, "way better than cow's tongue."

JAPAN, MY FOOT

A. C. HALL

SOME TRAVELERS remember trips by pushing pins into maps. Me, I have wounds. Baja California, Mexico: gash, left foot. Vietnam: strained tendon, right foot. New York City: tweaked elbow. Really, I should just stay home.

Instead, I was setting out again. It was January 2001, and I was preparing with my husband, Cliff, for three weeks in Japan, two in Thailand and, finally, four days at Angkor Wat, the magnificent temple ruins in Cambodia. The night before our departure, in not-so-neat piles around my brand-new backpack lay approximately eight pounds of clothing, three pounds of hiking boots and twenty-one pounds of naturopathic medicine.

"You can't possibly need all that," Cliff muttered in disbelief, almost chagrin.

I picked up the electric heating pad and refreezeable gel packs. "For hot and cold contrast, if I strain a muscle." I pointed to the instant ice. "In case there's no refrigeration." Arnica gel. "For joint pain." Chinese herbs. "Diarrhea." Different Chinese herbs. "UTIs." Homeopathic tinctures. "Allergies." Melatonin. "So I can sleep on airplanes." I had been injured enough to know that I preferred alternative modalities.

A former news editor, Cliff identified an inconsistency: a bottle of ibuprofen. I answered, "When all else fails."

In the face of such obvious logic, Cliff relented. Besides, I reminded him, I carried my own pack. Someone who couldn't carry her own pack shouldn't be on the road.

Our first stop was Tokyo. I spent four days showing Cliff choice spots I remembered from the three years I lived there in the late '80s. It's easy to bring the city down to manageable size by taking the subway, but walking is really the way to appreciate the Japanese capital. So, walk we did, through some dozen neighborhoods. We especially enjoyed Shitamachi and the vivid contrast it presented between modern high-rises and Ueno Park's tall pagoda, set back from Shinobazu Pond. I explained that in a few months, the brown chaff floating across the pond's surface would reinvent itself, growing green through the spring and summer, until the blue-gray water disappeared beneath a blanket of green leaves, white flowers and yellow centers—lotus blossoms.

In Harajuku, we edged delicately through throngs of youth battling to make the greatest fashion statement. Behind us the rockabillies promenaded in tight jeans and leather. And then there were the *yamanba,* named after the mythical witches of the Japanese mountains. These modern enchantresses sported dyed blond hair and blue eye shadow. Not a good look on these women, but not potentially lethal. What, on the other hand, would occur should a yamanba topple off the eight-inch platform soles of her shoes? Or worse, off the bicycle one clambered onto, eight-inch platform shoes and all?

Tsukiji Fish Market, another gem. Arriving at five in the morning, we wandered up and down narrow, cold, congested lanes, through booths selling anything you could want pertaining to seafood. Toward the back, near the docks, we saw whole, frozen tuna, each five feet long, being marked for auction, sold and dismembered—mostly by table saw, but a few Japanese Luddites used handsaws. Cliff and I nimbly skipped around a fish head the size of a microwave oven, discarded on the moist cement, no obvious torso in sight.

Perhaps it was the cumulative walking of the prior few days, or maybe the short leap I took in a laze-inspired attempt to avoid the stairs between the tuna corpses and the tanks of live octopi, but by ten o'clock, my right foot was hurting. By the next morning, it was officially on strike.

I refused to negotiate. That day we were scheduled to take the famous bullet train, the *Shinkansen*, to Kyoto, a city of more than two thousand temples and shrines. Our Lonely Planet guidebook listed three different walking tours; our Frommer's, four. I heated and iced in the morning, applied arnica gel throughout the day and tried to enjoy the gold, silver and red temples, the long hall housing one thousand statues of the Goddess of Mercy and the quintessential Zen image to come out of Japan, the rectangular garden of raked pebbles at Ryōan-ji Temple.

My foot hurt too much.

"You should go to a hospital."

That was Cliff.

"It's the same tendon I strained in Vietnam. I know what to do."

That was me, reduced to popping ibuprofen at a terrifying rate. Our third day in Kyoto, I woke unable to put weight on my foot.

Our plan that day was to head for Nara, a nearby city, famous for sites more ancient than Kyoto's. Walking is the thing to do in Nara: around the park filled with free-roaming deer, up a mountain for a view of the city, through the Daibutsu-den (the largest wooden structure in the world, built to protect and venerate Japan's second-largest statue of the Buddha). We had even arranged to meet up with an English-speaking volunteer guide.

I knew that if I went, I would walk. And I knew my foot needed rest. So, while Cliff came up with creative ways to allow me to visit Nara—find crutches, rent a car—I silently accepted that I would spend the day on my back with my foot elevated. I'd miss out on Nara, but hopefully win back the remainder of our trip.

"At least go to a doctor," Cliff argued when I finally convinced him it was really, really okay if he went to Nara without me.

While I still wasn't willing to stoop to seeing a Western doctor, I agreed to get some acupuncture. The previous day, I had spotted a small sign reading *Hari*. As soon as Cliff departed for Nara, I cried for forty minutes, then limped down the narrow wooden stairs to confirm with Matsubaya-san, the chatty lady who ran our inn, that the shop around the corner was an acupuncturist.

Matsubaya-san didn't recognize the word "hari," but she seemed to understand my pantomime of needles piercing flesh. I figured if I didn't find treatment, maybe I'd end up with a cool tattoo.

Off I hobbled, located the sign and knocked. The woman who slid open the door looked to be in her fifties. She wore a white lab jacket, kept her eyes closed and held her head at an awkward angle.

She was blind.

While I refused to see a simple allopath, I was fully prepared to pay a blind person I had never met to jab needles into my wounded foot. In Japan, the blind are often trained in the healing arts because, it is thought, the loss of one sense leads to greater ability with the remaining senses. Half an hour later, I was pain-free. Until I stood.

"Ow!"

I sat back down.

The acupuncturist, Saito-sensei, suggested I come for another treatment in two days.

In precisely two days, Cliff and I had a date with a friend we had not seen since she returned to Japan from Seattle three years prior. She lived two train rides, four hundred miles and approximately five hours away from Kyoto.

"Ah," Saito replied when I explained. "Your Japanese is very good."

The ultimate blow. It had taken me two of the three years I lived in Japan to realize I was not the wordsmith such a statement would lead you to believe. When a Japanese person says your Japanese is very good, generally, that is Japanese politeness in action. You'll know your Japanese is very good when you find yourself in conversations and no one mentions you are speaking Japanese.

I gimped back to our *ryokan* (Japanese-style inn), where I pounded the ibuprofen and prayed for a miraculous return to foot health until Cliff appeared. He sighed. The volunteer in Nara had turned out to be the president of the local guide association, and had come equipped with perfect English, a thorough knowledge of history and architecture, and . . . a car. She drove him all over Nara.

Cliff tugged on his beard, his habit when perturbed. "Why don't we rent a car, at least until you can walk without pain."

I forbade it. Our rail passes, over four hundred dollars each, allowed us two weeks of unlimited access to virtually every train in Japan. This was one of the few good deals in a country where a grapefruit costs six bucks and bargaining is not part of the culture.

Rather than rent a car, we decided that Cliff would carry *everything*. He stuffed the contents of his daypack into his main backpack, then donned the now sixty-pounder. Next, he hoisted my pack in front, covering his chest and stomach. With one free hand, he clutched my daypack. The poor boy looked like a pregnant dromedary on its hind legs, forced to carry a daypack. Every time he moved, he clanked and rattled.

"What *is* that?" he demanded, prevented from tugging his beard by the pack slung across his stomach.

I could hardly say, "Twenty-one pounds of ineffectual potions in individual glass bottles."

We took the train to Shikoku, the smallest of the four main islands making up the Japanese archipelago, to meet up with our friend. True to Japanese custom, Satsuki drove us everywhere and paid for everything. Allowed to rest, my foot stopped hurting constantly. It was painful only when I walked or stood.

I continued to refuse a visit to the hospital, so Cliff bought me a cane. After some trial and a lot of error, the cane seemed to work best when used in tandem with my hurt foot. Later, of course, I learned the cane should be used in opposition to the injured appendage. But as we traveled from Shikoku to the next island south, Kyūshū, then all the way across Kyūshū to Nagasaki, I used the cane in such a way that my foot didn't feel worse, but didn't feel better.

In Nagasaki, we lodged at Minshuku Fumi. *Minshuku* are family-run inns, but the family who ran this inn was not Fumi, was not even a family. Minshuku Fumi was run by one extremely sweet guy. He told me his surname several times, but between the unfamiliar Nagasaki dialect and the incessant throbbing in my foot, it wouldn't stick. I thought of him as Mr. Fumi.

Cliff thought I should ask Mr. Fumi if they might have a wheelchair at our primary destination, the Gembaku Shiryōkan, referred to by everyone but the guidebooks as the A-bomb Museum.

"I don't know how to say 'wheelchair,'" I whined.

"Just try."

I turned to Mr. Fumi and began. As soon as my sentence hit the word "wheelchair," I mimed rolling myself along.

"Kuruma isu?" queried Mr. Fumi.

Kuruma is Japanese for "car." Isu means "chair." I grinned and parroted, "Kuruma isu."

Mr. Fumi clapped with delight. "Your Japanese is so good!"

Mr. Fumi telephoned the A-bomb Museum, which indeed had several kuruma isu. What a relief, to sightsee without pain or worry, to sink into the blue cloth seat and fully enjoy the . . . uh, instant annihilation of seventy-five thousand human beings. My own minor suffering whipped into perspective. Wishing to honor the dead and wounded, I asked Cliff to push me around the statue-lined Peace Park adjacent to the museum. The park was sixty feet up a steep incline.

We hung around Nagasaki a day more than we would have liked, hoping my foot would feel better. When it didn't, we began gradually retracing our steps across Kyūshū, back to the main island of Honshū. Two days after leaving Nagasaki, I finally agreed to go to a hospital.

We were in Kurashiki, a city of five hundred thousand, known for its historic district of restored wooden buildings and a long moat surrounded by willows and crossed by bridges. An ideal atmosphere in which to amble, quoth the guidebooks. Our first stop was the hospital.

The doctor diagnosed a pulled tendon and *oba-use.* That's Japanese for "overuse"; I shit thee not. He prescribed painkillers and an ace bandage (note to self: add ace bandage to medical kit), then showed me the correct way to use my cane. When he suggested a minimum of three days' rest, I asked if the hospital could lend me a kuruma isu.

The doctor pushed back in his seat, crossed his arms over his chest and sucked air through his teeth. This meant what I had asked for would be very difficult. Fifteen minutes later, however, a wheelchair appeared. It must have been older than the shrines at Nara. The seat was brown, the leather cracked and the footrests rusty, but it got me around Kurashiki, despite the cobbled streets and museums lacking elevators. Forgetting my humbling Nagasaki epiphany, I developed a fierce resentment for those unaware of their own luck or the difficulties of someone in a wheelchair, trying to make her way through the narrow aisles of a crowded shop. With my cane, I poked meanly at their ankles.

"I hate to say it, but you're being," Cliff grinned through the beard he was tugging, "a bitch on wheels."

A break from Kurashiki was in order. We planned a day at Korakoen, one of Japan's "Big Three" gardens. This would require somehow getting the wheelchair from Kurashiki to Okayama. The train was our obvious choice. Kurashiki's main station had no elevator and no escalator, only a steep staircase and four able-bodied railroad employees. They surrounded me with the precision of a drill team, turned my wheelchair around and carried me, in it, down the steep stairs. Backward.

"This is a little scary," I told the team captain.

"Your Japanese is very good!"

I survived the descent. My next obstacle: finding a bathroom.

We found one next to Okayama Station, in Daiei, a department store akin to K-Mart. We were happy to discover that the Japanese love of technology had affected even the wheelchair-accessible dumping grounds of low-end department stores. I pressed a large red button to open the door, rolled on in and pressed a large green button to close it. Cliff thought it would be funny to play a trick we often played on each other back home in Seattle. He thought he'd turn the bathroom light off with me inside.

Unfortunately, instead of hitting the lights, my husband pressed the large red button. The door slid open, revealing me and my big, white butt.

I yowled as you might expect a person to, should she find herself in a foreign country with her anus suddenly on display. Flustered by the murderous caterwauling, Cliff proceeded to punch every button in sight. The door closed and the light shut off, leaving me in the pitch dark, half out of my chair.

After phoning divorce instructions to our attorney in the States, we left Daiei for Korakoen. Cliff, who had previously volunteered in the physical therapy unit of a hospital, tried to make amends by popping wheelies and accelerating to warp speed. All in all, being carried backward down a steep flight of steps at a train station was comparatively mild.

We learned that many of the larger stations offered wheelchair services. Suddenly, our journey back to Tokyo was looking more manageable. A few days later, I was sad to return my chariot to the hospital, but relieved to know that at the other end of the taxi ride waited a wheelchair and a station employee in a crisp uniform, cap and white gloves. He would meet our cab, roll me to our seats and radio to Kyoto, our destination, where a similarly dressed fellow would take over.

The long train pulled into the somewhat familiar, ten-story amalgamation of train station, department store and underground shopping arcade. Waiting on the platform was a white-gloved, uniformed fellow. He stood behind a kuruma isu, at the precise spot where the door to our car would open when the train stopped. Stop it did, precisely. We split up, Cliff to drop the excessive luggage he still carried in a coin locker and me to meet him at the Tourist Information Center.

As if by perverse plan, the moment Cliff disappeared, the uniformed fellow told me he could not take me outside the ticket gate.

"This is a Japan Rail wheelchair. It can only be used within the JR."

"But I'm meeting my husband at the TIC."

"Then you will have to walk."

"I can't walk." Hence the wheelchair, you lame-o.

The best of my grunty Japanese convinced The Uniform to take me to an elevator that left me fifty feet from a ticket gate. I reached into my fanny pack for my JR Pass.

I found not only mine, but Cliff's. He wouldn't be permitted to exit the JR area without the pass to prove he had paid his fare. He was probably being detained at one of the dozens of ticket gates. In this hyper-honest country, he was probably being bludgeoned as a thief.

I waited a few minutes, hoping Cliff would show up. When he didn't, I gimped over to the Reservations counter, a mere twenty feet away, and tried not to sob as I stood in line. When my turn finally came, I got out "husband" and "lost" in Japanese before the waterworks took over completely. The eighteen-year-old behind the counter shook in consternation.

I clutched my cane. If he told me my Japanese was very good, I would cave his skull in.

Eventually, I made it clear that I needed him to make an announcement. I hopped back and waited. Finally, over the muffled loudspeaker, I heard, "Would Mr. Hall A. C. please meet Miss Meyer Cliff . . . " in the accented English understood only by those who could also speak Japanese.

Really weeping now, I decided I simply had to walk to the TIC and wait for Cliff. I'd made it up the first flight of stairs and started across the long passage when I saw a single shining white forehead bobbing amid a sea of immaculately groomed black hairdos like a beloved buoy.

As it turned out, I panicked needlessly. The Uniform who pushed my wheelchair used a freight elevator that left both Cliff and me outside the ticket gate. I might have noticed that I was outside the ticket gate when I discovered I had Cliff's rail pass, but I was too busy being hysterical. Cliff, on the other hand, had calmly proceeded from the coin lockers to the TIC, as planned. When I didn't show, he set out to find me. That's when I spotted his forehead.

☠

We successfully used the wheelchair system to return to Tokyo, then to leave the country. Heading to Narita Airport from Ueno, one of Tokyo's mammoth train stations, the uniformed, white-gloved individual rolled me right up to the main escalator and chained it off behind us, forcing many harried commuters to take the steps. He stopped the escalator at a stair that opened up into a platform and loaded me onto it, all the while providing a constant stream of exquisitely polite narration: "I am now troubling you greatly by making you wait for the escalator." "I am now locking down your honorable wheelchair."

I traveled from Ueno to Narita, flew to Bangkok, changed planes, flew to northern Thailand and checked into our hotel in Chiang Mai, taking no more than forty paces. My pregnant dromedary trotted gamely alongside the whole way. He never actually complained about the extra weight he carried, though once or twice, he hoisted with a discernable *"Ooof."*

Two weeks later, we landed in Siem Reap, Cambodia.

I had spent two weeks in Thailand, not to mention two of three weeks in Japan, trying not to be the girl who dragged down the whole trip while urging my foot healthward. In Thailand, I passed on treks to hill tribes and sat while others roamed night markets for great bargains. I did none of this graciously; I did it because I wanted a foot at Angkor.

Angkor Wat is the name of the most famous of a massive series of temples and palaces located fifteen minutes by car north of Siem Reap. You pay twenty dollars per day to enter the historic area, where you can meander through and even touch what remains of royal mansions and estates constructed between the ninth and twelfth centuries. I couldn't imagine traveling all the way to Cambodia and missing out on Angkor because of my stupid foot.

Well, I arrived in Siem Reap, and my foot still hurt.

Our first afternoon, I forgot my worries as our car approached the ruins. In the back seat, Cliff and I pinched the tender insides of each other's forearms, as we are wont to do in moments of excitement. Behind a moat that had, in the heyday of Khmer power, been filled with territorial crocodiles, was Angkor. Five towers of gray sandstone, the tallest almost seven hundred feet from the ground, shimmered in the afternoon heat. For an instant, it felt as though a thousand years had not passed and Khmer culture still dominated Asia, from Burma to as far south as Indonesia. The archaeologist Louis Delaporte had not removed the finest statues in 1873 for "the cultural enrichment of France," the United States hadn't bombed, the Khmer Rouge hadn't used it for target practice. Angkor stood. I half-expected to see the god-king Suryavarman II, surrounded by the several thousand bare-breasted babes who purportedly attended him.

He wasn't home.

Instead, there were hundreds and hundreds of tourists. They walked and I limped along the five-hundred-meter causeway that took us over the moat and to the main gate.

I stopped twice to rest my foot. Once inside, a second causeway of similar length took us to steep stairs leading to Angkor's first level, a courtyard enclosed by high-walled, open-aired galleries, a kilometer square. In the twelfth century, Suryavarman II had the breezy stone walkways carved with bas-relief depicting scenes from Hindu mythology, his military victories and, of course, many, many babes and their fabulously bare breasts.

The bas-relief was incredibly well preserved. I managed the first of the four galleries before my foot would have no more of it. Dispatching Cliff to see the rest, I perched on a stone bench under a carved arch and tried to convince myself that when you've seen one twelfth-century Hindu epic carved into a quarter kilometer of sandstone wall, you've seen 'em all.

I'd stopped crying by the time Cliff returned. Clutching his arm for support, I made my painful way up the staircase to the stone courtyard that was the second level. Crossing it, we found ourselves at the base of yet another flight of stairs leading to the final level, the courtyard of the five towers.

Metal handrails lined these stairs. Without a thought for my dignity, I dropped to my knees and used my arms to help myself up the stone stairs.

Knees aching slightly, I sat in the shade of the mighty towers and watched Cliff clamber to the top. That must have been when he came up with his plan.

The next morning, my dexterous sweetheart rigged kneepads out of a pair of sweat socks, an ace bandage and duct tape. We headed straight for the complex known as Angkor Thom, famous for the huge, mysterious faces of Jayavarman VII carved into the crumbling stone. The first ruin, the Bayon, had no extended causeways. It was all stairs.

I went up on my hands and knees and slid down on my ass.

The other tourists gawked, as did the stone faces of Jayavarman VII, I am sure. I didn't care. I crawled and slid all that day and the next. At Ta Prohm—where a few months prior, Hollywood had filmed Angelina Jolie starring as Lara Croft in *Tomb Raider*—150-foot-tall trees grew right out of the dilapidation. I got to see that. At Banteay Srei, among the many chesty ladies carved in the pink sandstone, we spotted a few super-studly male figures, similarly objectified. I saw that, too.

Our last afternoon, I went back to Angkor Wat and crawled to the top of the towers I hadn't been able to climb the first afternoon. Stretched below, the temple's design represented a scale model of the Hindu cosmos. Beyond, the weird, flat, often jungly terrain of Cambodia writhed in the heat. I wept for the umpteenth time that trip, but for the first time, wept with joy.

AN AMERICAN IN VENICE

INGRID WENDT

THE SCENE is straight out of a Henry James novel, transposed onto Merchant-Ivory film: a sumptuous, ancient *palazzo* tucked off a narrow, pedestrian back street, away from busy canals, at the far end of a long courtyard protected by heavy, cast-iron gates. Faded, crumbling stucco walls, three stories high, give little hint of the elegant, stylish and utterly sophisticated rooms and furnishings and people assembled within. Silver trays of the largest strawberries I've ever seen—the first of the season, imported perhaps from Spain and frightfully expensive—float among clusters of brocaded settees and ivory-topped tables, antique desks and carved pedestals, sculptures and marble busts, gilt-framed mirrors and paintings. Flowers are everywhere: potted hyacinths, sunburst sprays of forsythia. Small clusters of people hold tall-stemmed glasses of champagne, poured by Jacob and Milton, our cultured, American-born hosts—also our landlords. Venetian writers, artists and aristocrats, English nobility, American and other expatriates of tremendous wealth, high-ranking government officials from several other lands—the guests are gathered in the centuries-old tradition of the European salon to enjoy a reading by the "celebrity" writers of the evening, one of whom, our gracious and impeccable Milton, will (he urbanely reveals) read his own poems, for the first time anywhere, in their indulgent presence.

And here we are, my husband Ralph and myself (the two other poets scheduled to read this evening), trying, in this prereading champagne hour, not to appear as awed as truly we are by the grandeur of our surroundings; to act as though we are used to chatting with such notables as Lady Daphne of England, or the American novelist whose latest book has been on the bestseller list for months, or the Queen of Denmark's personal jeweler. We're trying not to be unnerved by the long and fabled parade of literary geniuses we know to have left their mark on this city before us. Everywhere throughout the maze of streets and canals, in guidebooks or on metal plaques, are reminders of where they ate and slept, where they took their tea and evening pints—not only Henry James, but French novelist George Sand, the very English John Ruskin, America's Ernest Hemingway (putting Harry's Bar on the map), Mary McCarthy, Graham Greene, Muriel Spark, Thomas Mann, Johann Wolfgang von Goethe, Mark Twain. Here is the spot where Lord Byron swam, in full evening dress, in the Grand Canal. Here, the mansion where Robert Browning died. And not only the luminaries of literature, but also of music: Claudio Monteverdi, Richard Wagner, Antonio Vivaldi and Frédéric Chopin, to name a few. Igor Stravinsky, whose grave can be found on Venice's famed island San Michele. The opera house (recently destroyed by fire) where Verdi premiered his operas. What can we be thinking, we of Eugene, Oregon, adding the sounds of our own humble poems to echoes of such a storied place?

Still, we have our share of courage. And we aren't exactly Twain's idea of "innocents abroad." We've had, off and on, our share of experience: in London, for example, house-sitting for friends of friends; in Norway, where

Ralph once held a Fulbright research grant; in Germany, where I was a Fulbright professor for a year, and where Ralph had been the same, ten years before. Nor are we entirely new to Italy, having given poetry readings under U.S. Information Services' auspices in Parma and at the universities in Turin and Rome. We earned only enough to cover barest expenses on these ventures, but who could complain; these small "gigs" took us to places we'd otherwise have missed.

And we most certainly are not, like some of James's hapless young protagonists, unaware of the ways in which many Americans, with their disregard of class and rank and old-fashioned manners, and their impulsive (some would say "crude") ways, often offend the more reserved Europeans, especially those of some social standing. We know enough not to ask the typically American get-acquainted question, "And what do you do?" We know to keep our speaking voices steady and level, never shrill, and never, never loud. We know that most Europeans speak English and can and will understand us, if only we remember to speak slowly and clearly and use common-denominator English words whenever possible, instead of more specialized synonyms. We know enough not to gesture too much with our hands when speaking, a habit especially hard for me, born and raised in the American Midwest, to break (which explains, perhaps, why I never did study the page of Italian hand gestures and their meanings, passed out to our night-school language class the year before). And if anyone laughs when we speak in public, they laugh because we—experienced readers of our poems—have planned it that way. They laugh with us, not at.

To make sure we're at ease and let his guests know he and Jacob don't hold themselves above us in status and rank, Milton, bless his heart, has taken the greatest of pains to ensure that the evening goes smoothly. Days ago, he decided who would read first, second and third, in a kind of round robin. He asked what we planned to wear, shoes and all, knowing, of course, that Ralph's are Reeboks. Ralph packed no others, and he didn't pack a tie.

On this particular night, February 14, ten days after our arrival, Milton's program (mailed a week in advance on printed invitations, each adorned with a small, red Valentine heart) is a reading of original poems "by three American poets, on the theme of 'Love, Lust and Longing.'" That Ralph and I speak only the smallest amount of Italian is not a problem. That we'd planned our once-in-a-lifetime, three-month cultural immersion in Venice without bringing love poems from years and books and computer files past could have been a problem. But (ah, lucky Milton, lucky us!) Ralph and I each had, back in the States, stuck copies of our several books of poems into our suitcases—a practice we've developed over the years, knowing there may be occasions to give them as house gifts, or as gifts to university hosts.

So we do have poems with us. Milton's blind faith is not to be shattered. And we have found several poems in each of our books that can be teased into the category of "love, lust and longing," though having been married for nearly thirty years, neither of us has much to offer in the way of "lust" or "longing." (Or if we do, we certainly aren't going to read them in front of each other.)

"What poet writes love poems out of satisfied desire?" is a question once posed by a writer with whom I studied as an undergraduate. He was becoming terribly worried, as he entered a new relationship, that his creativity would dry up. What would he do without pain? One of the poems I'm planning to read tonight, a poem titled "Mussels," was written as a response to that college instructor of long ago. It is a poem intended to celebrate the beauties and complexities of married love of long duration. A tongue-in-cheek poem, playful yet tender. A poem whose surface content tells how Ralph and I, discovering together the natural wonders of the Pacific Northwest, were also discovering how to live with each other. How learning to gather and cook mussels, and all the knowledge that goes with it, was some-how linked with learning about, and how to survive, each other. The poem was chosen for an anthology of twentieth-century American women poets for the very fact of its being something of a rarity: a feminist take on the pleasures of long marriage.

Knowing the poem might well be perceived as unconventional, not only in its subject matter but also in its conversational, rather than formal, tone, my strategy tonight is to use introductory remarks to bridge whatever cultural gaps I can. I'll do what I usually do at readings—make some per-sonal remarks and give some hint of what to expect. I'll also make sure that certain key words are understood by those for whom English is not a first language.

The most important of these words, surely, is the title itself: "Mussels." Surely someone in Venice will be surprised to learn that in America, in the state of Oregon, we can pick our own mussels off the rocks (unthinkable in polluted Venetian lagoons). But what if someone doesn't know what a mussel is? (Do I know the word "mussel" in Spanish or German?) Or, even more likely, someone might hear the word "mussel" and think, and see, "muscle." A love poem on brawn? No, a love poem on mollusks! Clearly, my first job is to set all ears straight.

So here I go, my planned introduction: "This first poem, in keeping with our theme tonight, is a love poem to my husband Ralph. Its title is 'Mussels.'" So much for planning ahead. So much for conventional reading style. Instead of welcoming smiles, or smiles of anticipation, I see, after these first few words, and before I even launch into the poem, smiles that surely are—in any language—smiles of amusement. Clearly, there's some kind of linguistic confusion. Or am I seeing, in this modern-day Venice, a carryover of expectations bred from centuries of court scandals and intrigues, from the days when nuns served more earthly masters than the Lord and women of public standing kept themselves in funds through practicing the bodily arts? Is there an expectation, on hearing that this is a love poem, that it will be scurrilous? Or, who knows, maybe I've touched some cultural nerve. Or maybe it's the champagne. They want something light, amusing, entertaining. Or maybe one doesn't write love poems to one's spouse. "This is a serious poem," I continue, hopefully not beginning to plead. "This is a playful poem, yes, but also serious." And still I see amusement.

Another poet, less innocent, might have stopped there and launched directly into the poem. But, teacher that I've been and always will be, with my lifelong, dogged faith that all misunderstandings can be overcome with the correct words, I carry on. It must be that they don't know the literal translation of the word "mussel." They think I mean something else. "Mussel," I say. "This is the title of the poem. This love poem. Can anyone please tell me the Italian word for 'mussel'?" Someone unknown to me, a cheerful voice and face I will soon forget, calls out a word, which I promptly, politely (I'm sure; I'm always polite) try to pronounce. *"Cozza."* I'm quick. I'm good at languages. I like to get the audience involved. "Mussel," I repeat, in Italian, "Cozza. Right. Mussel. But plural. *Mussels.* A love poem."

But now the laughter starts to erupt. I must be trying too hard. Maybe poets in Italy are aloof. Or maybe it's just plain funny to think a love poem has been written around the subject of shellfish. Is there something funny in this? Well, yes, I did enjoy creating this basic juxtaposition—it's meant to be light, not Romantic with a capital "R." But *funny?* And the poem I wrote is wry, sure, and the mention of closed sea anemones hanging down from rocky ledges, like the "cocks of horses," is supposed to be tongue-in-cheek. But my audience doesn't know this. They haven't heard the poem, and already they're stifling laughter. Maybe it's my accent. I try again. "A love poem! Really. About mussels. It is!" And still they don't get it, they can't stop snickering.

Ah, I know. The homonym problem. "No," I say, taking the matter firmly, and literally, in hand, raising my voice (I have to, to make myself heard), lifting my left arm, bending my elbow at ninety degrees and raising my fist to the sky—the Communist salute, the picture on the baking powder box. I grab my strong left biceps and triceps with my strong right fingers and thumb. "Not *this* kind of muscle. I'm talking about shellfish!" That does it; I'm the queen of comedy. Heads turn, eyes contact other eyes, the laughter is loud.

It's said that pride goeth before a fall. If so, and if that's my problem, there must be a thin border somewhere between pride and self-confidence I still need to explore. How would anyone get up before a crowd of strangers to read a love poem without some kind of confidence? But have I been *too* confident? Assertive, yet sensitive—that's how I've tried to become, and in America, most of the time, it's gotten me by. But maybe here, in Venice, that mode doesn't translate. Never before has an audience laughed at something I didn't intend.

And never, as it turns out, have they heard a woman—American, of course (such an innocent abroad, they knew it all along)—tell them, in high company, in front of the whole crowd, that she's written a love poem with the title "Female Genitalia." For that, as it turns out, is the vernacular, street-talk translation of the Italian word "mussel." Which is what I learn after the reading is over, when two kind women from the audience (one Italian, one American) come up to talk, to praise the reading and to ask gently if I knew why people laughed. Ah, I hear it again, it rings in my head: "Love poem with the title 'Cunt.' Love poem on cunt. On cunt. Really. It is!" Not once, but twice, three, four times.

And not only that. Raising one's fist in the Communist salute is perfectly acceptable in Italy, where the Communist party is not only legal but very big—but grabbing the left upper arm with the right hand is a gesture (in Italy, the quintessential land of the gesture) used only as an insult of the greatest magnitude. Fuck you, up yours, to the max. Not in those words, of course, from these gentle women, trying to help. (Ah, those of you reading this essay, study those graphics passed out in night school.)

Still, there are always lessons to be learned from making a fool of oneself. Or maybe questions to be asked. Does it matter, really, if one learns to "pass" in high foreign society? And can it be done, really? All it takes is one slip of the tongue, one animated Midwestern gesture, to bring the whole careful facade tumbling down. And maybe it's not such a bad thing, after all, to show one's innocence abroad. Who knows, without the sympathy I called forth from those two dear women, who later become good friends, we might have stayed strangers.

And I might never have had the chance to savor the very short, rather amusing and dubiously flattering coda to this story. At the end of the evening, as we and other guests are leaving, I happen (or maybe it isn't entirely accidental) to approach the door at the same time as the rather good-looking Greek ambassador, who, flirtatiously catching my eye, asks Milton (with red bandanna "tie" inside his open-necked shirt) why we haven't been introduced before, and will he please do something about that.

Am I flattered? Well, yes, a bit. The Greek ambassador is, after all, dark and handsome (forget tall). Poised. Rich. And powerful, surely. A movie-star kind of man, the kind whose slightest attentions some women "would die for," and may well have already done. And he's attracted to *me,* a woman just turned fifty. Am I amused? Well, clearly the poem I've just read—for my husband of twenty-seven years—just didn't get through. And this is Venice, after all, just like the books, the movies. What do class and rank matter when one such as I can flaunt her hunger for sex with such daring, ingenuous aplomb? For surely it could have seemed I planned that whole faux pas, hoping for just this kind of attention. What truly "good" woman would dream of throwing herself at the public like that?

So, do I rise to the bait when Milton later calls to ask if I'll meet him and Mr. Ambassador for lunch somewhere? (So gracious, Milton is, so delighted to be the go-between in what could become the latest Venetian affair. For this is still a rather small town, after all, and matters of the heart, or of the flesh, are as entertaining now as ever they were in books of the past.)

End of story. I've read those books and their sad conclusions. Sat through those films. Eat your heart out, Henry James. Sorry, Mark Twain. And all you authors I haven't yet read. Innocent abroad I am and always will be. But not one to succumb.

Mussels
For Ralph

We've learned where the big ones grow,
to harvest not from the tops of rocks where shells
fill with sand

to follow the tide out to the farthest reefs we can reach
and still not get wet, where last time we found
giant anemones green-sheathed and dripping under

the overhangs like the cocks of horses, we laughed, or
elephants, having each come to the same conclusion,
fresh from bed and married long enough

to say such things to each other, again
to remember the summer we first discovered mussels
big as fists protecting Sisters Rocks.

Just married and ready for anything, even
mussels were game, black as obsidian, stubbornly
clinging to rocks, to each other, their shells

so tightly together we had to force them apart
with a knife, the meat
inside a leap of orange, poppy-bright; and when

three perch in a row took the hook you'd baited
tender as liver we said we must try them ourselves
someday, if they're safe, which they weren't

all the years we lived down south: red algae in summer
tides infiltrating our chance to experiment, food without precedent,
how would we know what to do?

Counting at last on friends who had been to Europe and now
are divorced, we waded waist deep to pick some,
scraping our knuckles raw on barnacles

none of us knowing to soak our catch two hours at least
to clean out the sand; the sand we took in with butter and lemon
cleaning our teeth for a week.

Now we can't get our fill of them.
Weekend vacations you work to the last, cooking
one more batch to freeze for fritters or stew.

Now we harvest them easily, take the right tools, wear boots
we gave to each other for birthdays so we don't have
to remember to watch out for waves

to feel barnacles unavoidably crushed underfoot
like graveyards of dentures waves have exposed, although
sometimes now I find myself

passing over the biggest, maybe because
they've already survived the reach of starfish,
blindly prowling on thousands of white-tipped canes,

or they've grown extra barnacles,
limpets, snails, baby anemones,
rock crabs hiding behind. As though

age after all counts for something
and I've grown more tender-hearted,
wanting you not to know about the cluster

I found today, for the first
time in years having taken time off from job
and housework and child care, sleeping so late

my feet got wet on the incoming tide, unexpectedly
talking aloud, saying look at that one, bigger even
than Sisters Rocks: a kind of language

marriage encourages, private as memories of mussels,
anachronistic as finding I miss you
picking mussels to take home to you

not the ones you'd pick if you could but fresh
as any young lover's bouquet and far more edible,
more than enough to last us at least a week.

SPARE ME

KRISTIN BECK

"I'M GONNA come down. Just wait up for me. I'll be there in six hours."

My plan had been fairly straightforward: Hang up the phone, get in the car and drive to L.A. This was fifteen years ago. By then I was driving my fourth car, the previous three sold for scraps due to my cruel neglect. I had no idea how to take care of an automobile; the cars I had destroyed outnumbered the years I'd had my license. Like so many teenagers, I believed that a five-hundred-dollar VW Beetle would suffice as long as it was a cute color and had a working tape player or, at the very least, stereo sound. This was the late '80s, the pre-ATM years (can you even imagine?), what we now think of as the information and communication Dark Ages. There were no real conveniences yet. Forget about cell phones—I still used a rotary dial phone. How luxurious it must have seemed back then in our simpler days to dream of talking on the phone in a car!

I jumped in my car and hit the freeway without stopping for gas—too busy. It was summer in Northern California, and I was floating down Interstate 5 to Los Angeles to see my boyfriend.

Ex-boyfriend. I couldn't tell which, so I thought I should just go and find out what was what.

When I called to announce my romantic plans, he acted very casual about the notion of a late-night visit. But I knew he'd been waiting for my call. And I supposed that he would be flattered and even excited that a woman in love would be frisky enough—brave enough, really—to attempt such a passionate journey. But he just said, "Hmmn. Okay. See you tonight." Was it his dark brown voice? The promise of illicit breakup sex? No, decidedly it was the fact that college boys try to appear unattainable but are very tender inside. I knew this even at my young age. He would pine for me while I drove, and by the time I arrived he would be in a love lather, ready for some kind of action. I really didn't care what kind, as long as he worshipped me a little. How could he live without me?

For four hours I listened to any radio station I could find, noting that even the most marginal song can seem incredibly moving when you're desperately ferreting your way through AM radio. I obsessively checked the dashboard meters, even though none of them worked. I had developed a good sense for both the speed and the gas tank level just by feel—a point of pride for me.

The car was practically vertical, creeping up the tip-top of Grapevine Pass, when I heard, *Psssssssh! Plup-plup-plup-plup* . . . As the car began to swerve, I still had no idea what was happening. I had wrecked plenty of cars by neglecting the oil meter or grinding my way through the gears, but I'd never lost control of one (which I thought made me a responsible driver). I tried not to flip out as I navigated my way to the shoulder. Once there, I stepped out of the car and looked at the anemic tire, certain that it would be mere moments before a nice police officer arrived to help me. I waited. There were no cars on the road. Not a police car; no trucks. I'd assumed that since cops were always there to see me pull some fucked-up driving maneuver, they would be imminently accessible, always watching, ready to serve and protect. I cursed traffic school. I bit my nails. I worried that my boyfriend would be concerned about my tardiness. Just then a semi chugged its way up to me. A capable-looking but coffee-addled teamster climbed down from the rig.

"Need some assistance?" he asked, patting down his hair and hiking up his jeans. He was so busy adjusting himself that I started to wonder if he hadn't initially pulled over to take a roadside leak. I answered, hopefully, "Yes, please, I need help. I think I've got a broken tire."

"Where's the spare at, hon?" he sighed, and looked around doggedly to see if anyone else was possibly pulling over to help. *The spare! Right!*

"Uh, I just couldn't tell you that, sir." He stared at me for a few beats, blinking in Morse code: y . . o . . u . . . i . . d . . i . . o . . t . . . "Well, I guess I'll just take a look-see in your trunk. That's where most folks keep their spare tires. You *do* have one, right?" he inquired, trying to appear gallant, but obviously annoyed by my extreme lack of vehicular sophistication.

"I honestly don't know," I whispered, then tried to cover up my colossal stupidity by adding, "This isn't my car. It's my, um, mom's." But anyone with half a wit would know this random piece of shit was no mom car.

Withering on the side of the road, enveloped in darkness and staring at the chew-tin-faded ring in the back pocket of this stranger's 501s, I actually prayed to God that there was a spare. I might die of mortification if he had taken this much time out of his route and . . . my prayers were answered. "Eureka!" he exclaimed. He'd found it. Once he had the tire in place, he warned me through clenched teeth that it might not be exactly the right size for my car. "Oh well," he breezed, "I'm off to deliver French fries in Burbank." I thanked him and he was on his way.

I returned to the car, weary but determined. I had experienced a minor setback, but I was very nearly there. Back in the groove, I drove no more than two minutes before I heard a loud *smack!* and the car began sizzling down the road, sparks visible from my rearview mirror. Holy fucking shit, now what? The back right side of my chariot clunked down. If I had never before experienced a flat tire, I had positively never had the pleasure of having a tire fly off the car. The tire popped off the axle as if it had been jimmied off with a crowbar. I needed to finesse a quick roadside deposit of the bucking, careening automobile. My legs went numb and my hands tingled and got all sweaty. With stiff fingers clutching the wheel, I somehow managed to stop.

I looked in the rearview mirror—no more sparks. And then my view adjusted: Look at that! I'm still alive. After a several-minute recovery, I stepped out of my lopsided car and surveyed the damage. The car was tilted dramatically to the back right, the smell of burnt rubber and sulphur still hanging in the air. I scoured the bushes for the ejected spare and tramped though the dirt. It was gone. I was keenly aware how few opportunities for help there would be. And now it was even later. No one would be on the road.

Hearing the sound of coyotes in the distance, I tried to dismiss them as too clichéd to be true, but their howls fleshed out the scene for me: I was vibrating with fear, having now officially assumed the starring role in my own personal teensploitation flick. I mused that maybe this was my punishment for ditching class, and for all of my other crimes. That I was living a charmed life, and had to pay for it from time to time. Since this had become a moment of reflection on how fortunate I was, it seemed a good time to vow to attend German at least three days a week. And to remember to turn off the lights when I left a room. And to alternate weekend drug use instead of indulging every weekend.

I also had plenty of time to go over the last few interactions with my boyfriend. Yes, I told myself (out loud, because no one was within twenty miles of me), he was three years older, a college man, but that didn't give him the right to be so tepid in the face of true love. And yes, it was kind of weird that he wanted to spend spring break with his mother—didn't he realize what he would be missing? But by now he must have been pulling his hair out, and so my fickle heart's pendulum swung back toward loving him. I felt deeply the panic he must have been hyperventilating through right then. Had he called the police? Had he woken his mother? Maybe she was up with him, pacing through the night in solidarity.

My mind was still on my boyfriend when a pickup truck pulled up. Four skinny ranch hands jumped out at once. At first they didn't say anything, just looked me up and down, kind of half-smiling. I tried to affect a tough-girl pose, like, "What kind of assistance can you offer me?" But really I was shitting my pants. If they wanted to drag me into the back of the truck, use me up and then toss me out the window, who would even know about it? It occurred to me that I was scared for a reason: I could be more busted than ever before in my short life. I became aware of the scene from their perspective: piece-of-shit car, a bumper sticker that read "Bumpersticker" with a red slash through it on the rear window, no rear bumper, tilted license plate, missing tire, eighteen-year-old girl in cutoffs looking tough but terrified. Nice.

"So, do ya wanna come with us? We're just over the hill in Valencia," the lead ranch hand asked through his drool. I must have been too vigorously shaking my head no, because he attempted to allay my fears by announcing, "We don't bite!" I thought of doctors who announce, "This won't hurt a bit," and then proceed to hurt you. I hadn't considered that these guys would bite me until they said they wouldn't. I imagined them biting me, ripping me apart with their incisors. Then I found the words: "No, thank you, I just need you to please call for help."

"Are you suuure? We can wake up our mother and she'll make you some tamales." Though I wasn't for one second certain if they were going to help me or lunge at me, I somehow managed not to cry as I reiterated my previous request.

"All right, then," they said, and got back in the truck, looking suspiciously uninterested in calling for help.

"Okay, okay, okay," I thought to myself, "it's a pretty fucked-up situation when you feel lucky that people who might help you don't kill you." I had to soothe myself and believe that I wasn't going to die.

An hour passed. At least it seemed like an hour. I had no way of telling time—no watch, and a busted car clock. I spied a flickering neon sign I had noticed in the distance earlier but had considered unbelievably far away—it looked like a Chevron station. Although it might not be open, it would surely have a phone. I could call my frantic boyfriend, allay his fears and ask him to come and get me. Reaching the station involved climbing a fence, crossing a dirt road and, scariest of all, entering real darkness. I had grown used to the relative darkness of the freeway, peppered with roadside lights. But this would be dark-dark, and I was terrified. I drew in a deep breath and, without exhaling, made the journey to the gas station. I was right; it was closed. There had been a phone, but it had been ripped out of the wall. Dreams dashed again. I imagined that the coyotes were getting closer and hungrier. I made my way back to the car, relieved to see my old, handicapped friend. I had calmed myself quasi-successfully when my heart rate spiked again at the sound of another approaching semi.

This time a pleasant if Hollywood extra–looking truck driver leaned his road-weathered face out the window and, to my amusement, actually tipped his cowboy hat in my direction and asked, "What seems to be the trouble, ma'am?"

After too many hours on the freeway in the middle of the night, my voice had risen up a full octave in pitch. "Can you please use your CD or CB or whatever it is to radio for help?" I squeaked. "I've been stuck out here for hours and my boyfriend is waiting for me in L.A." Looking up at the driver in this enormous truck, my blood curdled as I suspected that he wasn't being chivalrous . . . he was laughing at me. He chuckled and said, "Sure, little lady, I'll get on the ham and get you some company out here."

That was ambiguous enough to seem threatening to me. I was so paranoid by this point that if my own brother drove up, I'd be curious about his intentions to help. As the trucker drove off, I sank into an emotional abyss: Would I ever get off this road?

By this point it had to be four in the morning. Had to be. I decided that the only way to get to a phone would be to head on down the road, and I didn't care how long it would take. Resolved, I stepped away from the car. After just a few feet, a road-hogging eighteen-wheeler, all lights and whistles, pulled over and stopped. The trucker opened the passenger-side door and asked gently, "Do you need some help?"

I thought, "If I do not get into this truck, I might get killed. If I do get into this truck, I might get killed." Even though the driver seemed genuinely prepared to help me, my instincts were by now totally shot. What tipped the scales in the eighteen-wheeler's favor was the pressing notion of my terrified boyfriend. Calling him sooner was better than calling him later. I reluctantly climbed into the cab.

His name was John. He was on his way to Santa Monica with a delivery of strawberries. That did sound terribly benign. I was too tired and too scared to be charmed, though it was tempting to let down my guard for a minute. John said he would take me to the next exit so I could find a phone. As we chit-chatted, I noticed that he wasn't making the turn toward the off-ramp. "This is it," I thought, squeezing the door handle, "this is when I get killed." He must have felt me recoiling because he quickly assured me, "I think I'll take you to the Lyons Exit instead. More light there. More restaurants." I sat, paralyzed with fear, unable to talk anymore.

Finally, the truck came to a stop. It released its jake brake with a whoosh, and John turned to me and said, "Well, here's a phone, and it's under the brightest light I could find. I hope your boyfriend is happy to hear from you! Take care, now!" I almost embraced him for not killing me and, beyond that, for being so thoughtful! I slipped out of the high seat and ran, shaking, to the phone.

Of course I didn't have any change or a calling card, so I called collect, sure that he wouldn't be annoyed at me for such rudeness—just grateful that I was alive. The operator rang. A groggy, middle-of-the-night voice answered. Surely his mother couldn't be sleeping! She said she'd get him right away. To my horror, another equally sleepy voice whispered into the receiver. "Hi. What's going on?" he asked, irritated to be out of bed. He was totally asleep. He hadn't been worried that I wasn't there. My six-hour trip had already taken twelve, I hadn't reached L.A. yet and it turns out he was all tucked in, snoring away. My desperate effort to save him from worry had left me shaking and stuttering, while he was warm and snuggly. My anxiety dissolved into the flatline awareness that he really didn't care. We really were broken up. And I was a big idiot for chasing him, and risking my life to see him.

Now, all grown up, I believe that the state of one's car reflects the state of one's life. Each car after that derelict machine was more and more functional and, remarkably, so were my relationships. I stopped leaving the house with only my cutoffs for a long road trip. Now I take my ATM card and my cellular phone.

SAVING THE GUAYMI

LEA ASCHKENAS

GUATEMALA HAS Rigoberta Menchú and, in the northern rainforests, rebel guerrillas. In Honduras, Mayan ruins line the cobblestone footpaths of Copán. Nicaragua has the legacy of its Sandinista uprising and a clan of rebellious poets who live out the revolution's ideals on the communal Solentiname Island. And Costa Rica? Costa Rica, the fashionable gringo gripe goes, well, Costa Rica is just the tropics. It is beautiful landscape but nothing more. It has no revolutionary heroes and no oppressive military. Unlike its Central American neighbors, Costa Rica has no narrative of sub-jugation, no tragic struggle for independence, and thus (from the school of thought that misery + strife = art), Costa Rica has no culture. And even worse, I've heard many an expatriate lament, there are no indigenous people.

But in the southeastern corner of the country, at the border with Panama, there is a crescent beach whose name is a Spanish word for mosquito. Here, the rocky black sand will cut your feet and the heat will bake your wounds. And if you continue on into the jungle and hike five miles uphill through mud that pulls at your ankles like quicksand, you will come to a land inhabited only by indigenous people. For a few days in November 1995, they came out to greet a group of visitors, but after our stay I imagine they've become more guarded with their hospitality.

I was living in Costa Rica at the time, writing for a news magazine and forever seeking ways to escape the dreariness of the cockroach-infested converted garage that served as our editorial office. I had come to Costa Rica imagining coconut palms, gentle Caribbean breezes, waterfalls and dense rainforests. Even in town, I had expected to find mango trees and wild monkeys lining the streets. I'd thought I might be able to pick my breakfast from the tree branches on the walk to work.

Instead, I was living in the suburbs and working beneath the diesel-coated skies of San José, several hours from either the Caribbean or Pacific coast. For my first few months in Costa Rica, the only waterfalls I saw were those that poured from the skylight in my office during the afternoon rainstorms. In place of mango trees and wild monkeys, the streets were filled with flooded potholes deep enough to swallow a medium-sized dog.

When my boss entered the office one dreary afternoon and asked if anyone would be interested in tagging along with a European film crew the following week, working as an interpreter for their documentary on an indigenous group in the jungles of Costa Rica, I raised my hand and waved it wildly like an overeager school child. My boss's friend Roberto, whose organization was hosting the crew, had called for help when the regular interpreter canceled at the last minute. I jumped at the chance to see what the ecotourism brochures and the complaints of my fellow gringos had brainwashed me into believing was the "real" Costa Rica—as though the urban grind that I and a majority of the country's residents endured each day was an illusion.

I would soon learn that I wasn't exactly qualified for the interpreting job. In college, I had spent a semester in Spain, and now I was translating press releases on a daily basis in Costa Rica. But there is a big difference between painstakingly poring over a passage on my own time and having my voice recorded on film before an impatient herd of Euro-Hollywood types.

In the years leading up to our visit, something strange had been happening to the Guaymi, an indigenous tribe inhabiting northern Panama and a sliver of Costa Rica's Caribbean coastline. Their reputation as Costa Rica's token self-sustaining indigenous group no longer reflected reality. The community's crops had begun to wither and were largely abandoned and replaced by canned goods from the *pulpería* mini-mart in town. The Guaymi women, who traditionally wove baskets from palm leaves and crafted necklaces from colorful local seeds, had modified their artistry for market to the outside world. The necklaces, for example, were now being made from plastic Indian beads. The Guaymi had neither the skills to survive in the "modern" world nor those necessary to hold on to their conventional lifestyle. Many Guaymi didn't speak standard Spanish and few knew how to plant a crop. The elder designated as "master farmer" had apparently taken this knowledge with him to the grave several months back.

Disturbed by this trend, Roberto's organization, a nonprofit that focused on indigenous issues in Costa Rica, had put out an international plea soliciting funds to save the Guaymi. A European group had responded. And for the past year, their money had been funneled into agriculture seminars, grassroots discussions on how to run an effective bartering system, and classes to improve the Guaymi's Spanish and link them with the outside world. Through this multifaceted approach, Roberto's group had taken on the challenging, dubious task of integrating the Guaymi while simultaneously encouraging them to preserve the unique aspects of their dwindling culture.

The job of the film crew was to document the Guaymi's progress a year into this operation, to collect their stories and record the historic moment of a people reconnecting with their roots.

☠

From the start, things didn't go as expected. I met Roberto at his office and we drove to the airport to pick up the film crew at 10 p.m. I stood in the humid aftermath of the evening thunderstorms, waving a sign that read "Guaymi Group" at every tall, European-looking person who stepped off the plane. But three flight loads of passengers landed and quickly scurried past without so much as a wayward glance at the sign.

"I don't know where they are," a flight attendant told us. "It looks like they were scheduled to get in on the ten o'clock flight."

Just before midnight, they arrived. A short, middle-aged woman with shoulder-length, wavy brown hair stepped off the plane followed by three men, only one of whom fit the description of those I'd been flagging down with my sign. He was the youngest of the group, probably in his early twenties, and with his styled blond hair, perfectly poised shoulders and prancing gait, he seemed more accustomed to being in front of the camera than behind it.

After spotting our sign, by this time abandoned in a mud puddle at my feet, the woman came rushing over to us.

"Oh, you are still here," she said in English. "I would apologize, but it's not my fault. We missed our plane because this one was primping in the bathroom." She pointed to the blond boy, who shrugged his shoulders innocently.

"Cathy, let's just get going," said one of the older men, who proceeded to head off in the direction of the baggage claim.

As we lugged the camera equipment and recording devices to the rented jeep, I translated the conversation into Spanish for Roberto. He was a tall ponytailed man with an astigmatism in his left eye, which made it appear that he was always looking somewhere else and gave our conversations an eerie distance no matter how caught up in them I got. On the ride to the airport, Roberto and I had discussed literature. He told me about the Nicaraguan poet Rubén Darío and the writings of Costa Rica's former president Oscar Arias Sánchez.

"I don't read so many foreign writers these days," he said. "Sometimes their arrogance in the matters of Latin America frustrates me."

Playa Zancudo is reputed to have the longest wave in the world, regularly reaching a mile in length. Roberto told us that we would arrive just around sunrise and perhaps, before we hiked up to meet the Guaymi, we could catch a glimpse of the surfers attempting to catch this notorious wave. We were expected to meet a Guaymi named Eusebio at Playa Zancudo in eight hours. The beach was seven hours away, so we would drive all night. I was sitting in the passenger seat, and although I'd planned to stay awake and keep Roberto company, I drifted off around one o'clock.

I awoke when the morning sun poured through the windows. We were no longer moving, and I was alone in the jeep. Roberto was filling it with gas, and Cathy was walking toward us with the two older men. I watched in amazement as the blond boy strutted over to the bathroom in his Calvin Klein underwear and then, turning in the direction of the jeep, whipped them off for an outdoor hose-down shower. Without toweling off or covering up, he ran over to the jeep, penis flapping, following a loud, sharp whistle from Cathy.

"Come on, Rex," she said as if this were the most normal thing in the world. "Get your clothes on. We've got somewhere to be."

Back in the jeep, I fell asleep again to the steady bump of potholes and the static of overlapping radio stations. I woke to a shriek from Cathy several hours later.

"It's a strike," Roberto said. "The pickers are striking."

There was a bridge blocked off by about twenty or so men and women shaking bananas and holding protest signs that I could not read in my blurry-eyed early-morning state.

"No, this cannot be happening," Cathy announced. "We have been everywhere. We have filmed in Ethiopia and Cambodia." With gusto more appropriate to a revolutionary corporal than to the mission we were on, she declared, "We will not be stopped in Costa Rica."

One of the older men snorted in dissatisfaction and when I translated for Roberto, he shook his head in disgust. He left the jeep and went to talk with a man sitting in a truck bed and waving a banana over his head like a flag. When Roberto returned, he told us that the strikers planned to protest indefinitely and no one would be allowed to pass.

"What will we do?" I asked while Cathy tapped impatiently at my shoulder for the translation.

"We'll have to go another way," Roberto said. "But we'll have to back-track a good three hours to get to the turnoff."

Before I could translate, Cathy wound herself into a huff. The morning heat was building up, reflecting onto all of us through the jeep windows. Rex pulled off his shirt, and I felt a sharp flash of pain in my stomach, worrying that he might disrobe here in front of the protesters, insulting them and forever destroying our chances of getting across the bridge. But fortunately, Rex kept his pants on.

"Dan, Stan," Cathy said to the two older men. "Who's got their wallet on them?"

The man addressed as Stan warily handed over his wallet, pulling his hand back quickly as though he was afraid it might be slapped.

I translated what Roberto had told me, but Cathy shook her head. She held up a U.S. fifty-dollar bill and said, "Tell Roberto we have not come this far just to turn back. Tell him we will buy the bridge."

Roberto implored me to tell Cathy no, to inform her that this was offensive and would not work. But Cathy headed over anyway, waving the money above her head in a bizarre imitation of the man in the truck with his banana. I could hear Roberto inhaling deeply, but Cathy returned within minutes, empty-handed and triumphant.

We arrived at Playa Zancudo at 12:30 p.m. The beach arched delicately into the slap of the surf. The enormous wave was nowhere in sight, and all I wanted in that moment was to run into the clear aqua ocean and let the rhythm of its crashing drown out the morning's arguments.

But there was no time for this. A small man dressed in jeans and a white T-shirt walked over to our jeep and introduced himself as Eusebio, our Guaymi guide.

"We cannot go today," Cathy said, speaking for all of us. "There's no point. We won't even be able to film. Five hours from now, it'll be dark."

Picking up on Cathy's body language, Roberto did not wait for my translation and instead told Eusebio that we would take a hotel for the night and hike up the next day.

"But I have brought the horse," Eusebio said, motioning to a wobbly, malnourished-looking creature leaning against a shaky fence.

Roberto offered Eusebio a hotel room for the night so we could all hike up together the next morning, but Eusebio gave Cathy and her entourage the once-over and shook his head, smiling.

"I'll be back tomorrow," he said.

I spent the rest of the afternoon on the beach, playing in the water and slicing my feet on the rocky ocean bottom. In the evening, Cathy and Rex retreated to their room in our hotel, a ramshackle, weathered beach bungalow. Stan told us that Rex was just along for Cathy.

"He's a soap opera star back home," he said. "There's no need for him here, but the two of them have something going on, and Cathy is good at pulling strings to get her way."

Stan was the cameraman and Dan worked the lights. They were interesting guys, providing an evening full of stories about their adventures. We cracked open a coconut on the beach and toasted it over a bonfire as the sun set. I slept well that night, full of that quiet exhaustion that blocks out all preoccupations and replaces worry with calm.

Cathy must have had a good night's sleep, too, because she was awake at the crack of dawn the next morning, riled up and ready to go. A little after 6 a.m., a persistent thumping ripped into my dreams, replacing the calm sway of the ocean that had lulled me to sleep. It took me a minute to orient myself and realize that the noise was coming from my door.

Before I could stumble out of bed to attend to it, Cathy walked into my room and headed toward me, informing me in her harsh, accented English that she and Rex were on their way to the Guaymí's cabins.

When I asked if Eusebio had already arrived, Cathy shook her head.

"It doesn't matter," she said, annoyed, defiant. "We'll find the way. I need to get settled up there, and these men, they are such babies."

I rubbed my eyes, trying to determine if this was a real woman towering over me or just an angry apparition, part of a bad dream from which I hadn't yet woken.

"Dan and Stan didn't even answer when I knocked on their door," Cathy continued. "And Rex says he is tired and hungry. He believes he can't work if he doesn't eat or sleep. But look at me, I'm twice his age and I'm okay. We have the rest of our lives to eat and sleep. Right?"

I gave a feeble nod.

"Well, good," Cathy said, somehow oblivious to the fact that I was still in bed myself.

After she left, I fell back to sleep, not waking until Eusebio arrived a few hours later. Stan, Dan, Roberto and I hiked with him for nearly four hours uphill on a jungle path so muddy it stole my shoe more than once.

The packhorse, after falling twice in the slippery ground, took off running up the mountainside, leaving our supplies embedded in the mud.

We collected our goods and attached the soiled packs to our bodies—a duffel bag in the crevice of an elbow, one backpack on the back and another on the front like some sort of subterranean straightjacket—and continued on through the guava-scented jungle.

The scenery distracted me from my discomfort. Banana trees swayed in the air, which was so clear I felt energized from just inhaling deeply. From different points along the trail, I looked down over the crescent of Playa Zancudo and saw the sunlight glinting its way across the water's surface.

When we reached the Guaymi's land, a group of women and children stood up to greet us from their outdoor communal kitchen, which consisted of a makeshift stove and some benches beneath a wooden overhang to keep out the rain. A few men who were leaning against a long, ramshackle wooden house looked on with interest but made no move to come over until Eusebio motioned to them.

While the men were dressed in jeans and worn T-shirts, the women all wore crisp yellow and pink and blue dresses, traditional outfits that stood in stark contrast with the digital watches that adorned their wrists. A woman smoking a pipe introduced herself as Marta. Her son and daughter had wide, round eyes, and when they saw my camera, they asked in Spanish if I would take their pictures. They laughed as the metallic click went off, and then they retreated shyly behind their mother.

Cathy, who was pleasantly quiet and worn out from her early hike, was still arranging her equipment. I walked with Roberto and some of the Guaymi over to a stream that ran behind the long house.

"This is where we take an afternoon swim," Marta told us.

Before I was able to test out the water, Marta and two other women jumped in, their drenched dresses clinging tightly to their bodies. I jumped in the water with my clothes on, too. Shaded by the trees, the creek was refreshingly cold. I stretched backward to dunk my hair in it and floated like that for a while, listening to our hosts splash each other, breathing in the scent of overripe banana.

My days with the Guaymi passed in a sensory blur of timelessness. Something strange happens to a person when the days are separated only by sleep, when there is no external routine. Bodies and faces, scenery and conversations melt and merge like a watercolor wash. Although most of my conversations with the Guaymi took place in Spanish, in my mind they are already translated into English.

Several times during the trip, Rex pointed out to me that a proper interpreter doesn't wait for the whole sentence to be spoken but rather translates along the way. Cathy ultimately became frustrated with my slowness and often pieced together the few Spanish words she knew to glean her own meaning from the conversations.

At night, I slept a fitful, itchy sleep among the spiders and nibbling jungle bugs that inhabited the creaky wood plank floors of the longhouse. The house was used for community meetings. The Guaymi lived way up in the jungle, their bamboo and palm-leaf thatch houses dotting every small clearing in the highlands.

The Guaymi were kind and eager to share their stories, which all rang with a sadness I had not expected. The ideal of the simple, communal lifestyle proved either to be not so simple or to be so simple it robbed the Guaymi of any stimulation or sources of inspiration.

I met a woman in the highlands who told me her pig was dying and she didn't know what to do about it. The pig, or really a piglet with muddy pink skin, had an infected leg and was lying in the shade under a hammock, making an occasional high-pitched snort, waiting for sleep or death to ease the pain. The woman had six children. She told me both her father and her husband had abused her. Her husband was now living with another woman.

I tried to translate this story into English for Cathy, who had told me to ask the woman what her daily life was like. Cathy took my words and rephrased them into Stan's microphone.

"She says life has been difficult," Cathy said. "But she hopes that it will improve with the new education and agriculture programs."

Although these programs were supposed to be the heart of the documentary, it seemed that most of the Guaymi were not even aware of them. At first the Guaymi were excited to have camera crews. With no electricity, they had never seen a television, but they did have a battery-operated boom box. The soundtrack of my time there was filled with Madonna's "Like a Virgin" and a smattering of Michael Jackson hits.

The Guaymi's enthusiasm for the camera crew and their high-tech film gadgets diminished once they realized that the crew was not truly interested in hearing about their lives. Cathy wanted success stories, tidy tales of how everything worked out once the grant money came through. But the Guaymi told me that the agriculture and language instructors had gathered at the longhouse and taught only those who were there at the time. The class size had never really exceeded five or six people.

Commandante Cathy, as I'd silently nicknamed her, demanded scenes of horseback riding and outdoor language classes where students sat in a circle sharing knowledge like they did on grassy quads in college brochures. I explained this to Eusebio, who wrinkled his face in distaste, pointing out that their horses were too weak to be ridden for recreation. So we took some still shots of men on horses, supposedly stopping in the middle of the fields to chat. The children eagerly agreed to be filmed discussing Spanish grammar while they sat in grassy circles.

Rex grew bored and antsy during the down time between shots. He took to doing chin-ups, shirtless, on the rafters of the outdoor kitchen. He was anxious for the filming to be over so we could head back to the oceanside cabins for our final night, probably itching to pull off his clothes and run naked alongside the surf. Whenever I saw him, using his newly acquired Spanish, he would say to me, *"Vamos a la playa."* ("Let's go to the beach.")

Once a week, several Guaymi hiked to town to buy supplies. They washed in their creek with Ivory soap. Their boom box kept them company through afternoon jungle hikes, and dinner consisted of spaghetti and canned pasta sauce. The last evening at dinner, Cathy asked me to find out about the Guaymi's oral history. What types of stories did they share? What were their creation myths? We circulated the question around the table, each person shaking his or her head in confusion until finally an older woman, the widow of the Guaymi's last farmer, said her husband used to tell these types of stories, but she could no longer recall any of the details.

In the mornings before mealtime, in the afternoons before dinner, in the twilight hours before sunset, the Guaymi practiced an unnamed ritual that I could only describe as an exercise in waiting—waiting for boredom to abate, waiting for opportunity to arrive. They would stand at the glassless windows of the rundown longhouse and stare into the barren fields that met up with the jungle. They stared with such intensity, as though perhaps, just beyond the horizon, lay an answer to a question they were unable to articulate, or which I was unable to interpret for the film.

There is still something beautiful for me in my memories of these days, something calm about waking, not to the sound of the garbage truck outside my house in the city, but to the sounds of the outdoors—a cricket, a snake slithering through the grass. In a way, we lived out the ecotourism ideals: We left only footprints. We packed out what we packed in. And, despite Roberto's desires to return this community to sustainability, we really had little impact.

My most vivid image of the trip is one of the few that did not get recorded on film. As we prepared to hike back down to Playa Zancudo, Cathy reached into her purse to hand out presents she'd brought for the Guaymi. She passed around handfuls of key chains with tiny trinkets from her homeland attached.

"Mi país," ("My country,") she told them. The irony of the gift escaped her. Most of the Guaymi houses had no doors, and if they did, they certainly didn't have locks.

I waited expectantly, dreading the moment when someone would ask me for an explanation. But the Guaymi were more resourceful than I realized. By the time we had packed up our bags, a group of girls came running over to me.

"Muchacha, mírame," one of them said, asking me to look. And spinning from their pierced ears like a rainbow of kitsch were the colorful trinkets.

Eusebio and several other Guaymi joined us on the hike down, accepting Rex's invitation to "vamos a la playa." Commandante Cathy found it in her budget to treat us all to dinner and drinks, which essentially translated to a lot of cocktails. From the looks of the startled waitstaff, we were the biggest crowd they'd had in a while.

"It might take some time to prepare all the food," the headwaiter told us.

"Vamos a la playa," Rex responded, thumping his fist on the table. Cathy calmed him down by ordering a pitcher of piña coladas. The waiter moved together two long tables for us. Roberto sat next to the Guaymi, and I sat next to him. Rex sat on my other side, joined by the rest of the film crew. As people became more inebriated and started speaking louder and faster, shouting at me from all directions, I began to feel less like an interpreter than like some sort of human frontier between the Guaymi and Commandante Cathy's crew.

Finally I gave up trying to interpret altogether. When Rex leaned over and asked, "You're not a real interpreter, are you?" I simply said, "Hey, the documentary's over."

Perhaps the Guaymi had picked up some English during our stay, or maybe one of them had just said something funny. But either way, in that precise moment that I announced the conclusion of the documentary, a distinctive sound that needed no interpretation emerged from their end of the table. I don't know if anyone else noticed the small sound amid the chaos. But I noticed because it seemed the most appropriate ending I could imagine for this adventure. It was Eusebio. And he was clapping.

WHEN CUBANS BECOME VEGANS

TRINA TRUTHTELLA

IF YOU ever want to be treated like a celebrity, go to Cuba. When our tiny plane from Cancún landed on the island at two in the morning, more than two dozen children greeted us at the airport to celebrate our arrival with song, dance and cheers. With such a welcome, I didn't notice the filmy heat that clung to my bare skin until the children were long gone.

In summer 1997, I visited Cuba as part of the Venceremos Brigade, which travels every summer in defiance of the U.S. blockade and in support of the Cuban Revolution. Brigadistas collect and bring to the Cuban people basic necessities—toilet paper, aspirin, sanitary napkins. Things we take for granted but unavailable to them, thanks to our country's punitive policies toward theirs. For a week, brigadistas work side by side with Cubans, cutting sugar cane and building homes while dodging mosquitos. You know, the kind of stuff we find noble precisely because we don't have to do it every day. Then the following week, volunteers participate in whichever conference or festival is taking place, 'cause Cuba's always jumpin', jumpin'.

The trip was a pilgrimage for me, and like all pilgrims, I learned a lot, including much about myself. Some of it I liked, some I didn't. I learned a lot about what I called home and what I called utopia, some of it inspiring, some of it disturbing. But most important, I learned a lot about the people traveling with me, and well, you know, some of it I respected and some of it I didn't.

Our first week there, we stayed in a dormitory where we woke every day before dawn, showered with cold water, ate a small breakfast of eggs and bread and headed to a construction site. Even the roosters looked at each other as if to say, "What are these crazy *yanquis* trying to prove now?"

At the site we helped the Cubans who would eventually live there transport concrete blocks with nothing but our own hands and several rickety wheelbarrows. In the sticky Caribbean heat, we would break for a two-hour siesta of food and music, and then it was back to work. We put in long days in the hot sun, but headed back to the dorm for dinner long before our Cuban colleagues.

Now indulge me while I pause to say that me and my friends in the brigade? We were the bomb! As tough as it was, we got up every day and walked our talk. Not once did we bitch. Well, at least not in front of everybody.

Wish I could say that about everyone in the brigade. Unfortunately, there were a bunch of divas who just didn't get it. Whining about the food. Trying to get out of work. Why even go on a trip that's supposed to be about solidarity if you're not even going to try to check yourself?

Shit really didn't hit the fan though until we arrived in Havana, where each of us would stay with a Cuban family. In our old-fashioned school bus rambling down the one-lane road, I grew increasingly restless as the acres of plush fields gradually transformed into concrete streets lined with modest Spanish homes and Chevy Impalas from the fifties. Sure, I was proud to have put in my week-long stint of hard labor like a real trooper, but I was more thrilled to escape the crybabies who forgot that this wasn't some stop on a Carnival Cruise.

Our host families met us on the lawn of an elementary school. A woman came toward me with my name scrawled in marker across a piece of cardboard. One look at that frumpy housecoat and bad dye job and tears came to my eyes.

"Are you . . . Trina? What's wrong?"

"You look just like my mom," I blurted out before I threw my arms around her.

Her name was Gloria, and she and her husband Fausto treated me like a prodigal daughter come home. They sent their adult son to his common-law wife's home so that I could assume his bedroom in their small project apartment. And from what I'd heard from my friends who visited the island regularly, that's typical of the Cuban people. They have no quarrel with the people of the United States; it's our government that pisses them off. We don't take kindly to knuckleheads overseas telling us how we should live, and guess what? Neither do they.

So they doted on me—with a little help from the Cuban government, I soon learned. See, there was fresh meat and bottled water in Gloria's house precisely because I—the American guest—was there. Man, did that discovery mess me up. I was touched because what little these folks had they shared with me. But suspicious, too, because why should the Cuban government shell out these goods just because my yanqui behind was there? And guilty, because it probably wouldn't be an issue were it not for the U.S. blockade against Cuba.

It just so happened that another brigadista was staying with the family upstairs and couldn't have cared less. I'll call the sista Urbi (that's Egyptian for princess, hint, hint). Urbi was one of several siblings on the trip, the offspring of some no-joke movement legends. That said, you can probably guess that they were the most annoying of the bunch, trying to cash in on their parents' political legacy instead of building one of their own.

At the precious age of fifteen, Urbi was particularly priceless. See, she was a vegan. Anything that had ever had anything to do with any part of an animal, she wouldn't touch. Which woulda been aw'ight had she not been so damn righteous about it. Or if the girl had spoken Spanish, at least enough to explain her diet to her hostess. In my fractured Nuyoricanese, I tried to run interference for the kid.

"No le gusta comer nada que tiene qu'hacer con un animal," I said to *la doña. "Ni come chicle."*

Rough translation: "Yo, she won't even chew gum 'cause it comes from, like, pig guts and whatnot."

But all the lady of the house knew was that, after getting up to fry eggs for the girl's breakfast, Urbi would carve off the whites and push the yolk away in disgust. Eggs the government probably rationed to her just to accommodate her American guest. In other words, this family had next to nothing and what little they had, they offered to share with someone. Someone who wanted for very little in her home country. Someone who wrinkled her nose at their hospitality with no explanation.

Trust me, I know that when you purge something from your diet, eating it can actually make you sick. In no way did I think the girl shoulda put the Cuban health care system to the test (although I could write a whole other essay about just how much it actually rocks). While I felt she was being a little divaesque, I still felt a little bad for Urbi.

My compassion was amped by the opening march to the international festival. Thousands of people from all over the world marched to the University of Havana, wearing their national colors, chanting slogans in the their native tongues and waving banners championing their causes. For once, all the brigadistas felt unified, realizing again just what the hell we were doing in Cuba in the first place. We ran through the streets of Havana like a bunch of kids from the same block the day after school lets out for summer.

Well, that short-lived cameraderie was snuffed out when some of the brigadistas decided to unleash their inner Urbis full force at the most inappropriate time. Our itinerary was packed with visits to Cuban facilities and institutions. Schools, hospitals, farms, you name it—none of which have changed physically since the fifties. Although immaculate, they struck my modernized eyes as rustic, even antiquated, which to this day I am ashamed to confess that I equated momentarily with inferiority.

It's amazing what these folks have been able to accomplish under the stress our government has caused them. Who has heard of a nearly nonexistent infant mortality rate in a country where a child is guaranteed milk only until the age of seven? When you come from a country where one person can own two homes, three cars and a boat while thousands sleep in the street, it's humbling—even embarrassing—how much the Cuban people have achieved with so little.

So it really irked me when, during a Q&A after a tour of a biomedical facility, certain members of the brigade started dissin' 'em for animal testing.

"Yes, I have a question. The dogs and horses in the yard—do you use them for tests?" an animal rights activist directed to the tour guide for translation. She had an ill tone, already knowing the answer and having mad problems with it.

Poor scientist didn't know what the hell she was getting into. "Yes, we do."

"Well, why?'

"Because . . . " Sista was genuinely confused by the question, "we can't very well experiment on humans."

"But that doesn't mean you should experiment on animals. I mean, they have rights, too."

A few others put in their two cents, and before you knew it, things got tense. The scientist insisted that the animals were well taken care of and not put in any pain. I gotta give it up to her because she refused to allow these folks to shame her, and they came with a full-court press.

It's not like the Cubans were blinding cats to test mascara or to make some other crap we don't need. With the little resources they had, they were trying to make medical advances. Combat disease. Find cures. Save lives, goddammit.

At the same time, I wasn't cool with the hateful feelings I was developing toward some of my fellow brigadistas. Not that I was the only one who didn't care for the scene the vegans and animal rights folks made at the biomedical center. For the first time on the trip, my well-tempered, meet-people-where-they-are, conflict-is-healthy-when-processed-openly friends were pitching a fit on the bus trip home. Somebody said, "Don't they realize they're behaving like ugly Americans?"

"Talk about cultural imperialism," chimed another.

But I was particularly stank in that special way I can be. I said, "These PETA people would step over a homeless guy to feed scraps to a stray."

I instantly knew I had gone too far. Geez, I felt bad just *thinking* it. And not because I remembered how I hate it when people roll their eyes at me when I tell them I read tarot cards or practice aromatherapy. (Then again, I don't poo-poo anyone for not dabbling in my hobbies either, but later for that.) This trip wasn't about who drinks soy milk and burns sage, man. *It was supposed to be about solidarity!* I mean, the vegans and animal rights activists had the right to their lifestyle choices like anyone else, right?

Hell, there were probably Cubans who wished their circumstances allowed them to make the same choices. Not *la doña* upstairs from Gloria and Fausto though. Urbi had beaten me back home for dinner, and her hostess was seeking refuge on the front stoop with Gloria.

"Esa nena no come na'," she complained about Urbi's annoyingly birdlike appetite. You have to understand—picking at a meal in Latino culture is as rare as Mariah Carey belting out a power ballad without resorting to that irritating dog whistle.

I gave her a sympathetic grin. *"Que no come."*

Rough translation: "Let the bitch starve."

Okay, so my words were infinitely more diplomatic. But trust me, my tone was really, really clear. Gloria's neighbor laughed appreciatively. Ah, so exhilarating to find a home when you're far from home. Especially when you're butchering what's supposed to be your native tongue.

Eventually, the revelation hits: Not every lifestyle choice is a political conviction. A lifestyle choice is just that—a decision you make when you have *choices*. It's something that hinges entirely on your context. It derives its significance from the existence of alternatives. Being a vegan or an animal rights advocate in the United States is a lofty goal 'cause it ain't hard to say, look, I'm ordering a burger, buying a leather jacket and squashing bugs. It's much tougher to say, dammit, I'm going to eat tofu, wear hemp and shoo the roach out the window.

But veganism ain't an option for Cubans. And when the day comes that it is, it'll be long after they can enjoy other things. Now, we can argue about how free and happy Cubans truly are . . . after you've been there. But right now don't waste your time trying to convince me that eating pork is a critical issue for them when, thanks to the tactics of *our* legislators, cotton swabs are a luxury item.

Cuba's far from utopia, no doubt, but those folks do more to practice their political convictions than we do, that's for sure. Higher education is for everyone, not just those who can afford it. You get seriously ill in Cuba, and you go to the hospital and stay as long as you need to get well. Never does someone ask you for your insurance card. Homelessness is still rare in Cuba—more than a few folks sleep on the beach, but if you had flaxen sand, turquoise water and crystal heavens a short bike ride from your place, so would you.

A true political conviction should transcend time and culture. It shouldn't be something you have to be able to afford to do. And save the obvious—like the fact that there're no voting booths in the middle of rainforests—circumstances don't dictate whether or not you can express a political conviction.

So here's to the day when Cubans can become vegans. Maybe then I'll become one, too. Heck, in the world that allows that, we all should.

AWASH IN THE JUNGLE

KARI BODNARCHUK

I FIRST met Geri at a Javanese guesthouse, the week after I was nearly attacked by four Indonesian men posing as travel agents. The men had lured me into their "touristic office" in eastern Java—not a big challenge for them, given the 110-degree heat that day and my impending one-hour wait for a bus—and then offered me "insider" information on a popular hiking area nearby and a wildly overpriced ticket for one of their tours there.

When I refused the ticket, one man grew enraged. He began shoving me around, and then grabbed my shirt at the throat, crinkled it up in his hand and raised a fist as if he were going to punch me. His friends stood nearby, but none of them moved. I looked down at the angry man, who was several inches shorter than my five-foot-four frame, and shouted, "Watch it!" I don't know if it was my height or the colloquialism, but he instantly let me go and didn't even follow as I quickly left his office.

I was furious and frightened over the incident, yet determined to continue exploring Asia. After I met Geri and found out we were heading in the same direction—west through Java and then north through Singapore and Malaysia—we decided to stick together for safety.

We were the most mismatched of travel companions. Geri's an accountant from Ireland, who's up by 7 a.m. every day, goes to sleep by 10 p.m. and follows a steady routine in between. I'm a writer from New England, whose brain won't function before 10 a.m. and works best after 10 p.m., and I thrive on constant change. Geri is one of eight kids; I'm an only child. She hates the water; I love to scuba dive. She also prefers a slow, easy pace, while I thrive on pushing myself to the limit.

Despite our differences, Geri and I shared an interest in exploring, and we soon discovered that traveling in a pair opened up all sorts of doors: We felt more confident staying in strangers' homes, hitchhiking through Malaysia and trekking on our own through a jungle. Three weeks after meeting, we decided to do a nine-day hike through a Malaysian rainforest to climb the region's tallest mountain, Gunung Tahan. It was an eighty-five-mile trip, described by our guidebook as "the trek for the really adventurous," with elephants, tigers and spitting cobras. Adventurous we were; experienced we were not. Geri had spent time walking hills near her home in Ireland, but she'd never camped or taken any long-distance hikes. I'd camped dozens of times and covered quite a few trail miles, but my backcountry treks hadn't taken me far from paved roads. And all I'd ever encountered were cows, garter snakes and a feral turkey.

The Malaysian jungle would be different than the pine and maple forests of New England or the oak and birch woodland around Geri's home in Kilkenny. The jungle, we imagined, would be wilder, damper, muddier and more humid, with tangled vines, moss-covered trees and underbrush dripping with fungus and odd creatures. I figured I would be fine; Geri's only concern was maintaining her stamina for nine days.

Our hike to Gunung Tahan would take us through Taman Negara, a national park filled with palm trees, sandalwood, orchids and tualangs—some of the tallest trees in the world, measuring upwards of 250 feet. The park also contains deer, gibbons, geckos and birds, not to mention leeches, monitor lizards and forty-two thousand species of insects per hectare. It is home to Malaysia's Orang Asli, or "original people": nomadic hunter-gatherers who live off the land or trade jungle resources like sandalwood and rattan for rice, teakettles and tarps with local Malaysian businessmen. In exchange for other items the tribespeople wanted, like radios, flashlights and massive quantities of Energizer batteries, several Orang Asli men used to lead tours to Gunung Tahan for Malaysia's Department of Wildlife. (They no longer do so because the government is trying to move the tribes out of the jungle in order to "modernize and civilize" the country, according to several park rangers.)

The Malaysian government requires hikers to hire local guides to reach the mountain, due to the poorly marked route and tricky river crossings. But guides cost $250 per person, not including entrance fees and food, and Geri and I didn't want to blow our budgets. We figured we could make it on our own for forty dollars, tops. Since the monsoon rains were coming, it wasn't the best time to be in the jungle, but the region had only been experiencing short late-day showers so we weren't very concerned. It was also off-season, meaning we might be the only hikers along the trail. We talked to a few locals in Kuala Tahan, a small village at the start of the trek, at the southern end of Taman Negara: Saberi and CD, two friendly river guides in Taman Negara, and Ani, a thirty-year-old woman who was training to be a trail guide and had climbed Gunung Tahan three times. They had all grown up in Kuala Tahan, with the jungle as their backyard and playground. So when they told us we'd find our own way, no problem, that was all I needed to hear. This was an opportunity for adventure.

☠

We set off at eleven o'clock one morning from Kuala Tahan. Since we didn't want the rangers to know we weren't taking the mandatory guides, we slipped past the park headquarters office and made our way into the woods. We walked along a moderately level trail that proved easy enough to follow, despite the absence of blazes (trail markers) and other hikers. Taman Negara is the world's oldest and, in sections, densest rainforest. As we walked farther, large sections of the trail became covered in brush.

We had full camping gear and food for ten days, plus the only map we could find, a locally produced, hand-drawn, not-to-scale "artistic rendering," which was photocopied and given to backpackers like us—for free—by the manager of our guesthouse. It measured six by nine inches and contained sketches of hikers who appeared as tall as the mountains, and exotic-looking birds and butterflies three to four times larger than the hikers. The top of our mini map read, "An Unforgetable Vagation that is Close to Nature: Taman Negara." The most distinct element on it was a dark, thick line that cut straight up the middle of the picture—Sungai Tahan, a mountain-fed, green-hued river measuring about seventy-five feet wide (though it can double in size during the monsoons).

According to our plan, we would spend the first two days of the trip wending our way through the thick forest, then another two days walking alongside, crossing over and, where possible, fording the river. After that, it was anybody's guess—our map simply depicted a black line (the river), a triangle (the mountain) and an extraordinarily tall hiker leaping up the left side of the triangle in a single bound.

Geri and I took our time hiking that first day, stopping often to look at the unusual vegetation. One bush radiated fifteen-foot stems topped with leaves the size of doorways. Massive fig trees stood so wide it would take twelve people with outstretched arms to fit around each one. Others had twenty-foot-high buttresses that resembled fins on a rocket ship.

The first night, we pitched our tent in the middle of a steep, slanting trail, unable to find a clearly marked campsite. After a quick dinner of noodle soup, we rolled into the tent and used bags and bug nets to create level sleeping surfaces. We had accidentally left the tent unzipped during dinner, and as I lay in bed, I could hear dozens of jungle ants scuttling around inside our nylon dome. Jungle ants are big enough to leave footprints along dirt trails and an inflamed lump where they bite you. They are not something you want to sleep with. After evicting the last one around midnight, my makeshift bedding shifted underneath me, and I fell asleep in a ditch, sandwiched between two rocks, a root running up my spine.

Twenty minutes into our hike the next day, we found a campsite located in a flat, dirt-packed clearing next to a stream, where we bathed and topped up our water bottles. Then we set off for a grueling hike across twenty-seven hilltops on a ridge called Bukit Malang, or "Unlucky Hill." We were still having trouble deciphering our map, and it grew dark again before we found the next campsite. This time we pitched our tent beside the trail, on top of leaves, roots and moss-covered branches, and I lay in bed listening to a chorus of jungle sounds—cicadas buzzing, birds squawking and strange, unidentifiable chewing noises. I wished we were closer to the river. There is something very eerie about being deep in the woods, in an unfamiliar forest, with big animals and a bad map. I have always found being near or having access to water reassuring—not only to keep hydrated and clean, but also for the sense of space it provides and the sense, however false, of having an escape route from the forest. I barely slept that night, especially after hearing two dead trees tumble over nearby.

"We really need to scope out our campsites better before pitching tent," I said to Geri the next morning.

The sights along the way made up for some of the discomfort. We trekked through brilliant, sunlit forests with aqua-colored palm trees, bamboo stands and wait-a-whiles (long, prickly vines that look like whips covered in thorns—if you get snagged by one, you're supposed to "wait a while" and take your time unhooking yourself). We didn't see any elephants, tigers or spitting cobras—just as well, since we didn't have a defense plan figured out anyway—but we did spot a three-horned frog, a brown snake and a wild boar.

The end of day three took us through dense jungle and along a hillside where the narrow, steep path was slippery from wet roots and yellow, clay soil. Leeches were plentiful, so we had to do regular "leech checks" as we walked to see if they had planted their suckers into our legs. As the path wound down along the river's edge, walking grew more challenging. Leaves, fallen trees and big branches littered the trail, but it never occurred to us why there was so much forest debris along the embankment. Geri and I fought our way through the brush until we could eventually walk along a section of dry, rocky riverbed. When we stopped for water around four o'clock, I watched Geri slump onto a rock and fade.

"This is the closest I've come to hell," she declared, once she'd mustered the energy to talk. If she had known what lay ahead when we set out, she never would have followed me thirty miles into the jungle.

Geri sat hunched over on the rock, with her shoulders resting on her knees and a stream of sweat trailing down her face. Maybe her time as a bank accountant in Australia had softened her a bit. I had been traveling around the world for twelve months, lugging sixty pounds of essential travel items (don't ask what), so I had an advantage. I also had boundless energy that day and felt like I could walk at least another five miles.

"You're a wuss, Ger," I thought. But to Geri I said, "You know, this is a good place to stop. Let's get some rest. I'm sure we'll feel better tomorrow."

I brought Geri the stove, a pot and four packages of curry noodle soup, and she stirred dinner while I pitched the tent. We were now thirty miles upstream on the banks of the Sungai Tahan, which was about seventy-five feet wide here and flanked by thick jungle bush. The trees lining the river seemed almost desperate for space and grew at sharp angles, dangling out over the water. Thick brush, vines and other less fortunate trees hung in their shadows and created a wall of plant matter so dense we couldn't see into the woods beyond them. It was a calm, idyllic setting, though, and appeared to be the perfect place to camp.

With a steep, brushy slope on one side of us and ten feet of rocky riverbed on the other, there was just one spot to put the tent—in a manmade clearing at the foot of the hill, about thirty feet from the water's edge.

A late-day shower hit as dinner was served, so we ate in the tent, leaving the dirty dishes outside for morning (in retrospect, not a good idea, but luckily they didn't attract any animals). Geri collapsed from exhaustion while I fumbled with my journal, trying to record the day's events before light disappeared. Our "long-lasting" flashlight batteries had died the first night in the jungle, so we were forced to bed at sundown, 7 p.m. Geri can fall asleep before the stars are fully awake. I can't go to bed before midnight, regardless of how tired I am, which is why I took two sleeping pills around seven o'clock and then drifted right off to sleep. It seemed only minutes later when I heard a distant voice.

"Hey! Wake up!" *Blah, blah. Swish.* I fused these sounds into my dream. *Shhhh* . . . "Kari!" . . . *Shhhhh.* Was I dreaming of a waterfall? "Look!" *Blah, blah.* Of someone beckoning me to come see, as frothy water plunged over an embankment into a crystal-clear pool?

Cashoosh. Or maybe a flushing toilet?

"Get up! Get up! It's coming in here!" Geri now yelled into my ear, trying to snap me awake.

"What?" I asked, which was the only word I could form with my sleepy tongue.

"I said, it's coming in here! The river," Geri insisted.

"Oh, Ger. That's not the river," I said, as water gushed through the bug-net door and slapped against my sleeping bag. "We're too far away from the river," I thought to myself. "It can't be the river."

I lay in a dreamy haze, refusing to believe what was happening, but then, *swooshhhh*—another wave hit and my survival instinct kicked in. "My god, it's the river," I suddenly realized. I threw on my rain pants and jacket and scrambled to the door.

"C'mon. C'mon," I muttered, jerking and tugging at the rusty zipper. "C'mon. It won't open!" I yelled. Geri rustled around for a knife to slash our way out, but the zipper finally came unstuck. I yanked open the door and we lunged outside, like birds spooked from their nest. The river, once calm and soothing, was now a thundering torrent, carrying prickly vines, palm trees and logs as big as telephone poles toward us.

"Quick, Ger. Get the boots! We have to find the boots," I shouted over the rumbling floodwater.

Several short, scraggly bushes kept the debris from hitting us while we scrambled to find the smelly boots and dirty dishes we'd left outside under the rain flap for the night. Faint moonlight filtered through the trees, but our eyes hadn't adjusted enough to see. Frantically, we combed the water with our hands.

"I found one!" yelled Geri, chucking a boot onto the hill.

"Great! Just three more," I called back, still searching.

But within thirty seconds, the water rose from our ankles to our knees, and the current made it nearly impossible to stand. We had to escape. I threw on my backpack, ripped the tent out of the ground and ran—tent pegs, dishes and boots still floating somewhere behind us.

Barefoot and hunched over, we clawed our way up the steep, muddy slope behind our campsite. The igloo-shaped rental tent I dragged behind me was still set up, and I could hear poles snapping as I forced it between trees. When I looked back, Geri was about fifteen feet away, grasping for branches to pull herself up and struggling to see without her glasses.

"Whatever you do, don't fall," I yelled. She didn't know how to swim. And, truthfully, I didn't want to have to save her. With my luck, we'd both get swept away.

After Geri made it up the hill, we sat in the mud, staring down at the angry river.

"Good Lord!" she said. "Do you think we'll ever make it back?"

"Not a chance," I snapped. "We've trekked thirty miles into a jungle without a guide, we never registered or bought permits to enter the park, no one knows we're here and the path is long gone." I didn't know yet that our photocopied map was also completely soaked and illegible.

I fought to swallow the lump welling in my throat—a combination of tears, vomit and desperation—and hugged my knees so they'd stop shaking. Geri didn't reply. We sat in silence for a while, until I eventually gathered my courage and said, "We'll make it, but it won't be easy—especially without boots."

Along with our camp stove, dishes and tent pegs, three boots had washed away. We passed the one surviving boot back and forth, taking turns feeling and smelling it. It was definitely mine, we agreed. Then we curled up on top of the collapsed tent and wrapped ourselves in emergency blankets. Geri was understandably terrified of the rising floodwaters and had wet her pants while scrambling up the hill. The sharp smell of urine added to the brew of jungle odors. It was going to be a long night. The sky was now perfectly clear, moonlight dancing across the whitewater below and water dripping from the trees overhead, making a crackling sound as it hit our aluminum blankets. Chilled and exhausted, I hoped the sleeping pills were still in my system. Something, sleeping pills or shock, finally knocked me out, and I slept seven solid hours on a wet tent with my feet in the mud.

The next morning, the sun shone brightly in the clear blue sky, and the river, although brown with sediment, had partially receded. We slid down the mucky, chewed-up slope to survey the damage and do a full inventory of our gear. Amazingly, I found my metal cooking pot about ten feet from where our tent had stood. It was sitting upright, in between the exposed roots of a tree, half filled with sand and topped off with water. Without that pot, we'd have had to chew on dry rice and dehydrated soup for three days. The stove was gone, but we had fuel tablets and could easily make our own cooking platform.

As it turned out, the surviving boot wasn't mine. My $190 Garmonts were somewhere downriver. "That's that, so get over it," I told myself. But I watched with envy as Geri laced up her left boot, then put a thick, red sock on her other foot. Unlike Geri, who'd bought new clothes for the hike (this being her first big trekking adventure), I was wearing stuff I'd had for months. None of it was pretty, and most of it was just barely functional. I glanced down at my threadbare socks and then twisted them around until their holes peered up at me. We slathered our feet with salt to keep the leeches at bay, and then, after one more fruitless search for my boots, began our three-day, thirty-mile jungle trek back to safety—in four socks and one boot.

I enjoy walking barefoot—around swimming pools, on beaches or across soft grassy lawns. Otherwise, I am a footwear type of person. I wear sandals when I kayak in case I have to step on slimy rocks, and I don't touch bottom when I swim in murky ponds. Normally, I wouldn't dream of walking more than a few feet from a campsite without shoes. I was truly dreading the idea of hiking through a leech-ridden jungle, even with socks.

Although the river had receded somewhat, we were no longer able to cut across the riverbed as we had the day before in order to avoid the densely overgrown patches of trail along the embankment. Instead, we had to clamber over downed trees and piles of debris deposited at bends in the river by the flood (so *that's* how they got there). It took a while to climb over these four-foot-high mounds of tangled brush or scramble through thick vegetation to skirt them, yet we always managed to get back on track.

The path eventually led away from the river, along narrow, slippery ledges that hadn't seemed as treacherous with boots. One ledge was only wide enough for our feet; we had to shuffle along its slick surface with our backpacks protruding over the ledge. I lost my footing just as I cleared this section and fell sideways down a steep slope, saved from dropping any further by a thin tree.

At first, the biggest drawback to not having boots was that whenever I walked—especially uphill—my muddy socks crept down until about two inches of stretched-out, wet sock material flapped off the tips of my toes. That's when my mini bungee cords came in handy. They were also useful for keeping my socks in place during river-crossings. Overall, walking in socks wasn't as bad as I had expected, as long as we took our time and watched every step. And, at least the first day, the clay and dirt ground typically cushioned our steps. So we continued on our way, slipping, clutching branches, concentrating hard and stepping gingerly through the forest.

We eventually arrived at a campsite, which, judging by its corrugated surface and the washed-up trees, appeared to have flooded the night before as well. Geri and I prepared dinner and then pitched our tent in the highest spot we could possibly find—about thirty feet above the river—just before the sun disappeared and the thunder began. No rain fell that night, but we planned our escape routes and slept fully clothed on the hard ground inside the tent—just as a precaution.

The next day, the path led us deeper into the woods, where the trail was covered in roots and sharp stones. Dragging one's feet when tired is not an option when walking barefoot, especially on steep terrain; the rocks and thorny vines underfoot brought tears to my eyes, and I stubbed my toes—hard and painfully—several times. Just an hour into the hike, a huge splinter lodged itself into the soft cushion of my left heel. It was in too deep to dig out along the trail, so I spent the next four hours walking on the toes of that foot.

Geri's hurdle that day was getting over the twenty-seven hilltops again. She almost made it, but then collapsed on top of number twenty-six and lay motionless for half an hour. When she finally sat up, she vented her frustrations. She had taken a break from accounting work and set out to travel, she said, hoping to have a few adventures along the way. Now, she said in tears, she didn't think she could handle it.

"Ger, I can assure you this is not a typical adventure," I told her.

We spent the rest of that day in a worn-out stupor, sliding around the muddy track and tripping over fallen trees. Despite having the security of the one boot, Geri spent a good portion of the final hill on all fours. Finally, we slipped and tiptoed our way into the next campsite—another dirt clearing next to a small stream—where we would spend our last night. While I dug the splinter out of my foot, Geri repatched the tent poles and set up our oddly shaped "dome" on top of giant fern branches for added comfort. Then I realized I had gotten my period—two weeks early and totally unprepared—from the shock of the whole experience. I discovered this, of course, right after washing all my clothes in the stream.

Just as it was my turn to eat (we had only one spoon between us), it started to rain, so we dashed into the leaky tent and watched a puddle form in the middle of the floor. The downpour lasted only about an hour before the moon and stars came out, shining brightly on that calm night. Then we discovered how the whole flash-flood process worked. About an hour after the rain, we heard a distant rumbling grow louder and louder as floodwater came rushing toward us from upstream. It roared past us, driving up the stream's water level within seconds. Under the moonlight, we could see whitewater bubbling over the top of the embankment, but much to our relief, it never reached the tent.

The last day, with feet as swollen as sausages and numb to any pain, we hiked through a level, muddy forest where the leeches seemed much more prevalent and aggressive. Geri and I had different tactics for leech removal. I shrieked, cringed and then quickly flicked them off my legs. Geri, for some unknown reason, was a more appealing target, and therefore had developed a more mellow approach. She would sit down on a rock or tree stump and quietly talk to herself as she used matches to burn the wormy creatures off her calves.

That final afternoon, we collected more cuts, scrapes, bruises and blood-suckers, up and down both legs—good conversation pieces, we agreed—yet our spirits remained high. Just several miles from the trail's end, we came upon a foot-deep marshy area that could be crossed in one of two ways: by walking along a downed log that connected one embankment to the other, or by shinnying, hand over hand, along a rope tied to a tree on each side of the mucky bog. Geri chose the log. Given our experiences along this trail, and my sense of adventure that sometimes exceeds my luck, I should have known better. But since we were nearly finished with our trek, I was beginning to feel more daring again. With my pack on my back, I reached out and grabbed the rope with both hands, leapt up and swung my feet around the rope and, in an instant, plunged into the mud pool. I lay in the mud, back-side down, like a flipped turtle, and Geri and I laughed harder than we had all week. Two hours later, we made it back to park headquarters, filthy and temporarily scarred, but otherwise just fine. Recently, we've even talked about attempting the trip again, on a shoestring budget, with walking permits and two pairs of boots each . . . and water wings.

FÊTE DU MOUTON

RACHEL BERKOFF

THE FIRST clues came several hours after my arrival in Morocco, but I wasn't sharp enough to pick up on them. But given what was to come later, perhaps it would have been a shocker if I had.

The guy sitting next to me on the bus from Tangier to Meknes didn't speak French very well. Neither did I, but as it was our only common language, we butchered our way through a conversation. I asked him if there would be any holidays the month I was traveling; I pointed to the guidebook, which indicated that the Islamic New Year happened shortly after my departure. "Must be pretty cool," I said. "What happens?"

He began gesturing wildly. I gathered, from his animated expression and the few words I could pick up—*"mouton,"* for example—that on the New Year there was a big happy parade with cars in the street, and something about lambs. Sounded neat. I shrugged. Too bad I was going to miss it.

Little did I know that a week later I'd walk to the bus station in Fez at 5 a.m. to ensure that someone, anyone, would sell me a ticket out of town that day—preferably to somewhere calming. The events of the day before would be enough to guarantee that I could never see Fez again and still die a perfectly happy woman. Some travel memories simply shouldn't be relived in pictures (though, dammit, I did have the pictures, lest my friends even think of not believing me. . .).

Abdullah, the guy working the hostel in Fez, had prepared me a little bit, sort of, explaining that this thing the bus guy had described wasn't related to the New Year at all. The big Fête du Mouton—a mutton festival—was to occur the day after my arrival. Abdullah said that it was a family holiday commemorating the salvation of Ishmael. As the story goes, God tested Abraham's faith by asking him to sacrifice his son—Isaac, according to Jewish literature, and Ishmael, according to the Islamic books. At the last moment, God gave Abraham a ram to slaughter instead. It's basically a Divine psych-out. As I understood it from Abdullah, folks celebrated by praying and eating lots of lamb. As a Jew, I could absolutely respect this: A sacred event? Let's chow!

The next morning, I wandered up to the famous Fez medina, expecting things to be quiet. The big *souk* (bazaar) was usually packed with people buying and selling tomatoes, herbal remedies, Berber jewelry, imitation Nike shoes, Moroccan pastries, ceramics, hardware, umbrellas, caftans and the like, hawking and bartering fiercely in Arabic with a few French words thrown in for flavor. I figured that it would be pretty much closed down, since everybody would be home with their families, stuffing their faces with lamb tagine.

The first thing I saw was a bunch of kids standing around a huge fire in the middle of the narrow street. As I walked closer, I realized that the blaze might be a little bit more significant than just delinquents' fun.

In the street lay an old bedspring with a ram's head on it. Just sitting there, burning.

The scene resembled something out of a horror movie—Carrie buys a Lonely Planet guidebook. Yet everyone else seemed to feel that the burning, smoking item was perfectly normal, just needed a little tending now and again, a poke with a stick. After staring limply for a minute or two, the smell of burning flesh and my sense that I was not invited to this party propelled me along.

But as I walked down the narrow, cobbled path of the medina, I saw another small bonfire—this ram still had its horns. And then another, and then another. Ignited lambs' heads were everywhere. Suddenly, Abdullah's story and the weird bleating noise my friend on the bus had been making came rushing back, in full Technicolor. I began to have one of those moments like when the light bulb goes on over Dagwood's head or Sylvester gets hit with a cartoon hammer: Oh.

Right. Okay.

What happened is this: Tout la Fez (and probably tout la Morocco) had bought a live sheep the previous day, and slit its throat that morning. Or that afternoon—over the course of the day I saw a number of pathetic, bleating beasts being dragged out for execution. Mary's little lambs were really kind of gross and dirty—not nearly as cute as the ones on baby clothes and Easter cards—but I still felt sorry for them. The poor creatures were at the mercy of crowds of Moroccan guys ready to fête. I saw more than one run in circles around the residential parts of the medina, seemingly aware of their grim fate.

Fête du Mouton is also called "Feast of the Sacrifice," which not only refers to the Ishmael/Isaac story, but is played out for real in the medina— again, and again, and again. After the initial adjustment, I decided that the burning ram's heads weren't so bad—they were kind of intriguing, really. Even the blood pouring through the streets and the tough, red-splattered guys walking around with knives was okay for queasy, wimpy little me; it seemed surreal—or maybe just honest.

But as time passed, I found it less and less amusing to be in the midst of this scene. By midafternoon folks began to bring out the entrails. As a girl who used to close her eyes during the "graphic" parts of *M*A*S*H,* seeing the guy to my left cart around a large handful of lower intestine was not easy. Ditto went for skinning the carcasses. Evidently folks made use of every part of their woolly offering, which on one hand was kind of respectful and reassuring—Lambchop's death was not in vain—and on the other made for a whole lot of gore. By the end of the day, corners of the medina were piled high with ram's horns. I couldn't help but think of the Jewish New Year, where we used horns as musical instruments—though I didn't really want to blow in these ones. I had seen them on their original owners.

There was a certain anxious frenzy in the air, a fervor that extended beyond mutton-cutting duties to the way people talked with each other, moved through the labyrinthian curves of the medina, even the way they went to pray. A Swiss girl I met observed, "All year they issue the call to prayer five times every day, and nobody even bothers to move. But have a holiday where you chop up a ram, and suddenly everybody's Muslim." Another shining moment of cultural unity: Folks in Morocco are just as inconsistent about religion as Americans who barely make it to midnight Mass or the Passover seder. And she was right: The mosques *were* hopping.

And so were the eager young men; the fervor that seemed to possess one and all on Fête du Mouton didn't stop short of interactions with Westerners, especially of the female variety. I had grown to expect said interactions; that is, since my arrival in Morocco, I learned to understand the words "street harassment" in a host of new ways. Everywhere I went, a trail of guys—ranging in age from about nine to sixty-five—followed in my shadow, catcalling, trying to make conversation, inviting me home.

"Bonjour, ma gazelle! Ca va, ma gazelle? Where are you from? France? Italy? England? What do you like? I will show you nice Moroccan food, come to my house and we eat couscous. Why do you not answer? Hello? Ma gazelle, where are you from? [Now perhaps, a touch on the shoulder.] Where are you from?"

Refusal to answer yields more questions. Short, clipped answers yield more questions. If you're walking, you will be followed. If you're sitting, you will be joined. If you're sitting and then you start walking, you will be chaperoned. If you're looking at shoes in the marketplace, the young man at the first stall will follow you to all of the other stalls in the bazaar until you find a pair that you like. Probably he will be joined by an ever-increasing pack of friends. If there's a middle-aged guy following you from the bus stop and you duck into a store, he'll wait for you until you come out, even if you've told him to bugger off in every language you know. If you're tired, you'll be followed to your hostel. If you're in a good mood, you'll be followed around the museum. It's like being the pied piper, except you're never told the nature of the flute you're playing, or trying not to play.

I thought I had seen it all, but the boys were particularly randy on sacrifice day. They acted the way antsy teenagers do at midevening on Thanksgiving, when they're bored and fidgety and there's nothing much to do so they go out to make trouble. In Fez, rather than getting drunk behind the garage with the cousins, these kids—probably on a strange, sensual high incomprehensible to one who has never cut up a live sheep with her bare hands—decided to chat up the tourist girls.

I had to hide in an old Koranic school to escape one would-be suitor, and employ the largest French man I've ever seen to scare off another. Neither tactic worked for long. There were others. It was the first time I'd ever been propositioned by a boy with a bleeding, dripping ram's head in his hand.

It was March 17. I had to process. I emailed my friends: "While you're all buying bagels and beer turned some ungodly shade of green, I've been partaking of the last great animal sacrifice of the monotheistic tradition."

At the time, I wondered—and continue to wonder—if I had (and have) the right to write about my experiences as a hapless character in the Fez medina.

My unfamiliarity with Islamic rituals and theology aside, there's also the question of outsider representation. When I returned to the States, I didn't tell many people about my day of ritual slaughter; Islam gets a bad enough rap in the world, and I felt horrible knowing the story could easily slide into a misrepresentation of Moroccans as crazy savages. But as unsettling as it was to navigate the thickets of sacrificial carnivorousness, I've felt at least as uncomfortable at a frat party—and probably my safety was more at risk at the Alpha Alpha Alpha Orgy-Bowl Blowout. How could I tell this story to Westerners when we have such an overinflated sense of ourselves as civilized, despite the evidence offered by Jerry Springer, Olestra and the world's biggest gap between rich and poor?

Despite the country's profusion of adolescent-boy behavior, many of the Moroccans I met were a hell of a lot more "civilized" than the selfish, boorish, inhospitable, money-obsessed Americans I know. These people literally offered me the clothing off their back, the food in their homes, their time and their trust, just because they believed in the good in people.

And holidays are funny, complicated things the world over. What they represent and how they work in real life are often very different things. I don't know many Christians who meditate on the birth of their Savior on December 25. Ask a priest what the holiday's about and you'll get a very different answer than from the kid who tells you about the tree, Santa, going caroling and, yes, *the presents*. Who's right?

Knowing that the day of sacrifice I witnessed is actually called Eid al-Adha and marks the end of the *Hajj,* or pilgrimage month, knowing that families eat about a third of the meal and donate the rest to the poor, that each region, country and culture understands the holiday a different way, that there are variations in the animals sacrificed . . . yes, it helps. Knowing that the animals are slaughtered in a particularly humane way, that the holiday is seen as a time when people ask forgiveness of those around them—

knowing more about what the festival is really about—yeah, it helps. It gives a little bit of context to the experience, helps me understand exactly why what seemed so jarring to my eyes is actually a very deliberate ritual, imbued with layers of psychological, spiritual, sociological, theological, physical and historical meaning. Like any religious ritual that stands the test of time, la Fête du Mouton has a logic both on a lofty intellectual scale and in an intuitive way to the regular folks who celebrate it.

And I gotta say, as a religion geek who actually reads books like *Ritual Theory, Ritual Practice,* and as an observant Jew making a lifelong endeavor out of learning her own religious tradition, it was strangely liberating to be the clueless girl in Fez, to just soak up other people's religious activity with little context. Like the child of atheist hippies who only half-understands the Sunday-school version of Easter but can tell you all about hunting for colored eggs, I experienced ritual—in all of its bloody truth, with all of its nasty, mortal consequence—as an outsider, seeing just the action itself.

Back in Morocco, I wrote to my friends: "I can't imagine what it would be to kill and dismember an animal as part of your annual celebration. When the Jews sacrificed animals, the priests did all the dirty work, and even they had to do elaborate purification rites to prepare for it. Actually, today I don't feel so bad that the Second Temple got destroyed."

For one-thousand-plus years, the Israelites worshipped their God by offering bulls, goats, lambs and birds much more often than once a year. Like the way we offer prayers now, it was the primary means of communication with the Divine. Become ritually impure? Offer a bird. Need to expiate sin? Offer a goat. And so forth. I can't even imagine the smell surrounding the Temple, back in the day.

But seriously, I'd be lying if I said I didn't understand, at least in part, what they did in ancient Jerusalem, what they did in Fez, what people do in a million different places where sacrifice and God occupy the same space:

We take life, that we may live. Almost every major religious tradition is obsessed with surrogate death, with our mortality, with life's precious yet elusive meaning in the world. It's not about a careless disregard for the sanctity of life; it's about the understanding that life itself is the most sacred thing we may ever know. And to sacrifice an animal is to exert the most profound power possible—to play God.

And in many ways—as jarring as my Fête du Mouton was, as much as the holiday redoubled my commitment to vegetarianism (thank God for vegetable couscous), and though I may never see a sheepskin coat the same way again—despite it all, I think I'm grateful to have witnessed an honest sacrifice for once in my life. It doesn't come often, these days; the best Jews have nowadays is a metaphoric use of bread-as-offering and hearing sumptuous lines from Leviticus like "And he shall lay his hand upon the head of his offering and kill it . . . and Aaron's sons the priests shall throw the blood against the altar round about" while sitting in synagogue on Saturday mornings dressed in elegant, flowered dresses and smartly tailored suits, wondering vaguely if the rabbi's sermon will end in time to go home and see the second half of the ball game.

But then again, it's true that we Jews have cornered the market on the ultimate in passive-aggressive, backhanded sacrifice: the kvetching of our long-suffering, guilt-enabling Jewish mothers who tell us constantly that they sacrificed everything, everything, just for us. Which, when it comes down to it, doesn't hold a candle to the death and dismemberment of a lamb—the lamb gets off way easier. At least they slit its throat, first.

LOUSY DIRECTIONS

LAURA CARLSMITH

THE TRIP was a parting gift from my newly minted ex-husband. During our amicable split, he suggested I get half of the bazillion frequent-flier miles he had accumulated flying all over the continent while I had stayed at home with two small children, making trips to the local McDonald's Playland. And, because of his advanced degree in mileage redemption negotiations, he even volunteered to make travel arrangements for me. His only request was that I use the miles up fast, rather than parceling them out, trip by trip of middling distances. That seemed reasonable, as we were trying to wash our hands of each other, albeit in the most civilized of ways.

So that's how I ended up in United first class, bound for Rome, lifting a toast to Ex-Husband and his many good qualities. With work, kids, getting divorced and all, I hadn't had much time to plan this trip. All I'd done was rent some Italian language tapes and decide to wander around Rome for two weeks. Life was too hectic, with too many schedules, appointments and expectations. I spent too much time in my car, just one of the legion of young mothers speeding grimly to their child's next soccer practice or art lesson.

For two weeks, I wanted only to sit in parks and watch Italian parents take care of Italian children. I had no agenda, no urgency to see any walled cities or works of art and no reservations, anywhere. I would melt into whatever Italian scene I found myself in. It was the trip I should've taken when I was twenty-three. By the time we flew over Greenland, I had forgotten that I was just another late-thirties American woman emerging from her own private state of angst.

On the plane, reclining in my ergonomically pleasing widebutt seat, feeling its little mechanical knuckles kneading the small of my back and contemplating the complexity of the wine in a way I never do at home, I wondered why I had always felt so sorry for Ex-Husband when he'd get up at 4:30 a.m. to catch the 6:00 a.m. flight to San Francisco. I had thought I was the lucky one, getting to sleep in and spend the day and the next and the next . . . with a couple of toddlers. Through my little in-flight window I saw a new world that didn't have "mommy" written all over it. It didn't have anything written on it.

I couldn't wait to turn myself into an Italian. Short, feminine dresses and strappy leather sandals in the backpack. No cargo shorts bulging with cameras and snacks, no hyper-white Nikes or high-dollar, travel-specific outerwear to betray me as an American. I wasn't even packing deodorant. I had practiced phrases like *"Vorrei un' acqua minerale"* and *"Dov'è la stazione dei treni?"* and I knew my accent was good, although a strict interpretation would probably find it incredibly exaggerated. Without my normal accoutrements, I would be undercover. My motherhood, my country of origin and my marital status would be anyone's guess. Freedom was in the possibilities.

All through the flight, down the runway, into the Frankfurt terminal and on the subway to the train station, I was on an independence high. Then, there in the impeccable train station—the *Hauptbahnhof*—where every train left on time, it hit me: I was in Frankfurt. Not Italy. Not yet.

There was no one here to ask, *"Dov'è il duomo?"* Of course, it couldn't be helped—sometimes Mileage Plus can't get you exactly where you want to go. I knew that, because of course I'd *read* my own itinerary. It's just that I hadn't *internalized* it. A classic case of avoidance. I had been all psyched to be in the moment, but not this moment. Not in this country.

Here I was, ready to be an Italian at six o'clock on a German Saturday morning, and the train to Rome wouldn't leave until five that afternoon. What to do? It took only an hour to explore and exhaust the charms of the train station. Seven o'clock. Still too early to start drinking. All I really wanted to do was sleep. In Italy. I willed myself into reconnoiter mode; backpack stowed, I started walking. Adventure comes to those who walk.

As I emerged from the dark train station on that early summer Saturday, Frankfurt looked like a foreign film set before the actors take their places: fresh, clean, sunny and soulless. I picked up a street map from a hotel and tried not to look too obvious as I oriented it and myself in the forest of stolid stone walls. The occasional car speeding on the empty streets was filled with people laughing and lifting their morning cappuccinos. Probably off for a sunny holiday in the Alps, where they'd pick wild strawberries and exercise their healthy German lungs with irrepressible Wagnerian exuberance. Those zooming Volvos made me feel, with my lame little unfashionable purple daypack borrowed from my six-year-old, like an alien from Planet Awkward American Tourist.

Fatigue and interior whining were making inroads. I felt melodramatically alone. All the sternness I'd read of the German character seemed embodied in this city. Teutonic buildings marched in shoulder-to-shoulder solidarity to the brink of the sidewalk and stopped there, leaving no courtyards or alleyways for a hungry tourist to peek into. Even the coffee shops were shuttered.

After fifteen minutes or so, I stopped my aimless walking to rest and window-shop at a dress store for plus sizes. There I met my first German. Except he wasn't a *German* German. They were all either still asleep under their eiderdown comforters or, like the smiling Valkyries in their Volvos, heading off somewhere to build their characters. No. My German was an immigrant, a maintenance worker from Iran, sweeping out the invisible German dirt from the store entrance. "Good morning," I said in English, forgetting immediately, in my first foreign encounter, to disguise myself. He smiled and said, "Good morning," in perfect English, and motioned me away with a smile. "These clothes are too grande for you." Omigod. An Iranian person casually mixing English and French on a German street. It didn't get any better than this.

"Where is everybody?" I asked, somehow forgetting that it was only 7 a.m. on a Saturday and even the Germans have to rest from their strenuous reunification efforts. But he and I were on the same page, and he nodded glumly. "These Germans do not know how to have fun. Work, work, all the time." Really, we were both being a little unfair, but it was fun to commiserate together.

Yes, he acknowledged, there wasn't much happening right then, but he did have a recommendation, the *floh markt:* "That is where I am going after work."

"Markt" was clear enough. But "floh"? I'd spent three months listening to Italian tapes and pasting Italian words on every inanimate and nonperishable object in my house. I even knew how to say "tampon" in Italian. All I knew of German was *"Jawohl, mein Kommandant!"* and *"Auf Wiedersehen!"* from *Hogan's Heroes* and *The Lawrence Welk Show,* respectively.

"What is a 'floh'?" I asked.

My new best friend thought a minute over how to respond in English, and then explained, "You know the little bugs you get if you don't wash?"

As a veteran public school parent, I immediately made the connection. "Lice?" I guessed, with an instinctive head scratch for emphasis.

"Yes, yes!" he exclaimed, whacking his broom on the ground, evidently pleased with his trilingual success.

I wanted to tell him that, while I knew of people whose kids had gotten lice, of course, *my* kids had never been so afflicted. But that seemed to be irrelevant bragging, so I left off the disclaimer.

He gave me detailed directions to the floh markt, shook my hand firmly and wished me a good day. He would see me there, he called out confidently as I strolled off. His multicultural friendliness and having a destination cheered me, and I pondered this first bit of foreign culture. A lice market. What exactly would it be like? He seemed enthused about it. Foreign travel was so intriguing! My mood soared.

I didn't question the presence of a lice market in this spanking clean city, and I didn't hesitate to go there and investigate it myself. I was on vacation, by gum, and if a lice market was to be my first adventure, I was ready for it! Anyway, I figured the lice part was just a metaphor, like having butterflies in your stomach. Germans and lice don't seem to mix. My mother is of German descent, and I knew her opinion on the subject. A lice market must be some kind of charming, sly German joke.

I zigzagged from block to block for almost an hour, admiring the architecture of Frankfurt's many glass skyscrapers. Despite my eagerness to embrace any kind of European antiquity, I was impressed by the good modern design.

It was now after eight o'clock. Because I'd only listened to the first two sentences of the Iranian's multiparagraphed directions, it was clear that I'd long since been wandering aimlessly, and that my friend's confidence in seeing me at the floh markt had been sadly misplaced.

I gave up and lay down on a bench in a little platz that looked like something out of Shakespeare. Its medieval good looks were touchingly inauthentic, a near-total reconstruct after World War II, I later learned.

I stared hard at a darkened coffee shop. As a sometime-member of the Church-of-the-West-Coast, I knew the drill: Visualize the coffee shop with its doors flung wide, the aroma of steaming java wafting across the platz, irresistibly beckoning hordes of interesting people inside, people I could spend hours observing. Soon it did open. And people began to materialize. But they weren't heading to the coffee shop. They came and went through the platz in a distinct pattern, appearing at the north end, walking through it like ants on a food mission and exiting the south side.

No one seemed to be walking in the other direction. Perhaps I should investigate.

I waited for my chance and saw a group of auspicious-looking old women heading to the mystery exit. They were definitely tracking something. I slunk behind them. We exited the platz, climbed a charming stone footbridge over the Main River, and descended to the other side into a park. Some kind of street fair was taking place under the sycamores along the Main. There were food vendors and tables spread with housewares, used clothes and antique jewelry.

Merging into the crowd shuffling along the rows of tables, I was thankful to at last have a purpose for the next few hours. After my initial blunder into English, I kept my mouth shut, nodding and smiling with what I hoped was a friendly, intriguing and culturally nonspecific air to the vendors whose tables I perused. The anonymity experiment seemed to be working. The guy at the falafel stand where I had my first Teutonic meal mistook me for French, and one antique jewelry dealer held a bracelet to my wrist and began a fervent German sales pitch. I was elated! If personal transformation was this easy and I, just by keeping my mouth shut and dressing differently, could fool people, what were the possibilities? This day was looking better and better. Not yet two hours into my trip and I was getting a whole new perspective on my life.

Standing there, musing and absentmindedly flipping through a box of sepia post cards, I thought about my father. Many were the Sunday mornings he and I had risen at 7 a.m. to mosey around tables just like these at our county fairgrounds. It was the beginning of my lifelong affection for flea markets.

Flea market . . . floh markt.

Duh! How could I have been so obtuse? It wasn't a metaphor. There were no lice—not in Germany, for heaven's sake. I drew a few sympathetic stares as I laughed out loud. People looked over to see what the joke was, but how could I explain? I didn't speak German! I could only beam at my fellow floh-markters, loving them all for assuming I was anything but an emotionally exhausted American woman, and for their charming language and its gift to a tired tourist. I wanted to tell my Iranian-German buddy, but he was nowhere around.

For the rest of that morning, I wandered in and out of the now-open Frankfurt shops. Even all the expensive-looking shopkeepers in their fashionable eyewear seemed like old friends now, smiling back at me as I grinned and occasionally giggled over my mistake with the inappropriate timing of the truly fatigued. No lice here, and no fleas either. I wished I could stay a few days. But I couldn't, too bad, so I did the next best thing and went back to the lovely, clean Hauptbahnhof, watched the trains come in on time and started drinking some of that good German *Bier*.

Nowhere to Hide

Ginu Kamani

THEY SAY that there is no better entreé to a culture than taking a native as a lover, but I was skeptical of finding anyone who would suit my expatriate, cross-cultural outlook. An Indian immigrant to the United States, I returned to live and work in Bombay after eleven years away, and to my utter delight, within two months of moving back I found myself involved with a complex, talented and lovable local. Neither of us had encountered such an interesting Indian before. We spent long periods together, utterly absorbed in each other.

The news that my boyfriend's best friend was to wed in the capital, hundreds of miles away, came as an unwelcome invasion. I hate Indian weddings. If you haven't been to one, you wouldn't know what I mean: the guest list is always several thousand strong, money is spent like there's no tomorrow, the women turn up dripping with gold, diamonds and silks from head to toe, the men exchange stock quotations and boasts about business deals and the impersonal wedding ceremony is presided over by a priest droning incomprehensible Sanskrit. The bride and the marriage venue were in New Delhi. The groom and his buddies were in Bombay. The groom's party had hired a private compartment on the overnight train to Delhi, with the clear assumption that the group would be male. None of the men were bringing along their significant others.

I felt a subtle pressure in this arrangement, but was damned if I'd twiddle my thumbs in Bombay for a week. Wonderfully companioned, for the first time in my life I might even have *fun* at an Indian wedding. But the entire point of the overnight train trip was to hold a twenty-hour stag party, which I would ruin simply by virtue of being female.

Feeling deeply ambivalent, my boyfriend did not RSVP. A last-minute call from the fuming groom set up the perfect opportunity for emotional blackmail; thus, I was permitted to gate-crash the all-male group of child-hood pals heading north, but on the firm condition that my boyfriend and I organize our own sleeping arrangements. This banishment from a first-class compartment to "god knows what" we could wrangle "back there" in the rear was the ultimate rebuff to a scab who'd chosen to cross the line. My boyfriend was no wimp, but he accepted his ostracism without protest.

Indian society exhibits great ambivalence toward persons who are romantically involved. On one hand, Hindi movies are loaded with dra-matizations of romantic attraction; on the other, individuals go to great lengths to hide their amorous entanglements from friends and family. Sto-ries abound of newlyweds being kept apart by zealous family members—mothers-in-law particularly favor casually falling asleep on the couple's bed. Mockery, harassment and public embarrassment often accompany being "caught." Holding hands and kissing in public are regularly labeled "Western corruptions."

I doubt that this group of unsympathetic buddies would have con-ceded to the arrangement my last boyfriend, an American, had devised with his two roommates in our coed freshman dorm: In the lower portion of the bunk bed in his room, he hung bedsheets to block the view. Each night, for almost a year, I crawled into bed with him while his two roommates snored peacefully above and beside us, my presence forgotten.

The day of the trip arrived. I was looking forward to the journey, as I had pleasant childhood memories of overnight train travel. There was the mandatory purchase of chai and spicy snacks served up through the train windows and the equally de rigueur argument with other passengers on where to store luggage. Then the whistle blew and the train crawled out of the station.

We walked the length of the train to the bachelor compartment, where the friends were smoking and playing cards. The locking compartment door sealed them off from the rest of the passengers, but we were allowed to enter. The moment the train picked up speed, these macho guys shifted into high gear, passing around bottles of rum, brandy, vodka and whiskey with the idea of emptying them all in quick succession. Knowing the rules of a bachelor party—drinking and smoking until you pass out—my lover was still game; after all, these were his friends from childhood. I, however, was indifferent to the prescription. I drink to heighten my social interactions, not dull them, and combining different alcohols results in a crashing head-ache. Besides, the unrelenting jostling of Indian trains coupled with the poor aim of passengers quickly renders toilets unusable, and I wanted to make as few visits as possible over the twenty-hour journey.

I like to think I have all the makings of an amateur anthropologist, but I could not fathom why a man on his way to his wedding would display coolness to a pal and his girlfriend. This bunch of guys was as horny as the next, and I knew from my boyfriend's accounts that sex talk generally abounded in the group. I would have liked nothing better than to partici-pate in the scatological horsing around of twentysomething Bombayite mu-sicians, mavericks and computer whizzes, but sadly there was no question of such a discussion taking place in my presence, due to both my gender and class. I was assumed to be a mostly modest girl, even though I was coupled with a thoroughly irreverent member of their inner circle. As a therapist might have said, these men had clearly defined boundaries—too clear.

The choking cigarette smoke and ritual insistence to "have another drink" drove me out of the private compartment in an hour. I traveled down the length of the train to our reserved seats. In contrast to the private sleeper, my boyfriend and I had been booked into open berths—platforms that folded down off the wall of the train along one side of the main carriage corridor. I returned to my spot and read, happy in my certainty that when evening rolled around, my beau would prefer the warm, responsive body of his partner to the inebriated remains of his friends.

Attendants moved through the train car, tucking sheets around the hard platforms that doubled as beds and handing out the roughest wool blanket and the most unyielding pillow one could pay good money for. However, the items were all spanking clean, and the workers efficient and polite.

With the light fading outside, the world closed in on the train. With no view to admire through the windows, the inhabitants of the train switched their gaze onto one another. Suddenly it became clear that the berths we had been assigned were in the communal passage, open to the scrutiny of everyone passing through. There was nowhere to hide.

Public and private are essential categories in Indian culture, especially when it comes to gender. Women in the public (read: male) domain are looked over and under and through by passing men. In the Vedas, it is written that the gaze exchanged between man and woman is as erotically charged as if semen itself had been transmitted. I could swear some men have taken this up as a challenge.

Women not immediately classifiable as demure wives tend to attract a lot of attention in India. I knew this—after all, I had grown up in India until the age of fourteen—but felt safe with my boyfriend around. He returned from the bachelor party mostly sober and in a reflective mood, mulling over the changes of life and the lasting links between him and buddies he'd known since nursery school. We must have talked for hours, holding hands, entwining our legs or touching in some other way.

At some point it became clear that an inordinate amount of human traffic was shuffling past us. Just males—curious males—stopping and staring, then moving down the corridor and shortly thereafter returning to stop and stare some more. If we met their eyes, they would shift their gaze up—at the window or the ceiling—until we looked away; then back swung the spotlight gaze. We even looked out the window to see what they were staring at, imagining some interesting sight outside. It took us a while to figure out that we were it. We could as easily have been the casket at a funeral, given this silent, stop-and-go procession. Word seemed to have gotten around on the train that there was a free show to be had over by berths 121 and 122.

Staring back with extreme annoyance at these dawdlers accomplished nothing. We decided to turn off the overhead light, get under a sheet and continue our discussion in the dark. After all, how much could they see if we were hidden in the shadows?

There's a good reason why Indian traditions have survived for five thousand years. Tenacity is the culture's middle name. What my boyfriend and I imagined was a clever maneuver served only to remove any last bit of inhibition in our audience: Where previously they'd been sauntering past one by one, several men now planted themselves eagerly right in front of us, breathing hard through flared nostrils. They bent over us, hands clutching the overhead berth for balance, devouring us with that heavy-lidded gaze I knew only too well. They said nothing, since the situation had been telegraphed to one and all: WOMAN OF GOOD FAMILY SPOTTED WITH LOVER IN PUBLIC STOP WEARING SHAMELESS WESTERN DRESS STOP REQUEST ANY NUMBER RINGSIDE SEATS STOP

Animals in the zoo must feel like this. But with no bars separating us from our audience, their looming figures were more than slightly intimidating; they looked like they would pounce on us.

Locked in an embrace motivated mostly by indignation, my boyfriend and I watched these men watching us, like so many gleeful boys lined up at a keyhole. The air was electric, and slimy-moist, as though peppered with the spittle of an overexcited raconteur. Even though their stony faces revealed nothing, I could feel jumping-bean desire bursting through their skins. These were most likely upstanding, middle-class men traveling with their wives and children, all safely tucked into locking compartments. The spectacle of a couple engaged in bodily contact in the no man's land of a train compartment probably seemed just the antidote for their overworked lives.

Preferring to avoid confrontation, my boyfriend and I lay still in each other's arms. The men hung on our every motion. A slight adjustment in our position caused waves of excitement in the bystanders. We felt trapped, as though in body casts from head to toe. Even if there were any sexual energy under that sheet, acting on it in the presence of such an overbearing audience was out of the question.

We toyed with the notion of moving in with the bachelor party, but the idea was hard to stomach. The locked compartment was probably reeking by now with liquor fumes and stale smoke, not to mention certain bodily fluids common to the inebriated.

The impasse continued for several long moments. Would this go on through the night? Finally, it occurred to us that the troops might move on if my boyfriend went up to his assigned bunk, while I remained chastely in mine. The individual bunks were too snug a fit for a couple anyway, even one madly in love.

The parting would have come anyway when sleep overtook us, but this early separation aimed at disbanding the greedy masses brought on enormous resentment. Whether friends or strangers, all of India seemed to be conspiring to keep my partner and me apart.

The night passed in a tortured symphony of nasal rumblings. Every male in the vicinity, including the boyfriend above, snored at the top of his lungs. Purple night lights burned into my eyelids, whatever my position. The train slowed to a lurching, screeching halt every few hours. By morning I was extremely grumpy.

When asked why he hadn't warned me about the open berths, my partner said he'd never experienced anything like it. Apparently, no Indian woman of good family would have consented to such an arrangement in the first place; with no private compartment available, a woman in my position would have stayed home, or perhaps flown instead. In any case, there would have been little expectation of sharing intimacy of any kind—even inside a locked, curtained, private compartment.

Still sullen, when I probed further as to whether my boyfriend could have done something, male to male, to discourage the onlookers more directly, he shrugged and flatly said, "No." I knew that shrug and tone so well—the fatalistic attitude conveying that this was just how it was in India, and one simply had to accept these Indians (translation: "men" in this case) as they were.

The wedding went on without a hitch—just as ostentatious and forgettable as I'd expected, but my boyfriend and I had a fine time exploring Delhi and each other. I was glad I had insisted on accompanying him. When it came time to leave, by some miracle, two plane tickets fell into our laps, making the journey home short and sweet and bearable. Not once, however, did my boyfriend reach for my hand or shower me with soggy kisses. We traveled like a conventional couple, with a good foot of space between us. The spell of our entanglement had been broken.

On Being at Sea

Lucy Jane Bledsoe

WE THREW our duffels into the trunk of the cab and fell into the back seat. Pat brought out her best Spanish and told the driver we wanted to go to the old port, *puerto viejo.* He revved the engine, pulled out of the tiny airport and said, *"Si, puerto nuevo,"* naming the *new* port, thereby beginning a long argument between Pat and the cab driver. I agreed with the cab driver: By all means, let's go to the new port. If there was a new—as in modern, with all the trappings of recent human inventiveness—port, why would we use the old one, the one, judging by the cab driver's reaction, that was no longer in use?

I tried to clear up the misunderstanding by articulating, *"Challenge of New England! Challenge of New England!"* which was the name of the vessel we hoped to meet. Maybe a big American schooner would be interesting enough to the citizens of a country dabbed in the middle of the sea to merit note in the port. I was counting on his having seen our boat and knowing exactly where to take us, hopefully the *new* port. But Pat, sure of herself, pursued her puerto viejo line, over and over again, until the driver shrugged and fell silent.

Though no towns appeared after we'd left Puerto Plata, now and then we flew by festively lit cabañas, their colors a bright blur in the night. I saw men wearing dark trousers and white undershirts, holding Coca-Cola or beer bottles, and wished we could stop for a cold drink. Wished, in fact, that we could stay in this country and explore its beaches, towns, cabañas and native beers rather than get on the boat in whichever port and sail into the Atlantic.

Because we left home so suddenly, I hadn't had time to do any travel research. All I knew about the Dominican Republic was what I found in my atlas. First, that it didn't merit its own page. Second, that it didn't even merit its own island. The Dominican Republic shares the atlas page with a dozen other Caribbean islands and shares a tiny piece of land with even tinier Haiti. As we sliced through the night on a slightly paved one-lane highway, the hot, wet air washing our faces through the open windows, I was aware that the sea surrounded us, that we could not travel more than a few miles in any direction without encountering salt water.

I'm a land person. I like the earth beneath my feet. The idea of bobbing about in a wooden boat in the immensity of the sea frightens me. After all, we know more about the surface of the moon than we do the murky sea depths. Pat, on the other hand, loves the water and sailing second only to music and her trombone. She'd taught sailing for many years on Cape Cod and in England and had always wanted us to take a sailing trip.

The *Challenge of New England,* a replica of a nineteenth-century fishing schooner, belonged to a sailing school in Massachusetts, and was captained by Dan, the younger brother of a good friend of mine. When Dan offered this trip to us for free, save the airfare, Pat was ecstatic and I acquiesced. I bolstered myself for the trip by trying to think of it as just another kind of wilderness adventure. After all, I loved high mountains and deep forests. The sea would be a new wilderness challenge. Who was I to say no to the Caribbean? We had been promised island hopping, beachcombing, swimming and whale watching. I prepared myself for long afternoons lying on the deck reading books while the sails slapped lazily overhead and the wind ruffled my tank top.

So I gave in to this trip, and that's one of the things I love best about travel: the loss of control. The feeling of being truly on a ride. Of being at sea. Well, this time it would be literal.

The stretches between the lit-up cabañas grew longer and longer until there was nothing but black sky and thick vegetation, both threatening to swallow the road. I began to think that the Pat and Lucy show—with me shouting the absurd words *Challenge of New England* and Pat insisting on a puerto viejo that didn't exist—had finally met with a native who'd had enough of crazy American women and was about to dump us in the middle of the jungle to teach us a lesson. But then he pulled over, turned to the back seat and said, "puerto viejo."

The cab driver had tired eyes and baggy cheeks. His hair was wet with pomade—why would you need it in this muggy heat?—and a clump of it hung down his forehead. I could tell that he hoped we understood that this destination was our fault, not his. Peering out the open window of the cab, I saw a pile of old railroad ties and, looming in the near distance, what looked like a deserted warehouse.

For reasons I still don't understand, Pat was perfectly confident that we were in the right place. It wasn't until I crawled out of the back seat that I saw that there was indeed a port on the far side of the cab. A few boats rocked gently in the doll-sized harbor. One small wooden ramp led from the pile of railroad ties down to the inky black water. Then what?

Pat had her wallet out and was trying to pay the cab driver, who was hesitant to leave, when footsteps and then deep voices, clearly belonging to at least two big men, emerged from the blackness behind the pile of railroad ties. The cab driver yanked my duffel out of my hand and threw it back into the cab. "Get in, get in, get in," his hand motions urged.

Then one gravelly voice said, *"Challenge of New England?"*

"Yes!" we cried with relief.

"It's okay," I told the cab driver in English. "We know them."

Not exactly true, but true enough. Pat tried to assure him in Spanish.

The cab driver looked over the two burly men, who were now pulling my duffel back out of the trunk and taking Pat's bag from her hands. He gave his two crazy American women one last glance, scornful this time, as if he'd suddenly pitched his concern for us far out to sea, accepted his big tip and drove away.

I have not had great success in my traveling career with rendezvous. The idea that you can actually pinpoint a place in the geography of the world, a place small enough for two people to find one another, when you are thousands of miles and many weeks or even months from that place, always strikes me as impossible. When it works, as it did this night, I am not just relieved but amazed. These two big guys were ours!

They introduced themselves as Jack and Jake and told us that we were the last of the boat's hands to arrive. Passengers, they meant, not hands; I found the mistake charming in a boaty kind of way. They were the real thing, these sailors, with salty New England accents and what might have been called "coarse manners" in a nineteenth-century novel.

We followed Jack and Jake down the rickety wooden plank to the tiny dock. Up close, I could see that a rowboat was tied to the end of it. As instructed, I climbed in and took a seat at the back. Soon we were being rowed through the old Dominican harbor to a vessel anchored a couple of hundred yards out, and finally I opened up to the adventure. The old port, indeed! Why had I wanted anything else! Here there were no cruise ships, no tankers, no yachts, nothing but a couple dozen small boats, mostly fishing boats, anchored for the night in a port lit only by lanterns swinging off the masts. Merengue music coming from one of the boats spiced the warm air. As the *Challenge of New England,* the biggest boat in port, came into view, I dragged a hand through the water and realized how lucky I was. No matter who this Jake and this Jack were, no matter who else we would enjoy or endure on this seventy-five-foot schooner, I was in the Caribbean for two weeks.

A long rope ladder hung from the deck. I slung the handles of my duffel, hard and heavy with all the books I planned to read while lounging in the sun for two weeks, over my shoulder and climbed aboard.

"Challenge of New England?" one person after another queried as we reached the deck, certain that we'd stepped onto the wrong boat, until finally someone went to alert the captain. When Dan arrived, the others watched with undisguised surprise at his warm reception of us.

"Want to pick your bunks?" he asked.

I nodded and gave Pat a wary look: For the two weeks prior to the trip I'd been preoccupied with where we'd sleep. Would I be able to stretch fully out? Would it be clean? Would it be private? This was, after all, our vacation.

"Let's go see what's left," Dan said.

I didn't like that phrase, "what's left." Pat had promised me one thing about this trip and that was that I'd get to sleep undisturbed. I'd heard enough sailing stories to know that middle-of-the-night duties were not uncommon, but Pat assured me that while we might be called upon to help with dishes or, at worst, clean the heads, we would not be expected to do anything other than sleep at night. I imagined it being like Girl Scout camp— maybe we'd learn to tie knots and be required to memorize the Beaufort scale, that was all.

The fo'c's'le, which I'd been told was the best place to sleep, was already full, so we proceeded down the ladder to the main salon, where the rest of the bunks lined two walls on either side of the dining table. The galley took up one end of the main salon, and the cook was at work clanging pots and batting steam away from a big vat. A stench of hot, salty stew filled the small woody cavern. The boat was no luxury liner, that much was clear.

The benches on either side of the dining table doubled as dressing benches for the bunks. Dan showed us the two available berths, both bottom bunks and each with its own curtain, which could be pulled closed for privacy. Thank god for small favors. I pulled back the curtain to have a look. The bunk was a wooden pallet, or more like a wooden cradle, for the curving inside of the hull formed the back wall. I found it a little alarming. Was there nothing more than these hull planks separating the sleeper from the sea? I could hear little slapping sounds of water against the boat, which told me more than I wanted to know. The eighteen inches of vertical clearance explained why the top bunks were all gone and made it clear that I wouldn't be dressing in the bunk, probably not even sleeping on my side. I started to remove the huge duffel someone had thrown in my bunk.

"That's your emergency duffel," Dan said. "Everyone has one. It holds a life preserver and wet suit. It, along with all other personal possessions, must remain in your bunk at all times."

"I see." I patted the rock-hard duffel, which took up considerably more than half the bunk. About the size of a big body. So I wouldn't be sleeping alone. I threw in my own duffel, which also had to be stowed in the bunk, and eyed what little remained of the space. Maybe at night I could shove one of the duffels under the dining room table. I turned to eye that space just in time to see Dan squash a cockroach scuttling across the top of the table—a mere two feet from the head of my bunk. It made a hard crunching sound.

"Sorry," he apologized. "We have a bit of an infestation."

An *infestation?*

His flashed his boyish grin, then distracted us by offering beers, welcome on this hot night. My clothes, which I'd been wearing since I left home, were soaked through from the humidity.

As we climbed back up the ladder, cold beer in hand, two or three faces peered from behind bunk curtains. Were we *that* interesting?

On deck, where the air was hot and wet but at least fresh, we leaned over the railing. The sky was a soup of stars and as we talked, quietly, a big half-moon, as orange as cantaloupe flesh, rose over the island, fat side down and flat side up. We could still hear the merengue music faintly, along with the lapping of the sea against the boat's hull.

Dan told us about a seventy-knot squall the *Challenge of New England* had encountered a few weeks earlier. The wind had howled through the rigging at such a pitch that he and the crew had to scream in one another's ears to be heard. When Dan ordered the crew to bring down the headsails, he'd left the helm with a passenger for a moment, giving strict orders as to the boat's course, so he could go forward to help. When he felt the boat heading down—too far down—he raced back to the helm to head her up, but he was too late. The foresail jibed, and the foresail gaff cracked against the shrouds and broke in two.

"What a shame," I said, wondering what a gaff was. "Did you get it fixed?"

Dan pointed out the telephone pole–sized beam, one end torn raw, now lashed to the deck.

"That's the *gaff?*" Surely a part that size was not optional.

Dan agreed that this three-hundred-pound, twenty-four-foot log was a critical piece of equipment, but seemed cheerful enough. Another grin, one of those get-back-on-the-horse grins. I'd already learned that one didn't ask the captain too many questions, even if he was the little brother of your good friend. So I didn't ask again what sailing gaffless meant for us. Excited by last week's adventure, Dan told us more sea stories about boats "just like this one" that went down in years past and exactly how the disasters had happened.

His stories, and the somewhat disabled boat, made me reconsider my romantic view of the puerto viejo. Was our mooring here a financial decision? Was this where second-rate boats anchored? Were we hiding from more stringent inspections that might take place at the puerto nuevo?

Ah, but on a night like this it was hard to worry for long. A light breeze rocked the lanterns on the boats in the harbor, and the plump orange moon rose higher and higher. In a setting this mellow, a storm was hard to imagine. The merengue music begged me to loosen up, relax, take this trip one day at a time. Okay, I told the moon, the lanterns, the black sea and the music, count me in.

I liked being in the charmed sphere of the captain, how the crew and other passengers deferred to him, and by extension, to us. Only one eager young man with thick glasses tried to interrupt our enjoyment of the Dominican night. He butted in and introduced himself as Greg and his companion as Cynthia. Dan nodded, barely acknowledging them, but Greg persisted, clearly enamored with the captain, or at least with the idea of captain. He announced that he and Cynthia had been married yesterday and that this was their honeymoon, then looked expectant, as if someone would call for a bottle of champagne to toast them. Again Dan didn't reply, and I felt compelled to fill in the silence with a mumbled, "Congratulations." Greg leaned on the boat's railing beside us, and Cynthia hovered behind him, as Dan, Pat and I went back to our conversation that did not include them. I watched confusion cloud Greg's face. I imagined he had anticipated this moment of telling the captain this voyage was his honeymoon and had envisioned a more hearty response. I suspected that he was the type of man who often expected a lot. He had a Religious Right aura about him, a sureness of his superiority. To have the captain rebuff him was unexpected, and it rankled.

"We're having a meeting on the quarterdeck in half an hour," Dan finally told him, and Greg understood he was being dismissed. He and

Cynthia walked to the bow for one of what would be many romantic moments for all to witness and endure.

We left Dan to prepare for the meeting on the quarterdeck, then reported there a few minutes later, only to learn about the next hitch. After introducing the first, second and third mates, and also Pat and me as his "guests"—again I enjoyed the surprised expressions about the alliance between these two women with far too little hair on their heads and far too much on their legs and the handsome, cowboylike captain—Dan mentioned that the crew had all become sick from the last water they'd obtained in Puerto Plata. He didn't think it was a problem, but if we were fussy we had two hours to get to town and back with bottled water for the two-week voyage.

My throat contracted in panic. I love water. *Fresh* water. I drink a couple of quarts a day, and that's in a cool climate. Even if I could purchase six gallons of water, even if I could carry them up the rope ladder onto the boat, they would take up the last few cubic feet left in my bunk. Besides, I didn't want to leave the boat.

Following the meeting, Greg the newlywed officiously suggested that a handful of people be commissioned to go ashore for water. "Thanks for volunteering," I said. "We need three gallons." Oh, the power of being the captain's special guests! I loved the look on his face, the unpleasantness of doing the bidding of the likes of me and also the fear of displeasing the captain's friends. Greg was an authority-lover, and so he took the wad of Dominican money I gave him and set out in the rowboat for our drinking water.

As for the mere three gallons, somehow it would have to do. When they returned a couple of hours later, I stowed two of the precious jugs behind my emergency duffel and one behind Pat's. Finally, it was time for bed.

I was barely speaking to Pat by now—so far, the magical aspects of the trip fell short of making up for the cockroaches, broken gaff, poisoned water and company the likes of Greg and Cynthia—so I climbed into bed without even attempting an intimate goodnight. I lay in my sweaty bunk, which felt more like a bookshelf, suspended in a kind of wet stupor, and wondered how it was that I had a girlfriend who was happiest at sea level while I was happiest at ten thousand feet.

Periodically, I tried different positions with my bunkmate, the emergency duffel, until I fell asleep.

At 2:45 a.m. someone yanked open my curtain. A large man loomed in the space. Luckily I'm not trained in any self-defense techniques. It was also lucky that I was groggy and nauseous. Some tiny alarm went off deep in my brain—a man coming into my sleeping area in the middle of the night!—but my body had no resources for response.

Jack said, "You're on my watch. We're on at three."

He had to be kidding.

I managed to say it, "You have to be kidding." During the meeting on the quarterdeck Dan had called out the names of the different watches, but I was still working with the Girl Scout camp model and assumed that the formation of these watches was to give us the feel of being true sailors—the *feel,* not the real thing.

Jack moved on to the next bunk, Pat's, and gave her the same story.

"Let's go," he said, heading up the ladder to the deck.

Leaning out of my bunk, I glared at Pat. "I'm sleeping."

"You have to get up," she said.

This was the captain thing again, ship protocol. One didn't say, "No, I don't feel like it." This wasn't Girl Scout camp.

"You're kidding," I tried one last time, waiting for the heaving in my stomach, a result of the boat's motion plus being awakened in the middle of the night, to subside.

"It'll be fun. Come on." She pushed me up the ladder to the deck.

The moment I hit the deck, I revived. My boxer shorts and tank top were soaked through with sweat, my nose stuffed with the rank air of the main salon, but the night air up here was cool and plentiful. The sky was full of stars, and the sea looked velvety. We reported to the quarterdeck, where the first mate, Mary, explained our duties. One of us was to be stationed at all times at the bow on the lookout for other ships, which of course was not necessary tonight as we hadn't left the harbor. We were to take turns making hourly boat checks, which included checking each of the heads and bilges. The bilges, she explained, were a particularly important point of inspection because there was a leak somewhere in the boat.

"What?" I woke up a little more.

The strict look she fastened on me conveyed another ship lesson: When the first mate was talking, it wasn't a discussion—it was instructions. "The bilges are filling too quickly, ergo a leak. Got it?"

I resisted the urge to salute.

As she continued with directives for our four-hour watch, I obsessed about "ergo a leak." Was this a usual thing? To be at sea with a leak in the boat that filled things called bilges? I looked at Pat, who refused to look back at me. Mary assigned posts and charged me with the first engine check.

"Do you need help?" she wanted to know.

Help? Oh, no, I've been a boat mechanic for years. I'll "check" the engine, no problem. "Yes, thank you," I said as servilely as possible.

Mary marched off toward the engine room and I followed. We descended into the belly of the ship, ducking through narrow passageways, until she opened a small door and stepped onto a tiny, cramped wooden platform, barely big enough for the two of us. The engine, an elephant-sized piece of machinery covered with knobs, handles and dials, looked like a sea monster encrusted with barnacles. Mary yanked a huge pair of earmuffs—padded vinyl—off a hook and popped them over my ears. I read her lips as she said these were to protect my ears when the engine was on, which it wasn't tonight, of course, because we were still on the anchor. She rapped her knuckles on the steel body and I yanked off the earmuffs in time to hear her say, "When this baby's on, she's hot enough to sear your flesh." I could just see it: The boat hits a wave, I'm tossed onto the engine, where my skin grafts to the steel. Talking fast, she pointed to the dials and gauges and switches, explaining their importance and how to read them. I was to record all my findings in the notebook attached to the clipboard that hung on a nail next to the earmuffs. I pretended to understand every word of her instructions so I could get out of that claustrophobic pit as fast as possible. I did try to concentrate on which switches to flip when and which set of numbers—all the instruments seemed to have several—I was supposed to record.

"Got it?" Mary asked.

"Sure," I said.

"Okay, then go ahead and do the first engine check."

"But we're not moving. What's to check?"

Another withering look. Okay, okay, I'd do the engine check.

I spent the rest of the watch marching up and down the deck "keeping an eye out." For what, I couldn't imagine. I was dying to go back to sleep. How was it that I suddenly found myself in this minuscule harbor off a tiny island in the middle of the Caribbean Sea performing paramilitary duties?

At seven we were finally sent below for sleep. I crawled into my damp, sandy bookshelf and passed out. By the time I emerged several hours later, the dawn had bloomed into a gorgeous day. No sooner had I rubbed my eyes and taken a few experimental steps on deck than Captain Dan ordered the anchor raised and the sails hoisted. The crew hustled to get us underway. The sails snapped into place, sunny and bright, and we clipped along at a good pace out of the harbor and into the open sea. The cook climbed the ladder to announce that he'd made a fresh pot of coffee, my dearest wish come true, and I sipped a big mug of it as the Dominican Republic shrank and finally disappeared off the stern. I went below to get my notebook and pen, then found a place on deck where I could nestle out of the wind to write. Now and then I heard Pat's voice, enthusiastically volunteering for a variety of activities, as happy and carefree as I'd seen her. She hurried by on the heels of the first mate to help pull some line, and I loved her in spite of my bondage on this adventure of hers.

I applied a layer of sunscreen and tried to write up the details of my first twenty-four hours on board. The unwieldy sky and sea made it hard to concentrate. I felt as if my mind expanded to fill the space, spreading my brain cells too thinly for solid ideas to form. I wrote a few words— "cockroach," "engine check," "miraculous dawn"—hoping they would prompt full sentences later, then gave in to the daze.

I had reached a catlike state of meditative napping when I heard the first mate's voice calling from the other end of the boat, "All hands on deck! All hands on deck!"

I was a guest, not a hand, so I stayed nestled where I was.

"Lucy!" Mary the first mate appeared, pointing. "All hands on deck."

Wait a minute. Wait just one minute. I thought I had been *invited* on this voyage . . . But I could no longer ignore the obvious. Apparently, I was indeed a hand on this trip. Which meant work. It was a bitter moment.

I barely had time to duck below and stow my notebook in my bunk. As I ascended the ladder to the deck, someone tossed a sponge at my chest. A bucket of water splashed at my feet. "Deck swabbing," Jake informed. Over the course of the next couple of hours, we scrubbed every inch of wood on the deck. A couple of lucky sailors had the fun job of rinsing everything in sight with water pumped from the sea through fire hoses, but the rest of us worked like dogs.

The wind picked up and my stomach began tossing with the waves. Wind, of course, was something to celebrate on a sailboat, but by the time we finished scrubbing the deck, I felt sick. The boat rocked and heaved, a motion that back home I'd fantasized as being nurturing, soothing, hypnotic, but which instead was one of the most unsettling feelings imaginable. We'd been instructed never to vomit in the heads, but to weave our arms in the ratlines, to avoid going overboard, while delivering the contents of our stomachs to Neptune. Now, as I watched my fellow shipmates hurling their lunches into the sea, an extreme nausea overpowered me. I wasn't about to barf in front of all these New Englanders, so I charged down the ladder to the main salon and, thank god, found the head unoccupied. When I was pretty sure I'd finished, I pumped the head empty and managed to get into my bunk. I hunkered there hoping no one would summon me for more labor.

The nausea I felt was akin to the kind that accompanies a migraine. The boat tossed and the air was fetid, a kind of chili-flavored salt stench. I felt both greasy and sticky; my eyes were crusty and I was exhausted. At some point Pat came to get something from her bunk, and I waved an arm out my curtain. She poked her head in, grinning, apparently having the time of her life. How could her perfect day be my nightmare?

"I've never sailed in such an ideal breeze," she enthused.

That did it. Couldn't she tell I was barely making it? Her euphoria was like gas on the fire of my discomfort. I demanded, "Land. Now."

Pat tried to pet my hair but I swatted her hand away.

"You tell Dan. You go tell him now. First island. I'm off this boat."

She nodded, thinking.

"I mean it. I can't go on."

"Okay, honey."

"Don't 'okay honey' me. I'm not joking."

"Okay, okay."

"You'll talk to him? You don't have to get off with me. I'm sure they have an airport of some sort on all of these—"

Here it came again. I bowled her aside and charged to the head. In use. Up the ladder, gagging, spitting, I stumbled across the deck, heaved over the railing. So much for not barfing in front of the New Englanders.

"Your arms in the rigging!" First mate Mary, whose eyes seemed to cover every inch of this seventy-five-foot boat, corrected my vomiting technique. She yanked one of my arms off the railing and jabbed it in the rigging for me. That time I vomited correctly.

Having come to terms with the fact that I was a hand and not a passenger, I made it through the next few days. No one put me ashore as requested, and I didn't ask again. I even had some good times. Like the day Captain Dan ordered all hands in the sea and we jumped overboard for a swim—oh, to rinse the salt crust and galley grease from my skin!—in the middle of the Caribbean, no land in sight, the bottom two and a half miles below. Mary the first mate climbed the mast and stood lookout while we swam. "Lookout for what?" I asked. "Sharks," Dan grinned. I wrote "sharks" in my notebook that night.

More highlights followed. We spotted whales, Pat played her trombone on the bow at sunset and I climbed the rigging. I guess it was an adventure-girl kind of thing, something I had to do to prove to myself I was still tough. The sails were up and we were clipping along at four or five knots. Captain Dan went first. As you go up, the ratlines narrow. I put one sneaker on the rope crosspiece, pulled with my arms and kept climbing. The boat was heeling over at a nice angle and when I looked down, I saw a thirty-yard drop to the deep blue. On deck, the crew and other hands craned their necks, watching. Finally, three-quarters of the way to the top, I froze. Up here, the ratlines were four inches apart, barely room to stuff my sneaker toe between them, and nothing to lean my body against. Dan, now standing on the platform at the top, shouted down for me to hook my harness to the rigging. I shouted back that I wasn't letting go of the ratlines to hook anything. He looked surprised—at my talking back—but just laughed.

On the fifth day, the main starboard spreader broke. This piece of equipment spreads the shrouds and supports the mast, even less optional functions than those once performed by the broken gaff. Dan and a couple of crew members spent five hours rigging a makeshift replacement. The skies darkened over the course of that afternoon, a rat was reported to be on the loose in the fo'c's'le and the bilges were filling more quickly all the time.

And my watch had another graveyard shift coming on that night.

By now I was slaphappy from the total loss of control over my destiny, that drunken feeling of being able to do absolutely nothing about the situation in which you find yourself. I was in the hands of Dan, our cavalier captain, and in the arms of the *Challenge of New England,* our disabled nineteenth-century replica. I'd come to be grateful for the rule-book first mate, but didn't really think her sharp adherence to ship protocol could make up for the leaks and broken parts. Not to mention poisoned water, cockroaches and rats.

So Pat and I approached our upcoming 11 p.m. to 3 a.m. watch shift with a little unrestrained joviality. "Party watch," we told the other hands at supper, "at eleven o'clock. All comers welcome!"

No one laughed. Oh, these New Englanders would drive me out of my mind.

By the time we finished supper, the breeze had quickened to a more challenging blow. The sky was a palette of grays, billowing figures sculpted from clouds. I'd never seen a sky so actively in motion. Pat and I hit the sack right after supper to be as rested as possible for our party watch. By the time we were awakened at 10:45 p.m., the boat was really heaving. The waves pounded the hull next to my head and all the timbers were creaking like some Halloween opera. When we arrived on deck, I was surprised to find that only a light rain spit down on us and the wind causing all that racket below wasn't as forceful as it sounded. The sea, however, roiled like a bad mood.

"Would you be comfortable at the helm?" Mary asked me.

"Uh," I said, "well, I'm not sure, uh . . . "

"It's not a multiple-choice question," she snapped. "Yes or no?"

I remembered Dan's story about the passenger at the helm when the gaff broke. "No."

She assigned the helm to Jack and sent me to the front of the boat for lookout. "Stay off the bow," she warned me. "Wrap your arms in the shrouds and watch from there. We don't need anyone overboard in this weather."

The boat rose on the crests and plunged into the troughs, rocking from side to side like an enormous cradle. Each time the boat's bow crashed back down, a spray of seawater rained down on the deck. I stood with my arms woven into the rigging—vomit position, although I no longer felt sick— and stared into the black storm. Did Jack know how to steer a boat? Shouldn't someone wake the captain when the sea gets this rough?

Occasionally Jake stumbled forward to check on me. Once he pointed into the mess of sea, rain and cloud. "Puerto Rico," he shouted to be heard. "We're about fifteen miles off its lee shore."

"What happened," I wondered, "to the coconut beaches? I distinctly remember hearing about a wonderful Puerto Rican market where we were going to shop." When was the island-hopping portion of the trip going to begin?

By one in the morning we were ripping along at about nine knots and plowing through eight-foot waves. I pressed my chest against the shrouds and rode the ship like some giant beast. One squall after another blew through, and I held on, staring as deeply into the night as I could, looking for any red, green or white lights, signals from other ships at sea. I kept hearing voices and turned time and again, expecting Pat or Jack or Jake, but no one was ever there. I heard a dog barking, too, as distinct and clear as if it were a few yards away on deck. I shook my head and tried to focus on my task. But the harder I tried to concentrate, the more active my imagination became. Or was it my imagination? Songs, animal sounds, whole conversations wafted from the rigging and sails and deck planks. It was as if the ship were inhabited by a multitude of poor souls, permanently lost at sea, in some kind of purgatory, and they were taking refuge on the *Challenge of New England* for the duration of the storm. "Bad choice of vessel," I wanted to tell them. "You're likely to experience a trauma similar to the one that trapped you out here in the first place." Nevertheless, I was happy for, rather than spooked by, the company. After a bit, I tried to sing and bark along.

Then the waves began cresting the side of the boat and splashing onto the deck. We weren't playing at sailing now; these were real squalls, each one blowing fiercer than the one before. I might have been frightened, except that as each wave receded and the water spilled back into the sea, the entire deck glittered with blue-green sparkles. The water was teeming with bioluminescent critters.

Once again, I corrected my attitude. All the labor performed so far was worth this magical sight. When the next wave doused the deck, I scooped up a handful of seawater, and the organisms pulsed in my hands like tiny stars.

"Do you see that light?!" This time the voice was real. Mary was at my side.

"They're beautiful," I said, dreamy and mesmerized in spite of the largest wave yet crashing onto the deck, knocking me away from the shrouds because I'd taken my arms out to gather up the seawater in my hands.

Her voice felt like a slap. "Not the deck," she shouted. "That light. Out there." She pointed off port side of the bow at the sea-sky, for on this stormy night it was all one.

"What light?"

"That's a ship. It's your job to spot anything coming and let us know."

I peered into the black wetness of rain and waves and saw nothing. I couldn't see a ship, a light, anything out there. I honestly couldn't. Besides, I wanted to know but didn't dare ask: Didn't they have instruments to detect oncoming vessels? I mean, I knew we were simulating sailing in another century, but didn't they hide a computer in one of those antique cabinets? Just for safety's sake? Were they really depending on me to avoid a collision in this squall? Surely the *Challenge of New England* was equipped with modern instrumentation.

Exasperated, Mary strode back to the quarterdeck. I was impressed with how she could walk, without lurching or staggering, on a boat this wildly in motion. A moment later, Jake appeared to replace me. I reported back to the quarterdeck, where I found Jack and Pat sitting on the deckhouse quietly cracking jokes while a few yards away Mary stood at the helm. "Party watch," I said and the jokes got louder. The rain pummeled our slickers and the waves swept onto the boat, but still we laughed, then began singing, until Mary told us to shut up. The captain was trying to sleep.

At three o'clock, the party watch was released, and we went below to bed. The storm sounded much scarier down here, the timbers groaning and squealing, the salt and pepper shakers, stored in a little slot on the tabletop, sliding back and forth, back and forth. It sounded as though the boat were breaking apart, and I had every reason to believe by now that this was possible. Upon crawling in my bunk, I discovered that half of my duffel was soaked, the half that lay against the inside of the hull. I quickly checked my two jugs of water. Both were capped tightly, upright and bone dry. The water soaking my duffel had come from the sea, through these hull planks, into my bunk. I thought of the ever-filling bilges, and then decided that if we were going down, I wanted it to happen in my sleep. I didn't run my hands along the planks to look for leaking water. Instead, I nestled up to my two duffels and willed myself to lose consciousness. As the waves battered the planks at my ear and pitched me back and forth in the bunk, my last thought was to wonder how long until the planks busted open and let the sea in.

When I returned to the deck around noon the next day, I found gray skies and a strong breeze but easy seas. Captain Dan and I had a cup of coffee together, and I learned that the storm had worsened after my watch. He'd finally arisen and taken the helm. I realized, listening to his immense relief, that I should have been more scared than I had been. Then he announced that we were close to Charlotte Amalie, the harbor at St. Thomas.

"You mean a few days?"

"A few hours."

I was floored. How could that be? We had signed up for a two-week sail. This was the beginning of day six. What happened to coconut islands? Beer under cabañas? After a brief moment of feeling cheated, I switched to joy. Oh, get me off this barely floating pile of planks!

Information had been hard to come by on the *Challenge of New England,* but Dan now allowed that we'd sailed straight through, as fast as possible, because of the condition of the boat. He planned to pull her out on the British island of Tortola and look for the leak, or leaks. We'd made incredible time during the storm and here we were, nearly at our destination. Dan was still in a hurry, though, because a big swell from a gale in the North Atlantic was quickly heading our way. He wanted to get in the Mona Passage before the twenty-knot easterlies, headwinds for us, stopped us dead.

"It's no problem," he said. "You and Pat can stay on board after we pull out. A little daytime help sanding and painting the hull, and you can have your bunks and meals for free."

I almost laughed in his face. Only Dan could present his access to our free labor as advantageous to us. By now the truth about our role on this trip had become all too apparent. Dan had needed a couple of extra hands. Presented to us as a gift, our coming aboard turned out to solve his labor problems. For free. We even paid our own airfare. And now we were going to be stranded for eight days in one of the most expensive places in the world.

Even so, I'd be damned if I was going to sand and paint a boat hull, in tropical heat, on my vacation. Or sleep in that stinky main salon another eight nights.

"I don't think so," I told Dan.

"What do you mean? You're deserting us?" His tone implied we'd taken the goods and refused to pay, like we owed him.

"Not deserting," I said firmly, "disembarking. In St. Thomas."

The next day we motored into Charlotte Amalie and dropped anchor. While Dan took the dinghy into customs with all our passports, I leaned on the boat's railing and gazed at the town. My feet throbbed with desire for land.

However, it was evening by the time all the arrangements had been made with customs, and we would have to wait until morning to disembark. That evening at supper, which we all ate in the main salon because it was raining again, Dan called a meeting. He wanted to organize a watch schedule for the time we were in the harbor. Since most of the folks on board expressed an interest in going ashore to drink, I volunteered to watch the boat until midnight.

Dan said, "That'll be from seven tonight until seven in the morning. Harbor watches are for twelve hours."

I said, "Sorry. I offered the evening. Someone else will have to do the late shift."

A strange smile, part amused and part enraged, settled on Dan's face and his body stiffened. It seemed like a small matter to me, my pointing out what I'd offered—kindly, I thought, accommodating the desires of the others—but the tense reaction of the entire crew and the volunteers let me know that I'd stumbled into dangerous territory. You just don't say no to the captain—no matter that he's your friend's baby brother, no matter that you're getting off the ship in twelve hours.

His voiced strained, sounding like a sea lion's bark, "Lucy and Pat on watch from seven until seven. And check those bilges every hour. You'll probably have to pump them."

"Oh, come *on*," I said. I understood the importance of a strict line of command while at sea—the necessity of a stringent set of procedures, how these save lives—but we were anchored in the harbor at St. Thomas. We were talking about who got to go into town to drink and for how long. There were twenty-five people aboard. Why were we the only ones to work the entire night?

"Galley duty goes to Lucy and Pat, too," Dan said. "Meeting's over."

"No!" My voice boomed out once again. Dan turned to talk conversationally with one of the deckhands and ignored me. The meeting was over.

He wasn't through, though. Before getting into the dinghy to row to shore for the drinking spree, Dan told me and Pat that we had to stay up on the deck for our watch. In a harbor like this, he said, you have to stay alert. For twelve hours, he expected us to pace the deck, in the rain, and check the bilges hourly.

What he didn't know was that by then I was so angry I'd have *helped* the *Challenge of New England* go down. I went right to bed and slept through the night.

Early the next morning, Mary the first mate, looking hung over, asked me how the bilges held up during the night. "How many times did you have to pump them?"

"Wouldn't know," I said. "I never checked."

The look on her face satisfied my revenge. I didn't get to enjoy it for long though, because Pat jumped in to assure her that she'd checked the bilges hourly.

By now I owed Pat big time. Not only did she keep watch on deck throughout that harbor night, taking catnaps in between the hourly bilge checks and one pumping, she also helped the drunk crew reboard at midnight when they returned in the dinghy through a pouring rain.

After reassuring Mary, we went to find Dan. Having slept off at least a portion of my anger, I found myself feeling mixed about saying goodbye. We agreed to find him on the island of Tortola sometime in the next week. We'd have dinner, hang out. The idea of it, whether we followed through or not, felt good. Then Jack rowed us to shore.

Not even eight hours later, Pat and I sat in our bathing suits on a white sand beach. How quickly one's fortunes flip-flop when traveling! We'd found this campground on St. John where you can rent your tent and cookware, buy supplies from a little store and bask on a beach surrounded by thick vegetation rather than high-rise hotels and condominiums. The island is a national park, and not only was it inexpensive, it was the most beautiful tropical setting I could imagine.

Pat poured another round of homemade rum punches from our water bottle, and I pushed my heels through the sand yet another time, making sure it was real. Yes, this was earth. I was seated on solid ground, the Caribbean spread out before me as blue and luscious as ever, only this time where it was supposed to be, on the outer edge of my personal geography, not directly below it.

EXPOSURE

NANCY COOPER FRANK

BEHIND A camera, I'm blind to all distractions, from oncoming traffic to the crumbling edge of a cliff. The world vanishes, save for a fragment perfectly arranged within the rectangle of my viewfinder. To coax that precariously balanced image onto film, all I need to do is play with the focus, tweak the f-stops and shutter speed, remember to remove the lens cap, hold my breath and step back an inch— no, wait, another inch. (Did somebody mention a cliff?) I know I can do it. After all, if I've already discovered most of the ways to mess up a shot, there must be at least as many chances to get it right.

I didn't know there was such a dogged and recklessly engrossed stickler for perfection inside me when I casually picked up my first camera with more than two buttons a few years back. Since then, my favorite non-idiot-proof camera has turned hundreds of stunning scenes into murky, underexposed images, but until that afternoon in Munich, it had never landed me in trouble.

I was supposed to be in German class that day—my main purpose for staying in Munich. But as much as I love *knowing* different languages and using them in my travels, the fumbling process of *learning* a language doesn't inspire me the way the trial and (mostly) error of photography does. So instead, I was taking pictures along the strip of park that follows the east bank of the Isar River through the city.

I caught the play of sunlight and shadow on the broad, milky green river, capturing the clumsy beauty of its ornate stone bridges and the gaudy mustard-yellow art nouveau tower over the riverside Müllersches Volksbad ("Folk Bath," or "Public Swimming Pool"). As I walked along the shore snapping away, each new composition more inspired than the last, the memory of the botched pictures I'd taken on past trips faded. The smudgy, anemic sunsets, the cockeyed horizons, the blurry heads sprouting blurrier trees—all were forgotten. For the present moment, while the film was still in the camera, safely undeveloped and unprinted, I was a champion photographer.

I'd been hard at work for over an hour and was adjusting the focus for one last brilliant shot of the Volksbad tower when I first heard the shouting. When it became too loud to ignore, I turned and saw a skinny, ponytailed man of about thirty in dirty shorts and T-shirt. He was running toward me, stumbling in his ill-fitting flip-flops, flailing his arms and sputtering something in German.

Soon enough I could make out the words: "Shame on you! Taking pictures of naked men! I'm calling the police!"

I couldn't imagine what he was hollering about, but he seemed only moderately crazy (as a former New Yorker, I know all the gradations) so I kept walking on the tree-lined path along the shore, determined to avoid eye contact (New York again). He scrambled after me, from time to time interrupting his rant about naked men to accost passersby: *"Hat jemand einen Handy?"* ("Does anybody have a Handy?") That's the German word for cell phone. "Sure," I thought, not too concerned yet, "it would be *very* handy if he'd call the police for me."

If the people strolling along the river ignored his frantic requests for a cell phone, they also ignored my growing discomfort. I turned to a graying citizen in a business suit and attempted to explain my predicament. (My German is hit-or-miss, though better than my camera work.) The dapper gentleman in the suit said, "Don't worry, my dear, you cannot get in any trouble. It is permitted to take pictures of naked men here." He laid great emphasis on the word "permitted." Without thanking him for his legal opinion, I started walking even faster.

I was intent on getting to the Volksbad, where I knew there was a café. We were in a close race-walk now, my noisy pursuer and I, scuttling through the park past a pickup soccer game, a couple of kids flying kites, a picnic, past blank and baffled stares.

Suddenly the noise stopped. While trying not to lose speed or collide with any people or trees, I glanced back. For once, the man was not shouting; his mouth was set in determination, and as I turned toward him, he fixed his eyes on my chest—that is, I quickly realized, on the fat Minolta with zoom lens dangling from its strap.

He lunged and got half a grip on the lens before I yanked it away. That was his signal to crank up the volume again: "You took pictures of me naked! I saw you!" I ran on, cradling the camera in both hands. Furious at losing his hold on the offending piece of equipment, he snatched at my backpack. But it seemed that most of his strength had gone into his lungs. "Halt!" he hollered, louder than ever before. "Halt! *Polizei!* Handy!"

All yelling mouth and skinny, flapping arms, he stuck with me the whole way to the Volksbad café. Standing my ground at the perimeter of the crowded outdoor section of the café, I shouted, *"Lass mich in Ruhe!"* ("Leave me alone!")

I was actually kind of pleased with myself, coming up with an apt idiomatic phrase at such a moment. But after that, I was forced to improvise, with a speech that came out more or less like, "I do not have them! The photographs! Of naked you! Go away, you understand, I have not the naked photographs!"

The chic coffee-sippers giggled. As far as they knew—or wanted to know—on this sunny afternoon, we were both street performers.

The man scrambled in through the café door right behind me. He made a scene, I made a counterscene, and the waiters chased him out. I planned to wait in the indoor part of the café until he gave up, simmered down or forgot about me and my camera. After all, to get to the street, I would have to walk a small section of semisecluded park lane, and, scrawny or not, "moderately" crazy or not, he wasn't worth the risk.

I ordered a pot of tea; he frowned through the window from beyond the rows of outdoor café tables. My tea arrived; I looked up at the window again and he was gone. I concentrated on my drink, trying to gather the calmness and nerve to walk out the door.

I'd downed a cup and a half before the man marched in again, frowning even harder now, two policemen at his back. Relieved, I started mentally rehearsing the German phrases for my testimony against him.

In bad German, I told the policemen, "My German is bad."

"Das macht nichts," ("No problem,") they assured me.

It was then that the interview took a wrong turn. "So. You've been taking pictures of this man."

They were polite to me, those two earnest, very young men in uniform, but they were taking his complaint seriously. They weren't impressed by my tale of how he had chased me and grabbed at my camera. I heard myself trying, rather lamely, to convince them that I hadn't been taking such pictures. Didn't they understand I had bigger aspirations as a photographer, bigger subjects in my camera's sights than the private parts of Bavarian men?

"He said he saw you taking the pictures," they repeated.

I was vaguely aware there was supposed to be a men's nude beach on the shore opposite the Volksbad, not as famous or nearly as well attended as the big nudist scene in Munich's English Garden. I was forced to conclude from the policemen's account that the man probably had been sunworshipping on the other shore when he saw me point my camera in his general direction. I pictured him throwing on his clothes—which, come to think of it, did look like they'd been put on in a hurry—and charging across the long, narrow footbridge.

Then I had another vision—of the cops asking me to hand over the film. Surely, any bodies that had found their way into my errant viewfinder would be mere specks, barely recognizable in gender let alone in personally identifying features. But all these two boys wanted to see was my ID. For good measure, I showed them a business card boasting of an advanced degree, along with my Florida driver's license containing proof of my advanced age (I'd just turned forty). Hardly the typical profile of a pervert, I thought, let alone one who specializes in snapshots of irritable, underweight types in bad need of a haircut.

"What are you doing here in Munich, Frau Frank?"

"I'm taking language courses at the *Goethe* Institute"—I placed reverent stress on the great German writer's name. They nodded approvingly. I didn't think it was necessary to add that I had cut classes for my photography outing.

Then one of them unwittingly touched on my true secret fantasy when he asked, in all seriousness, if I was a professional photographer. "No," I said (mentally adding, "And I've got the pictures to prove it"). Brushing aside my denial, he warned, "You must not publish these photos in a newspaper, magazine or any other form of publication."

"You may, of course, keep the pictures for your own private use," his partner said in the same earnest tone.

I was distracted from their good-cop/bad-cop routine by the sight of the sunbather a few feet away, shifting his weight from one flip-flop to the other and glaring down at where my camera had hung before I'd stowed it in my backpack. "I'll need you to walk me out of the park," I told the pair. They seemed a bit surprised, but with an air of catering to a whim they offered to drive me to my apartment across town, "if it would really make you feel better."

Back in my tiny Munich apartment, I paced, fuming at the baby-faced officers and my would-be nude model—and at myself, for letting them violate my right to feel safe, and reasonably dignified, while taking possibly award-caliber pictures of the landscape in a public park.

Still, the day hadn't been a total loss. I had traded bleak hours of class-room grammar for a chance to capture with my camera the perfect light of a summer afternoon. It's true I hadn't bargained on all the extras: the bracing jolt of culture shock, the real-life immersion language lessons, my fifteen minutes of fame as Frau Frank, freelance pornographer, or the private tour of Munich in a police squad car.

I only hoped the cops wouldn't contact my teachers at the Goethe Institute.

Under the Golden Arches

Mielikki Org

INSIDE ANYONE who's ever experienced wanderlust is a travel muse, and like certain other errant deities known for agitating strong desires, muses tend to work their powers on us at the most inopportune moments. In the comfort of our ordered lives, they permeate our brains and slip vague thoughts of escape into the depths of our subconsciouses. Suddenly, we awaken with inexplicable urges to travel to places as different as possible from our current global latitudes—Tanzania, for example, or in my case, Sweden.

Inspiration hit me unexpectedly one lazy summer evening as I sat on my boyfriend's couch relaxing to some Miles Davis. I'd been searching for work as a freelance writer for months, trying hard to conquer recently acquired habits of joblessness and homelessness. I was quickly developing status as a parasite—albeit a loving and grateful one—to the boyfriend, my most recent host. Glass of red wine in hand, I sat at my computer, hoping some brilliant alcoholic encouragement might summon the opening lines of my Great Novel, when I was overcome by a series of powerful sensations. Davis's version of "Dear Old Stockholm" was playing, and as his trumpet wove languid notes I envisioned city streets lined by gothic buildings and a river illuminated by the moon above. Suddenly the idea of taking my guitar to the streets and trying my luck at performing, as I'd dreamt of doing for years, seemed a lot more fun than staying in this room-turned-prison, wed to a computer and fax. I decided I would travel from Scandinavia to Greece.

Though I'd never been to Stockholm, I imagined it would be much like other European cities—vibrant, international, full of cozy dives, complete with a fantastic music scene. I knew Stockholm, like Paris, had been the post–World War II stomping ground of expatriate jazz greats the likes of Thelonious Monk, John Coltrane, Quincy Jones and others. I could almost feel the cobblestone streets beneath my feet and see café windows full of people smoking, chatting and reading. I could hear the notes of a baritone saxophone smoldering.

About a month later, equipped with a freshly purchased Euroline pass, I stepped into that fabled reality. A gust of clean, warm August air greeted me after the sixteen-hour ride from Copenhagen. Guitar over my shoulder and backpack comfortably secured behind, I emerged from the overwhelmingly modern train station onto the streets, eventually winding my way through the corridors of a mosaic-covered metro station. My ears tickled with the resounding echoes of street musicians' violins and accordions up ahead; it was just a matter of time until I would join them on the pavement.

After leaving Stockholm's labyrinthine subway tunnels, I passed the river, where the city's silhouette was framed against the sparkling blue water and the peach blush of a sunset. I walked along the streets, taking in the amber café interiors and stylish, angular buildings. After consulting my guidebook I decided to head toward the oldest district, Gamla Stan, full of narrow, winding streets, stone buildings and, I would later realize, expensive hotels catering to well-pocketed American tourists.

As I explored, I was led higher and higher above the city until I found myself on a bridge, gazing at the shadows of magnificent steeples lancing the sky. Below, glints of ebbing sunlight darted in the ripples of the river and a dragon-bowed boat made its way slowly across the water. At one edge of the bridge, a woman sang an English jazz solo, her throaty voice ricocheting eerily down the hill. Forgetting about lodging, thieves and time, I dropped my bags and guitar and leaned out against the banister.

"Stockholm is awesome," I said, firmly renouncing my atheism for just a moment to embrace the possibility that a higher deity might have guided me here. But within a matter of minutes my fate was to take a hairpin turn. Stockholm, as it turned out, had plans for me that evening.

I should have had a premonition when back at the train station the tourist office had sported a thousand variations of Go Away signs. No Rooms Available, read an assertive hand-written sign hanging from the velvet rope divider where excited tourists normally queued. *"ALL rooms booked for the week-end,"* said another menacing card on the counter. "Reservations for *after* the weekend *only,"* read a note on the window. "Office closes at 6 p.m. sharp," piped up another on the door. The frazzled tourist office employees might as well have posted the opening of Dante's *Inferno* above the door. "Abandon hope, all ye @#%!$ tourists who've been entering here all %$#!@ day. Stop harassing us and please &^!@ go find your own *&%!@ room. Have a wonder-ful @#!&@ day in Stockholm." In my excitement, I'd ignored the postings and headed out to explore, thinking that I still had plenty of time to find a room.

Hours later, I trudged, downtrodden, back to the tourist office. The girls working there, despite appearing harried, were really quite sympathetic when I finally made my way back. They smiled as I walked up to the counter ten minutes after they'd closed. "The pope is in town," I thought they might explain cheerily. It turned out that an international women's marathon was responsible for every room in town being booked solid.

"Is there *any* place I can go if I can't find a room here?" I asked.

The girls smiled weakly. One brightened a little and said, "There's an all-night McDonald's across the street." The same girl pointed the way. I felt like Ebenezer Scrooge being directed toward his fate by the bony finger of the Ghost of Christmas Future. Like Scrooge, I went through an initial state of denial—there had to be a room *somewhere* in the city. Another girl said she would phone one last place. After a brief exchange in Swedish, she looked up from the receiver. "They have one room left," she said, breathing a sigh of relief.

"Great!"

She inquired in Swedish about the rate. "One hundred fifty dollars is okay?" she asked, holding her hand over the receiver. She was a billboard of innocence. She hadn't even blinked. She must have seen a lot of desperate people that day. It looked like it was going to be an overpriced room or no room at all. I wondered how I'd look stretched out on a McDonald's booth cushion. "Thanks," I told the woman, trying to ignore a growing sense of doom, "but I think I'll try to find something else."

My boyfriend could usually be consulted in these times of crisis, but as luck would have it, at the current moment he was in California. Plus it was still near the beginning of my trip, and I didn't want to make him worry. He was miserable enough having to work forty hours a week for the first time in his life while I gallivanted across Europe, trying to earn back my travel expenses playing guitar and singing.

I called him anyway. "You should probably find a room," he said. "Oh, I know! I have a great idea. Why don't you—" And then we were cut off; my phone card ran out.

I meandered some more through subterranean Stockholm. The basement floor of the metro station was full of stores, restaurants and people—tourists whining as they pushed their floral suitcases, businessmen with briefcases, teenagers eating fries and shakes, anomalous scraggly characters. Stores were closing. Pizza Hut was closing. Even the metro ticket booths were closing, violet blinds drawn down one by one. All the while, Destiny's Child crooned from the video screens suspended above islands of wood benches, as if things were right and groovy with the world.

And for a lot of people in Stockholm, they were. After all, it was Saturday night; the rest of the city was ready to party. I returned upstairs and peered across the street. There it was, the slick neon-yellow *M* of the despicable Golden Arches, in one of those streaked, flashy fonts, beckoning like a pimply guy with smoker's teeth hitting on me at some smoky bar. I could barely stand to look at it. I called a few more places, but it was hopeless— the response was always the same: "No vacancy" or "Sorry, we're full." Someone suggested that I try one of the boat hostels by the river. "Not for tonight," said the proprietress. She called a few other boats, but they were all booked.

Then I remembered: On the bus, a suspicious-looking middle-aged man had approached me and asked if I had a place to stay in Stockholm. He'd scrawled an address on a piece of paper. "Cheap, very nice," he said. At this point, I was willing to try anything. The place turned out to be a frilly, homey, women-only hostel. The reception desk was closed until nine, so, sweaty and tired, I plopped down my grubby backpack and settled into a floral couch, attracting some unfriendly glances from some athletic women huddled nearby.

"Hi," I said. They said nothing. One snorted.

"Sorry," the nice woman said when the office opened. "We're booked. But if you want to use our phone . . . " I thought about accepting her offer, but had a flash of myself yanking the phone off the wall and spastically hurling it at the closest female athlete.

Back to the train station. I passed the yellow *M* again, my stomach still turning at the idea of staying there. In desperation, I began scoping out the ground-floor lobbies of a few fancy hotels. I decided to try to sneak in—I had done it before in the United States, although not for an entire night. Some of the lobbies, I remembered, had constituted mini luxury suites complete with cozy, overstuffed couches.

I hurriedly stashed my bags in a luggage locker at the train station. Before closing the door, I selected my "nice" clothes: a black vinyl jacket, a blue sweater and a pair of beige drawstring pants, which I'd shortened using my usual traveler/caveman tailoring tactics—ripping the hems off. My sandals, however, couldn't be helped: Bright green dental floss was visible just below one of the leather straps, where they'd broken and I'd mended them.

I paced outside Embassy Suites for a while, trying hard not to attract the suspicion of the doorman. Finally, I gathered my confidence and walked into the lobby.

"May I help you?" a woman at the desk asked as I tried to walk by. She knew I wasn't a customer. I lost my gall. "Oh, hi," I said, feeling a snobby, dignified accent creep into my voice. "I was just wondering if you had any rooms for tonight." ("What, me? Sneaking into your posh hotel? Preposterous!")

At the Hyatt, I got as far as the elevator. The doors closed. "Home free," I thought, pressing a floor button. But the elevator didn't budge. Trying to open the doors, I panicked when I realized I needed a hotel key card to get out. Trapped! I imagined sounding the alarm button: Security guards would yank the doors open, I would run out, and guards would chase after me. After a few unnerving minutes, the doors finally opened, and I rushed out.

The possibility of mugging a hotel employee for her outfit began to seem plausible. Or I could try to enter with a large group of people. Or maybe find a back entrance. But with all of my pacing outside the same hotels, I think the employees were beginning to raise eyebrows. Two suited, stocky security guards stood just outside the rotating glass door of one of the hotels I'd just cased; one leaned over to tell the other something and tittered a little while pointing at me. Maybe it was because I was female, or maybe they could read the intentions on my face. They'd probably seen scruffy tourists trying to pull off this sort of thing a thousand times before.

Hotels abroad, it turned out—at least in cities with high numbers of desperate backpackers—had much stricter security than their U.S. cousins. Each time I managed to creep past a counter, I was shot with suspicious looks. There was no way I would get in with my ripped pants and dental-flossed sandals. It was getting late, and I needed to find another option. Fast.

Wandering the cold streets and feeling pangs of envy at the sight of any lobby with a couch, I began to understand how this sort of forced expulsion onto the streets could change a person. I'd become civilization's unwelcome rat, with no place to rest—let alone sleep. Even finding a place to pee took on criminal connotations. Meanwhile, the yellow *M* glowed triumphantly at me from across the street. My franchise foe was winning, preparing to rub my face in its victorious grease. That's what I got for proselytizing to countless foreigners about the evils of McDonald's. For years I'd tried to start a movement against them: Death to the fry, I'd resolved. Never again the Filet-O-Fish! Never again shall I let cow flesh be aped into the avuncular, neighborly palatability of a McAnything! (Such dietary restrictions, alas, were destined to fail. I had a dirty little secret: I *loved* fries.)

I finally resigned myself to my last resort. It was ten o'clock. The McDonald's was still busy. I settled into a corner with my guidebook, trying to appear absorbed, when in fact I was just rereading the same paragraph in the Lithuania chapter. I tried not to fall asleep, silently muttering, "Please, please, let no annoying, obstinate or dangerous men approach me tonight."

The powers of my protective mantra lasted about two hours; then an unwelcome stranger sat at my table. Reeking of alcohol and other smells I couldn't place, he was in his late fifties, had an unkempt gray beard and wore a tattered brown leather jacket.

"Where are you from?" he asked in thickly accented English. I thought about responding in Chinese, but he had probably seen my English guidebook. Trying to fool him might just piss him off, and I didn't want a wounded drunk on my hands. I decided to be aloof and ambiguous.

"The U.S.," I said, not looking up from my book.

"Oh. What part?"

"California."

"Oh, California! *Beautiful* California!"

Silence.

"I always wanted to go to California."

Silence.

"So what do you do in California?"

"Oh, stuff."

Silence. Then a grumble. A quick scooting of a chair, and finally, peace.

Before long, it was midnight. Testy girlfriends with freshly washed hair waited for their late boyfriends. A pungent cocktail of shampoos, lotions, colognes and perfumes spiked the air. I thought the commotion would die down after a few hours, but it never did. It continued strong all night, as noisy as undisciplined fifth-graders in the presence of an inexperienced sub.

As the night wore on, techno music blared from the speakers. I stood in line for a cup of coffee. In front of me, women with long, lacquered nails hungrily plucked fries from brown bags as they waited for the cashiers to finish putting together their greasy order. On my right I spotted some long-haired, leather-clad bikers who looked ferocious but sounded like the *Muppet Show*'s Swedish Chef.

Behind me in line were spiky-haired clubheads decked out in black and chains, and a man in a velvet hat, black cape and blue velvet bowtie. I suppose I should have taken some comfort in knowing that all-night McDonald's the world over shared an ability to draw out the same kind of freaks as myself. Outside, men clutching liquor bottles stashed in paper bags swayed from side to side in a feeble attempt to rally the crowd into rave-party spirit.

It became more difficult to find a quiet, solitary corner to call my own. On my way to the bathroom, I slipped on slimy ketchup and smashed fries. Around 3 a.m., I spotted some other travelers forced to take refuge, suitcases and backpacks by their sides, looking miserable and bloodshot amid the buzzing crowd and heaps of McTrash. I began appreciating the common ground I shared with all of these people at three in the morning. McDonald's gourmands or not, we were all connected, living our lives as human beings subject to similar pain and distress. Who knew what social interludes or crises had brought these characters to this place at this insane hour: Maybe some of the couples were having illicit affairs. Maybe that tired woman in the corner in the midst of a serious conversation with her friend just ran away from her husband. Maybe the old woman methodically eating her fries had just learned she had cancer. In my fatigue and delirium, I felt compassion for the people around me. Hanging out in a McDonald's in the early morning hours seemed not so awful after all.

Seeing my surroundings in the clarity of daylight, however, changed my mind abruptly. When the soft pink light of dawn began to filter in, I saw the true horror of McDonald's the day after. Where was the floor!? You could hardly make it out, so abundant was the accumulation of cartons, napkins and spilled food. The tables were smeared with grease. When I tried to reposition my chair, I heard the legs unstick from the floor tiles. It was time to go.

The nightshift staff members were frazzled and visibly exhausted. I don't know how they mustered the gumption to sweep and mop all of the putrid night-shrapnel from the floor. I suppressed an urge to jump in and help them— I knew that they'd repeat this cycle again, very soon.

Outside, people started to appear on the sidewalks, and I felt an elated sense of relief. They were benevolent, prophetic birds who had been sent to tell me that my overnight internment was over. In less than twenty-four hours, I'd made a swift trek from heaven to a neon hell, and I was sure my body would remember the journey for days to come.

BLOOD, MILK AND MILLET

PATRICE MELNICK

AT DUSK Vikki and I began to look for a village. My sister wanted to sleep outside. She dragged her high-top, high-tech turquoise tennis shoes along the crumbly dirt road. Her back sagged under the knapsack loaded down with our cameras. Water bottles hung by strings off the side. Vikki brushed the sweaty bangs out of her face and sighed.

Vikki and I were traveling in Niger, and had decided to take a fifty-kilometer walk through the country to get a closer look at the landscape and to meet people.

We had chosen Niger in a rather haphazard way. I had lived in the Central African Republic during my two years in the Peace Corps, and I wanted to go back to Africa with Vikki and see a different part of the continent. One night while discussing our options, Vikki laid the map of North and West Africa across the bed, grabbed her Siamese cat, Puma, and tossed her onto the paper continent. We agreed that we would travel to the country on which Puma sat, as long as no war raged in that region.

Puma walked around and around, nervous at the crinkling sound of the map beneath her paws. She stepped lightly over the

Congo jungles, her pads sifted through the Sahara, edging away from Senegal, over Mauritania, and finally she started to settle very slowly, confidently, as if she owned a big chunk of Africa. She shifted side to side, settling like sand, her haunches lowering slowly, slowly, like a queen, lowering like an airliner, like storm clouds just above the Sahel, until she finally settled right down on Niger.

Vikki was the only person with whom I would travel. She had once worked as a cook in Israel and was used to heat and foreign languages. When I visited her there, we took a three-day excursion to Cairo. Though the guide-books warned against riding Cairo buses, Vikki ignored the warnings and took me onto those buses crammed with sweaty, tired people, buses that zig-zagged through the honking, steaming, shrieking, howling, blaring traffic.

From our map, Niger looked dry. I told Vikki that food and water might be scarce and her skin would dry out like parchment. But my sister said she was ready for anything, stroking Puma, who lay stretched out over Niger.

We packed gifts for people we hoped to meet—plastic toys that whir and fly, hair mousse, a plastic soprano recorder, perfume, photographs of the States and tourist postcards of a Texas cowboy saddling a seven-foot-tall jackrabbit.

Inspired by the advice of self-proclaimed "ethnofunkmusicologist" David Amram, we wanted to use songs as a way to interact with people. A friend taught me a couple of songs on the recorder and we each brought penny whistles in hopes that we could coax others to play or sing for us.

But the colorful countries on that map had disappeared, and now we trudged along hard-packed, parched ground, our musical fantasies slowly shriveling up like the spent leaves of a tree. I didn't like the idea of unrolling our blankets outside; there were no trees to sleep under, just the same brittle scrub brush that we'd seen all day. I scanned the subtle beige hills for a village. I was afraid we'd get rained on without shelter, or that strangers might be tempted to steal our clothes and food; we had heard rumors of "bandits" rambling along this very route.

On a nearby hill, several straw huts were clustered together like bee-hives. I left Vikki near the road and approached the closest hut, where an older man sat on a mat. I shook his hand, and he smiled a friendly wide grin and stared at me. Right away I realized he didn't know French, and I cer-tainly did not know his native language, Djerma. I gestured "sleep" by hold-ing my hands together like a pillow next to my ear. He spoke and threw his arm in the direction of a woman—his wife, I assumed—who was outside a nearby hut.

Four babies surrounded the woman. She sat on a mat on the ground, her knees bent to support a suckling infant. I gestured "sleep" again, and she grinned and nodded her head dramatically. She would let us sleep in the village. It was then that I noticed just how thin she was and realized that the village was probably very poor; food was hard-earned in this dry region. I thought she might try to offer us some of her family's precious food, and while I didn't want to take their food, I also did not want to offend her by refusing her kindness. I tried to smile a hearty thanks for the invitation, and stood up and walked away.

I walked about a quarter of a mile to another group of huts. This clus-ter wasn't quite large enough to be a village. All the nearby huts probably sheltered extended families that included parents, aunts, uncles, grandpar-ents, first cousins and second cousins.

In the center of this circle of huts, two women expertly pounded meal together. Each held a heavy, four-foot club in her hands, and between the two women sat a deep wooden bowl with a heavy base to hold it steady. The women alternately pounded the rounded ends of the clubs into the bowl with single methodic strokes: *thud . . . thud . . . thud.*

I repeated my sleeping charades and tried to indicate that Vikki was also with me. I swept my hand over an area outside one of the huts, trying to indicate that we would sleep outside. The two women looked at each other and spoke for a moment in Djerma. The taller woman nodded. I started across the field back to the road where Vikki was waiting.

After I retrieved Vikki, I followed an older woman up to the collection of huts and laid out our blankets beside one to show that we didn't expect them to provide beds for us. The two younger women continued to beat millet. We sat on our bedrolls to stay out of the way and observe our surroundings. I hoped they wouldn't offer us food. Though they were not starving like the other family, they were still quite poor, a "one-cow family," as Vikki called them. Vikki and I had bread and sardines that we planned to eat.

We rested in the late-afternoon shade; I was dozing off when suddenly six towering, slender men strutted into the camp. They shook hands with the women and then unrolled their mats as if they owned the village. They stared at us as they shook our hands. Vikki and I knew that they were Tuareg, a nomadic desert tribe. We had read about the Tuareg in guidebooks and had met some in Niamey several days earlier. Five of the men wore traditional tunics, beautiful drapes of fabric and turbans. Cloths hid their faces, leaving only their alert and inquisitive eyes visible. One of the men looked older, strands of gray hair showing from beneath his veil. Another man looked more modern, having left his face visible. He had a thick frizz of hair beneath the baseball cap that he sported, and he wore a T-shirt over his loose drawstring-style pants. I admired his angular face, his thin nose and handsome, deep-set eyes.

We were in a Djerma camp, not Tuareg, so I wondered why they had come. I doubted that these travelers were related to anyone in the village, but I guessed that in the desert, people depended on each other regardless of kinship or ethnicity.

All six Tuareg men sat in a row across from Vikki and me. They stared at us for a few minutes, which felt like three hours. Every now and then the man with gray hair would laugh and whisper into the ear of the man with the baseball hat so that we wouldn't hear him—as if we might have understood Tuareg.

In Africa it's not rude to stare. You can peer comfortably at some tall guy with shiny clattering jewelry around his neck until your eyes fall out. As you study a person's curly soft hair and his green, red and blue goat-leather sandals, he has his eyes on your flowered shirt from Sears. The guy in the sandals checks out the bright red cowboy bandanna hanging out of your pocket and the glittering hair tie at the end of your braid. Sooner or later your eyes meet and you both laugh.

Our stares never strayed.

"Bonsoir," said the man in the baseball hat. The six looked like a panel of experts fielding questions. But they asked the questions. One of the Tuareg men said something to the one with the hat.

"Vous venez d'óu?" said the Tuareg with the hat. He seemed to be the only one who spoke French; hence, he was the spokesman for the group. I wondered what their backgrounds were, if the translator had studied in a city school while the others were raised traditionally, as herders, craftsmen, merchants or nomads. I translated his words into English for Vikki as best I could. Meanwhile, I kept an eye on the older woman. I didn't want to ignore our hostess. She didn't notice us as she busily stirred a large bowl filled with a thick, lumpy mixture.

I told the panel that we were Americans and had walked from Niamey. The translator chuckled with disbelief. He told the group and they guffawed.

"Really, we walked. You walk. We can walk, too," I insisted. They nodded.

"Where are you going?" the spokesman asked.

"Say," I replied (pronounced "sigh").

"But why didn't you take a bus?"

"I told you, we wanted to walk," I answered. "Where are you going?"

"We're going to Say, too." I translated for Vikki.

"Ask them why they're not taking a bus," Vikki said.

"Why aren't you taking a bus?"

"Because we walk."

"You'll get too tired. You should take a bus," I said.

He translated my advice to the others. They yelled back to him.

"We don't have money for a bus," he said, "but you do. You shouldn't walk. You'll get tired. We're going to Say like you. Can we walk with you?" he asked.

In spite of their scolding, they seemed to like the fact that we were traveling on foot, too. Only we wore closed leather walking shoes, and they walked in tasseled sandals.

"No, you can't come with us," I told him.

"Why not?"

"Because we want to travel alone."

"But we can travel together."

"We have no food or money to give you," I said, thinking that maybe they were asking to be our guides to earn money. We did not want guides.

"We will share with you everything we have. We have food. We will give you money. We can share." He seemed sincere and I felt badly about my assumption.

But Vikki and I agreed that we should continue to travel on our own.

"We want to go with you. We can carry your pack for you," he said again.

"No, it's too heavy for you. Only a woman is strong enough to carry this pack," I said.

"No, he's strong enough," said the interpreter, gesturing to the long-armed man in the middle. "He ate three kilos of mutton today."

"He is too weak for this heavy pack," I said.

The mutton-eater began talking quickly, his brow wrinkling as he held up his arms, demonstrating his strength.

"I think he's getting upset, Trecie," Vikki said.

Some of the others smiled and shook their fingers at me for teasing the man. I could see his square shoulders shaking angrily in the dark. When he noticed the others laughing at him, he became quiet, his shape sagging with embarrassment.

From behind Vikki and me, more strangers walked into the village. "Bonsoir," said three young men. They greeted the people of the village cluster and the Tuareg men, who had begun talking among themselves in their own language.

Even in the fading light I could see that the young men were dressed in cotton button-down shirts. They were barefoot, with trousers rolled up above their ankles. One asked Vikki and me where we were going, speaking in well-accented French.

"We're students at the university in Niamey," one man in a light-blue shirt told me. "We live in that village over there. Why don't you come with us? You can meet our families."

"We are already here," I answered.

"How can you talk to these Tuareg?" he continued. "They don't know French." I wondered if the college boys were jealous that Vikki and I directed our attention elsewhere.

"We like them. One knows French and translates for the others."

"If you come with us, we have a place inside for you. You shouldn't sleep outdoors." He seemed irritated when I turned him down for the third time.

"The Tuareg are not to be trusted," the college kid said. "Sleep on top of your packs. They will steal everything you own. Everything." They seemed disturbed that we would turn them down to visit with uneducated nomads. But we had met plenty of college men; never before, though, had our paths crossed with veiled men who sauntered expertly through the desert, gliding across the sand.

I looked at the Tuareg men to see if they had understood the boys' insults, but they sat calmly with their backs to us, looking at the sky.

"Don't you want to come with us to our village?" one of the others offered for the last time. "It's on over there. You'd be much safer with us." Finally the Djerma college boys walked away, dragging their feet.

The Tuareg men regrouped on the other side of the camp. The old woman called us over for dinner and we gave her some bread. She looked pleased and handed us a gourd half-filled with lumpy porridge. The woman showed us how to scoop it up with our fingers.

"Mmmmmm," I said.

"You haven't even tasted it yet," Vikki said.

"I said it in anticipation." I brought a pinch of the mixture to my mouth but could barely swallow the grainy, sour glob. It was probably millet, an acquired taste.

"Mmmm," Vikki said. "This is really good. I want the recipe."

"You like it?"

"I'm trying to be polite," she murmured.

The old woman seemed content to hear us "Mmmmm" back and forth.

"Qu'est-ce que c'est?" I asked the woman.

"Lait et Sang," she answered. I thought I had misunderstood. I'd watched National Geographic TV specials about cattle herders who made small slits in the necks of their cattle to drain out the blood. Then they'd mix it with milk for a meal. But I thought this was the custom of the herders of Kenya or South Africa—not the Djerma people of Niger.

"We're eating millet with blood and milk. Put that in your recipe files," I told Vikki.

"Oh God," she said. "It smells like bone meal, like the stuff Mom puts on her pansies. It tastes exactly like that. Do we have to finish?"

"This is wonderful, mmmmm. But we are very full," I said to the old woman in French as I patted my belly, then held my arms out as if the meal had expanded my stomach to the size of a beach ball.

"She'll think you're pregnant," Vikki said.

"Shut up, Vikki. I'm doing the best I can."

The woman didn't seem offended. She set our bowls aside, then rested her elbows on her knees and watched us.

"Ask her if she knows any songs," Vikki said.

"Savez-vous des chansons?" I asked. She looked puzzled so I hummed. She smiled, thinking we had offered to sing to her, and waited for a song. We sang "Barges" to the old woman, a song we had learned in Girl Scouts. *"Merci, merci,"* she thanked us. We were quite a hit.

The Tuareg man with the T-shirt asked us to sit with him and the others on the mats. He had taken off his baseball hat and started giving us a lesson in the Tuareg language while another man made tea in a small blue teapot placed in a wire basket of coals. The Tuareg carry very little as they walk in the desert, but the teapot and glass are never left behind. The man poured green tea into the pot, added water and put the pot in the coals. When it began to boil, he poured the tea into a tiny jigger-sized glass. He poured it back and forth from the teapot to glass. Then he put a handful of sugar cubes into the pot and put it into the basket, like a bird in a glowing nest. When the tea boiled again, he patiently held the pot high in the air and let the tea stream down into the glass, then poured it back in the pot and repeated the process. He poured so many times that I lost count. He handed Vikki the glass. She took a sip, then passed it to me. I took a sip of the powerfully sweet liquid, and passed it on. The glass was passed until the tea was gone. All that work for a sip of tea! Later, I would see the small blue teapots heated in wire nests of coals in every household I visited.

"Do you know any songs?" I asked.

"We don't know much French," he answered.

"In your own language. We want to hear a Tuareg song. We'll sing you a song if you'll sing us one."

The translator told the others what we said. They began to bicker with each other. Three stood up, as if to leave.

Then a deep voice began to sing. The tone was so thick it seemed to thump against the ground. In the dark, I recognized the singer as the older man by his small-waisted silhouette. The other voices followed and I tried to see into the men's faces, but could only see their dark forms swaying. The three men continued standing and the other three knelt in front of them as if posing for a family portrait.

The kneeling three sang and clapped quick rhythms as the standing men raised their knees, one by one, in dance. Their hands pulled at the air, hand over hand over hand over hand. The mutton-eater stood in the center of the trio. His tall shoulders kept the rhythm as he swayed on his knobby legs and sang the fastest part of the song.

The man with the baseball hat stood. His high, wailing voice cut through the deeper ones like wind squeezing through a canyon. He made a snout out of his hands and turned to the mutton-eater as if singing the lines of a play. His knees jiggled, his shoulders jumped and all the singers' heads began moving up and down in the dark.

The mutton-eating man sang his song louder and louder. Medallions clashed around his neck and leather-tasseled necklaces shook like a mane. Lighter voices twisted around the deep ones, and shadows of harmony blended like vines, leaves shaking and clapping in the wind. The song felt as comforting as rain beating against the desert.

The song softened, shadows of harmony untwisted, and the rhythm slowed. The men folded the leaves of their voices and lowered their dark heads in a subtle bow.

Then the three on their knees stood up, and they all began chattering happily to each other in Tuareg, barely glancing at Vikki and me, as if they had just done something slightly embarrassing. Vikki and I applauded, but they pretended not to notice.

"What was that song about?" I asked.

"It was a song we sing."

"I know, but was there a story?"

"Yes, it is a Tuareg song."

"Tell me the story."

"You can't understand it. It was in our language."

"That's why I want you to explain it to me. Was it about animals?"

"It's just a song. Sing us a song."

Vikki sang "Donkey Riding," and then I sang a rap version of "The Three Bears," a Girl Scout favorite. The Tuareg men smiled and told us we were very good, which we weren't. One of the young men tried to talk to me in Tuareg, using sign language. He pointed one finger to his friend, one toward Vikki, and clasped his fingers together. Then he pointed to himself, to me, and clasped those fingers together again.

"I think he wants to marry us," I said.

"I got that," Vikki rolled her eyes.

The translator told me in French that he wanted us to be together. He didn't define together.

"Vikki, he asked to sleep with me."

"What'd you say?"

"I told him no, but I said you would."

"You told them *what?*"

"I said you'd do it."

"Bullshit," Vikki slapped my shoulder.

"What are your names?" the translator asked us for the second time that evening. I told him. All six men, who were lying down on their mats, began to sing again. As they sang slowly, quietly, they integrated our names into the lyrics. While they were still singing, Vikki and I went to the other side of the camp to get into our own sleeping bags. I liked feeling the clean desert breeze and listening to their soft harmonies.

We slept lightly that night, overwhelmed by the unfamiliar surroundings, in a village of strangers who spoke different languages, who walked and gestured and moved so differently from what we were accustomed to. I kept thinking about the warnings of the Djerma college boys. Surely their accusations that the Tuareg were thieves had no basis: They had been so kind to us, closing the evening with such a melodic song of prayer. But a small part of me began to wonder. As I sunk my feet deep in my sleeping bag, that small part wondered if thieves would sift through our luggage in the night. I woke up twice to the sound of sand creeping past my ears. Would we wake up early in the morning, after being taken in by the attention, songs and tea from the night before, only to find everything gone? I put my head down on the sand, closed my eyes and hoped that my intuition to trust was right.

As we slept, the wind and sand prowled around us. Lightning lit up the horizon, and the sky flashed pink and red. The moist chill of the wind licked the nape of my neck. In my sleep-thick state of mind, I realized a sandstorm was approaching us, for the second time during our voyage.

Vikki and I had encountered the first sandstorm in Niamey, the capital city, our third day after arriving. We were in town shopping the crafts markets, and Vikki was saying that the breeze felt good on her sunburned arms. Then, wind swirled the street dust, and the sky developed a band of red that crept up over the three o'clock sun and clouds like a rose filter. Vikki and I watched the grit-filled sky gradually deepen to maroon, then violet, then to the hue of dusk. We should have started back to the hotel when the wind first began blowing and the vendor kids were packing up their family businesses and finding shelter. Two stupid, ill-prepared tourists in a sandstorm.

The sand blew cool, then everything went black, eclipsed by sand. We headed for the hotel, holding our heads down against the grinding of sand and wind. Women passed us holding cloths over their faces. Men tucked their faces into their shirts like birds hiding their heads under wings. Cars jerked frantically through the street with headlights dimmed by the flaming sand. The air blew cold and wet as sand and drops of rain fell. Children broke out of the sandstorm into the headlights and sprang through streetlights like spirits undecided on which world to choose. Dark lines flashed in the sand and grit flooded our eyes.

"Prenez un taxi!" a man shouted at us. He grabbed us by the elbows and shoved us into a waiting taxi. He closed the door and hurried away. Fat, muddy drops smeared the windshield, but by the time we reached the hotel the rain had almost stopped and the cool air felt clean and refreshing.

This time, there were no taxis, no hotel rooms to which we could escape. Wet sand coated my face, and in the darkness I couldn't see Vikki, couldn't see the village huts, couldn't see the Tuareg men, couldn't see my hand in front of my face. Then I felt a strong, callused hand take mine, the grip of the kind old woman. I felt a moment of panic, wondering where Vikki was. I tried to find her during the quick lightning flashes. The woman helped me gather my sleeping bag, backpack, shoes, bandanna, journal and socks.

"Vikki!" I called out, but only heard the roar of rain, wind and sand. My sandstorm guide shouted something to me, but I couldn't understand. I gripped her fingers as we walked through the black storm. I was led into a hut, where Vikki was already sitting with her arms wrapped around her knees. Two other village women were there as well.

I sat on one of the two cots with Vikki, wondering if the Tuareg had been buried in the sand. The rainwater seeped in at my feet, and I could feel the wind through the gaps of the woven straw hut. The walls shook and shuddered, and I feared they would blow apart and we would again be sitting in the open.

Soon, six tall dark figures walked in. I lay on one cot with Vikki, and the translator lay down next to me. I was glad to be between him and Vikki, hoping to ease her discomfort, though she didn't say anything. I felt awkward myself next to this stranger, but there was no choice; we all needed shelter, so we shared. The others lay on the other cot or the floor.

My body ached, curled against the cold. I felt the bony chest of the Tuareg man at my back. I moved closer to Vikki. But he inched up against my back again and rested his hand on my hip—he was obviously taking advantage of the situation. I wrapped my fingers around his wrist and lifted his hand off my hip, then moved away another inch. No translation needed. I was nervous that the Tuareg man would move against me again. I could feel his knees tucked behind mine, as though we were a nice yuppie couple spooning in our mauve-and-teal bedroom in Suburbia, U.S.A. Was it his hipbone that I felt against my thigh? His groin?

Another fire-flash of lightning, a brush of wind across my cheek, and I realized that despite my discomfort, I felt safe inside the shelter with these desert-wise men and kind women. Vikki and I were frightened children, but we were safe.

Sleep came to me in small bits only, as I watched lightning wink between the gaps in the walls. I wondered how the straw mats kept the rain out, and I felt sorry for the men who had to sleep on the floor in the cold, wet sand. I heard a chorus of steady breathing. For the others, this was routine.

Soon, light penetrated the walls of our hut. "It's morning, you have to leave now," said one of the tall Tuareg. I was still tired.

Vikki and I sat up and repacked our wet, soggy clothes. The lanky men shook our hands and walked away, shoulders high and confident, out into the bright light of the desert. Two of the men carried goatskin bags under their arms and two others had straw mats on their backs. We noticed the man with the cap carried nothing.

Vikki lifted our pack onto my back—it was my turn to carry it. I stumbled under the load. She held it steady, helping me pull the straps over my shoulders. I buckled the waist strap and chest strap and shifted the pack until the weight felt bearable. I could hardly see the Tuareg men in the distance. They walked fast and effortlessly toward their next destination.

The older woman of the village wished us well on our journey ahead. I offered her a couple of tins of sardines. She tried to hand them back. I had never seen anyone turn down sardines, an expensive and coveted food in Niger. She was afraid we needed them more than she did. I was sure she needed them more. I assured her that I had enough to spare, and then Vikki and I left her, following the path the Tuareg had walked.

THE OCCURRENCE

MARILYN ABILDSKOV

It HAPPENED early one Saturday morning about three months after I'd moved to Japan. A knock at my door. A light tapping that I could hear from beyond a dim and sleepy state. I rationalized that it must be Jehovah's Witnesses, since they were the only ones bold enough to make house calls at such an ungodly hour. Missionaries were the last thing I needed in this, a Buddhist nation where I spoke too little of the local language to have a decent conversation, let alone debate. I believed more in sleep than salvation anyway, particularly that morning, having returned late the night before from a weekend trip. Ignoring the knocking, I turned over and attempted to go back to sleep.

But the knocking had done it. I was awake. Awake and cranky and crawling out of my futon and making coffee and brushing my teeth and then, certain that the missionaries were gone, floating toward my apartment's heavy, metal, prison-like front door to pick up the English-language newspaper, *The Japan Times.*

Stepping into the *genkan,* a surprise mess: a layer of water covering the whole of the entryway, starting to seep into the tatami-mat living room floor. I grabbed what I thought was a big towel (a friend later informed me it was part of the futon bedding) and spread it out as if shaking a blanket for a picnic. The towel immediately soaked up most of the water. Next, I checked to see where the water sprang from and traced it as best I could to the toilet. But nothing about the toilet seemed unusual. In fact, the toilet appeared just fine. The water, an annoyance, had been easy enough to clean up. A quirk, I thought, as I started back to my futon. A bother, but no harm done.

But then, again someone knocking, just a light tap-tap-tapping on the apartment's metal door. When I opened the door, there stood Yumiko, my neighbor from across the hall and one floor down, an English-speaker and, as such, City Hall's designated caretaker of the sole *gaijin* (foreigner) in the building.

"Something happened . . . an accident," Yumiko said. She struggled to find the right words in English, an awkward foreign tongue. "Please come," she said, pointing downstairs to Mr. Kanai's apartment. The look of panic on her face had me worried now, too. I slipped my feet into tennis shoes waiting in the *genkan*, not bothering to tie the laces, and followed Yumiko downstairs.

Mr. Kanai lived directly below me. Straight out of junior college, he worked as the secretary at Meizen Junior High, one of three schools I visited every few weeks as an assistant English teacher. I didn't know Mr. Kanai well, but I liked him because sometimes he gave me rides to school in his tiny car, a car that my large *gaijin* body seemed to fill to capacity, so much that I worried my very presence would slow us down. Along the way we'd chat in simple Japanese about the weather, how hot it had been or how cold our town of Matsumoto would become. But then an awkward silence would grip us, and I would spend the duration of the ride trying to stare straight ahead through the windshield, avoiding looking at Mr. Kanai, who had a prominent Adam's apple that bobbed up and down, and which, I was sure, was bobbing up and down nervously right then. I felt sorry that Mr. Kanai's kindness had put him in this situation so filled with tension, but I was nevertheless grateful not to be making the hour-long bike ride to Meizen or waiting to catch a bus.

Walking into Mr. Kanai's place the morning of the occurrence, I gasped at the sight: water dripping from the ceiling, pots and pans positioned to catch the run-off; soggy futons pushed up against the walls; wet tables, soaked boxes, sprinkled clothes and soon-to-mildew books piled to the side of his small living room.

Mr. Kanai turned to look at me and nodded with as much politeness as the situation could bear. Then he went back to rushing around, trying to gather up the rest of the contents of his bedroom, squeezing a handful of blankets and pillows into a corner of the counter in his small kitchen, which seemed the only room that wasn't leaking all over the place.

And throughout this chaos, the continuing sound of gentle rain. *Ping, ping, ping, ping.*

"My . . . toilet?" I asked. My toilet was situated right above Mr. Kanai's *genkan*. And it was through the ceiling above that entryway that water had clearly sprung.

Yumiko and Mr. Kanai nodded rapidly, smiling all the while. I couldn't believe their tact, the way they smiled instead of yelled. And I couldn't believe one ordinary toilet could produce such a large amount of water, which in turn could become such a disastrous flood.

"I'm sorry," I said.

I didn't know what else to say.

"I'm just *so sorry.*"

Seeing Mr. Kanai's apartment turned to rainforest made me want to swim away, slink into a corner, disappear into the soggy cracks of his tatami mats where I would live in moldy peace for the months to come. At that moment, I wanted to be anywhere other than my neighbor's apartment in a small city in central Japan and anyone other than the *gaijin* I happened to be. That I had been out of town, that I hadn't used my toilet the three previous days, that I had no idea what had *happened* to make the toilet overflow—none of that mattered. In that moment, all that seemed clear was this: I had facilitated disaster. I didn't belong. I should never have come.

Blushing in embarrassment as if my neighbors had caught me *on* the toilet, I apologized again and again. *"Honti ni gomennasai, honto ni."* ("Really, I'm so sorry.") And I was.

But nothing could undo the fact: In shame, my toilet and I became one.

Matsumoto had been just a name on a map before I arrived in Japan. I'd heard it was a beautiful little city surrounded by the Japanese Alps, only thirty minutes from Nagano, site of the 1998 Winter Olympics. I arrived during monsoon season but was told by the cadre of dark-suited men from City Hall who greeted me at the Tokyo airport not to worry about monsoon weather, that soon the monsoons would end and everything would be okay.

Those same dark-suited men took me on a tour of Matsumoto that very first day, beginning with a crow-black castle in the center of town. Perched on top of the seven-story site, I scanned the city from small portals designed to protect inhabitants inside from bullets and bayonets, and wondered not what life had been like in ancient Japan but what *my* life in this modern country and city would be like. I figured I would be living in a shoebox-sized place. I figured I would come to love eating rice. I figured I would become fluent—if not quickly, then at least over a period of time.

That first day, the future was—as the future always is—nothing but sweet mystery. I watched the city from the top of the castle, and then we all went to a soba restaurant for lunch. The city officials gave me a guidebook-like explanation of the food and reported that this prefecture was famous for its buckwheat noodles. They poured glass after small glass of beer, telling me my gold hair was beautiful and teaching me the simplest of Japanese words, the kind I'd practiced before coming but failed to grasp. Thank you very much. *Dōmo arigatō*. Good evening. *Konban wa*. Sake, please. *Sake kudasai*. I felt drunk and pretty and enamored of the sound those slender phrases made in my newly arrived and eager mouth. I thought my life in Japan might be okay, maybe even more than okay.

After the castle and the soba, we stopped at my new apartment: two six-tatami-mat rooms, plus a kitchen, bath and toilet, located in a building old enough that the officials apologized to me each time the subject of apartments came up. We'd been riding in the official van, getting ready for the second half of the day's tour, when I realized I needed to find a restroom.

"Is there," I asked, in the kind of polite English that officials would not be able to easily decipher or comprehend, "by any chance, might there be . . . Is there a restroom I could use nearby?" Eventually I would learn to strip my language of all but the basic necessities, asking in Japanese, "Toilet, where?"

For now, though, I asked in words cloaked in confusion. The men whispered with one another, sucked in air and looked perplexed.

So I tried again.

"A *bathroom?*"

Silence.

"A *toilet?*"

"*Ahh,*" the men cooed. "*So-so-so-so-so.*"

Mission accomplished. Almost.

The city officials pulled the official van up to a three-story cement building alongside a river and handed me a pair of keys, saying this would be my new apartment and perhaps it would be quicker to stop here than to find a public restroom somewhere else.

And so, I ran up two flights of stairs to my new place and pushed the key into the lock, glancing around to see an apartment much larger than the tiny dormitory room I'd envisioned. What pleased me, though, wasn't the size of the apartment but this: the sight of a toilet just to the right of the entrance.

"Anyone with a taste for traditional architecture must agree that the Japanese toilet is perfection," says Junichiro Tanizaki in his essay, "In Praise of Shadows." Built from the same white porcelain as typical Western toilets, squatter toilets are essentially oblong bowls built into the ground. To use one, you straddle the porcelain sides and go into the kind of deep knee bend that you might also employ for a tea ceremony, though the former is less delicate than the latter to be sure. Tanizaki writes eloquently about the old-style Japanese squatter toilet located apart from the main house, a toilet situated in a grove "fragrant with leaves and moss" where one can look out "upon blue skies and green leaves."

The toilet in my Japanese apartment boasted surroundings far less pastoral. The tiny stall smelled of new paint, not fragrant leaves; the window overlooked a parking lot, not trees. And it wasn't an old-style Japanese toilet at all, but a Western one. The officials at City Hall, it turned out, were so worried about their new American English teacher's reaction to this crummy old apartment that they painted it and installed a Western toilet.

At the time, I didn't care one bit about the difference between toilets, let alone the paint on my apartment's new walls. I had read about but never used or even seen a Japanese squatter toilet. I would come to love squatter toilets because they solved the question of whether or not to sit, whether or not to risk putting your skin in contact with public porcelain. Your butt never touches anything but air when you straddle a squatter toilet. I liked that. And except for one mishap when I misfired and peed on a pair of karate pants just before going into the *dojo*—human error, shall we say—I never had a bad enough experience with a squatter toilet to complain.

That day, though, I wouldn't have complained about *any* toilet at all, because my period had unexpectedly and annoyingly begun. If I hadn't found a toilet soon, I would have been in big trouble—big, embarrassing, female trouble, in the presence of a group of foreigners, meaning men.

So there I was, thrilled to be where I needed to be. A girl's gotta go when a girl's gotta go, as the saying goes. Or so the saying ought to go. And go I did. Happily. Blissfully. In gratitude for—and how did this happen?—the fact that I'd packed some tampons in my bag.

I took care of my female business quickly and expertly, feeling less vulnerable than I had two minutes before, feeling my age, thirty, once again, and not an adolescent, not fifteen.

Until someone knocked on the door.

"Marilyn-san?"

The voice sounded like Mr. Iguchi's, one of the dark-suited men assigned to show me around, the head English teacher at Meizen Junior High School where I would start teaching the following Monday. Mr. Iguchi had the best English of the men assembled for my introductory tour. They must have sent him to inform me about some emergency.

"Yes?" My voice sounded as small as the teacups we'd been drinking from earlier that day. Small and unfamiliar and fragile and ready to break.

"Is . . . is Miss Marilyn okay?"

"Yes."

There was a long pause, one I couldn't interpret.

"Please hurry," Mr. Iguchi said.

"Oh, yes," I said. "Of course. I'll be down in just a minute." And I was. Not in ten minutes or eight minutes or even two minutes, but literally within sixty seconds, as long as it took to finish my duties, pull up my underwear, pull down my skirt and fly out of the building, down the steps and into the van, where, with the engine still running, the men waited.

"We have many things to see today," Mr. Iguchi said, as I climbed into the van, and for a moment, I flushed in embarrassment, imagining he meant *me* taking an indelicate pee, that the men had *me* to see. "We must hurry."

"Yes," the others clucked, repeating after one another in English and in Japanese, "we must hurry." They checked their watches. Sucked in nervous air. The driver sighed a heavy sigh and stepped on the gas as if he couldn't believe how flaky Americans tended to be. They all shook their heads nervously. I nodded as if I understood, though in truth, I didn't understand at all. *I'd needed a restroom. I'd taken a couple of minutes.* It all seemed simple enough. What was the hurry? And why did I feel so embarrassed and guilty, as if I'd already loused things up by altering the schedule by a few minutes?

Later I would come to appreciate these and other cultural differences. I would not only accept them, but revel in them—in the way that parties in Japan began so promptly, with someone announcing that the partygoers would now begin their fun; in the way that taxicab drivers would show up not on time but early; and in the comforting predictability of schedules and systems and rigidity that gave way to precision. I came to love the strict rules of Japanese flower arrangements and the perfectly folded origami boxes and birds. I came to love listening to Japanese drummers, whose discipline and strength, it seemed to me, were byproducts of what, in earlier months, I might have overlooked as rigidity instead of creativity.

That first afternoon, though, I felt confusion, not pleasure. And so, as the tour continued, I sat in the back of the van, watching as all the images flashed by: houses with blue tile roofs next to shops with neon *katakana* signs, rice fields next to 7-Eleven stores, boys and girls walking home from school in stiff dark uniforms. I couldn't help but wonder what was to become of me in this place—a place where already the public and private spheres had bumped up against each other in such an unsettling way; a place where something as simple as using a restroom, taking care of one's most private bodily affairs, had seemed to cause an unnecessary ruckus; a place that felt very much unlike home.

After the occurrence, which is to say my unintentional ruination of Mr. Kanai's apartment—"You really *rained* on *his* parade," my best friend from the States snickered over the phone upon hearing about the incident—City Hall sent a plumber to my place. The old man demonstrated how to flush the toilet, how to clean the toilet and, most embarrassingly for me, how to *use* the toilet, meaning how to *sit* on the thing. The implication was clear: I didn't understand this contraption and had caused it to overflow. It was pointless to try to tell the old man that I hadn't used the toilet prior to the incident; my Japanese was insufficient to explain that I'd been out of town until late the night before.

Besides that, a strange surge of nationalism ran through me, a surge that felt toxic but impossible to deny. I wanted to shout out, "This is a *Western* toilet, you moron! My people *invented* it!" But the plumber spoke no English and wouldn't have understood. Moreover, I had no idea who *had* invented the Western flush toilet, or any toilet for that matter. And at that moment, I felt newly embarrassed for myself, shamed at this sudden impulse to draw the lines more clearly between us, tell the old man what *my people* could claim—McDonald's, sarcasm and sit-down flush toilets—and what belonged to his—compact cars, kimonos and squatter toilets. I was embarrassed at how badly I wanted to say *something* to set the record straight. Instead, I remained mute, having no vocabulary—a restriction I'm grateful for now—for this newfound strain of jingoism pulsing through my veins.

I thought the humiliation of the plumber's visit would be the end of it. I continued watching my toilet with careful concentration each day as it flushed, but nothing seemed out of the ordinary, nothing amiss. Meanwhile, city officials continued phoning and finally called a meeting, though I wasn't informed it had anything to do with the incident involving my toilet or Mr. Kanai's apartment.

At the meeting there was a great deal of small talk and much drinking of green tea. The old men sucked air between their teeth as they spoke haltingly, using lots of long pauses, as the translator tried to explain to me what the officials were trying (unsuccessfully, it seemed to me) to communicate. With or without a translation, I remained confused.

"What's going on?" I asked.

"Muzukashii," the translator said, sucking air between his teeth as a sign of discomfort. It was as if I'd just poked him in the eye. *"Difficult.* It is difficult to explain."

More tea. More sucking of air. More awkward pauses. More confusion on my part. The meeting came to a close. The week went by. Another passed. Three weeks had come and gone.

Finally, the message was communicated, something vague and puzzling at first, but an idea I could grasp. *Mr. Kanai must be sad? Perhaps Miss Marilyn could do something, something for Mr. Kanai. Mr. Kanai must be sad about the accident. Perhaps Miss Marilyn could . . . what is the word? . . . offer com-pen-sa-tion?*

In a nutshell: I was to pay Mr. Kanai directly for the damages caused by my "misuse" of the toilet.

I was stunned, and not just because I was expected to pay for something that I didn't perceive as my fault, but because it had taken so *long* for the officials to tell me what they wanted. Had Mr. Kanai been expecting money from me all these weeks? What had my neighbor Yumiko been thinking? That I had been irresponsible? Cruel? That all Americans were irresponsible, not to mention a little thick when it came to using toilets?

I can't account now for what had been going on in my mind then, save some wishful thinking that the incident would just go away. I must have had, I suppose, some notion that insurance would cover the damages to Mr. Kanai's belongings. But when the officials informed me that there was no such thing as rental insurance in Japan, I realized that I had not even bothered to ask.

Still, the official request touched a nerve among my expatriate friends.

"Don't give them a nickel," an American friend, Sandra, said. "Not a single yen. They should buy *you* a new toilet. Ask them. Demand it. Remember, the squeaky wheel always gets the grease."

Sandra, who, like me, taught English in Japan, was all for drawing a line in the sand. If she had been in my shoes, she would have done exactly that—consequences be damned. But I said I couldn't rationalize that, that doing so seemed wrong and extreme.

"My toilet's *fine,*" I told Sandra. I was worried about Mr. Kanai. How must he feel? And what had he been sleeping on these past weeks?

I still felt like a guest in Japan and wanted very much to do the right thing, whatever that was. Naturally Mr. Kanai had become nervous around me, always looking the other way when we passed in the hallways at Meizen. I had done the same. Once he whizzed past me in his car as I waited for a bus. I had felt momentarily rejected but understood. What would we have talked about if he had stopped to pick me up? How well his futons had aired out? How well my toilet was doing these days?

Maybe I felt guilty. Maybe I didn't believe that the squeaky wheel deserves all the grease. Or maybe I'd just lived in Japan long enough to come to appreciate the elegance of a submissive posture, the virtue of an apology, forced or not.

And so, in a spirit of shame and humility, I put the equivalent of three hundred dollars in an envelope and gave the money to Shirahata-sensei, a teacher-friend at school, to pass along to Mr. Kanai with my sincerest apologies for having taken so damn long. If roles had been reversed, Mr.

Kanai, I knew, would have done the same. I only hoped that at this point—three weeks now after the incident—he wouldn't be angry I had waited.

As an aside, I also told Shirahata-sensei that I was embarrassed to have caused so much trouble. And in a moment of genuine sorrow coupled with a dose of characteristic hyperbole, I blurted out: "Maybe it would be better for everyone if I just went back home."

Shirahata-sensei laughed, and I thought she understood I was just being a little dramatic, that maybe that's how most Americans were.

But then, a few days later, a note appeared under my door from Mr. Kanai, a note that suggested my friend had passed my words along in all seriousness. For Mr. Kanai's note bore clear, earnest letters that must have taken him hours to construct:

> *Dear Marilyn.*
> *Occurrence cannot be helped.*
> *Don't mind. If you will come back*
> *in America then I get angry.*

I kept the note long after I moved to another apartment in Matsumoto, a place with more space than the old, better insulation and a toilet that, unlike my first, went about its business quietly without causing anybody any trouble.

In fact, I kept the note long after I moved back to the United States. It served as a reminder not only of the strange occurrence when a toilet mysteriously malfunctioned and rainy chaos ensued, but of what happened later, when the paper-thin walls between public and private worlds momentarily collapsed and one neighbor looked out for another in a simple and kindly way. The note's sentiment moved me—and moves me still—and nudged me over that line separating stranger from something else: someone who felt very much at home.

LAST DATE IN THE CZECH REPUBLIC

CHRISTINE SCHICK

NOT LONG ago I spent a summer studying Czech in Prague. While writing my dissertation at a West Coast university, I'd received a grant to visit the Czech Republic to research famous avant-garde art, and I needed to learn Czech in order to negotiate documents and archives. I was thrilled; I had never been to the Czech Republic before.

Prior to visiting, my knowledge of the country consisted almost entirely of intellectual lore. I was aware of Prague's reputation as the Left Bank of the '90s, and I'd met a few Czechs through the Slavic department at my university, all of them well-educated, liberal and urbane. Mostly, though, through hearsay and from literature, I'd developed a vision of the Czech intellectual, the dissident, the quietly bohemian poet who smoked in cafés and argued with friends about literature.

At Charles University, where I studied, people more or less fit my expectations: My teachers were well-read, well-traveled, well-informed people, most of whom had spent one or more years abroad. They were progressive, opinionated and intelligent, with little resemblance to the type of stuffy academic I'd so often found in the United States. They knew their stuff, but liked more than anything to crack jokes over a long evening of many beers, where the conversation ranged from the German occupation of Sudetenland to the French preoccupation with Jerry Lewis. While I soon recognized that not everyone in the Czech Republic was like my teachers at the university, nothing I had seen in the country could possibly have prepared me for my first Czech dating experience.

I had been in the Czech Republic for about a month when one night I met a good-looking Czech guy at a friend's party. I flirted with him conspicuously, and successfully, it seemed, for by the end of the evening he was exhibiting several sure signs of being interested in me—he employed, for example, the time-honored strategy of following me from room to room. We arranged to go on a date some days later.

Our first date was a trip to a beautiful teahouse that seemed to be obscured in a side passage of some mysterious labyrinth. Later that evening we went dancing at a tiny, darkly lit underground bar with a dance floor the approximate size of a chessboard, on which people sweated and bumped elbows in their gyrating trances. It was a largely successful date. Jarda, my date, was fairly tall, lean, with dark brown hair and green eyes. He carried himself with the boyish, slightly naïve enthusiasm characteristic of people with degrees in the sciences, and he took obvious pleasure in showing me places I would never have found on my own. We arranged a second date at another place I would never have found on my own: his apartment.

The place was classically Eastern European in design, with intricacies of construction and furnishing you just don't see in the States. His kitchen had no sink; dishes were washed in the sink of the adjacent bathroom, which in turn did not have its own faucet, but shared a showerhead on a hose with the bathtub. But his kitchen *was* equipped with a special deep fryer, which he put to use immediately, making me a very Czech supper of fried cheese and French fries served with tartar sauce. Such a bohemian aphrodisiac of a meal must take its toll, and so it goes without saying that Jarda and I eventually ended up entangled in a makeout session on the couch; things got sweaty, shirts came off. Jarda was an enthusiastic if subexpert macker, and I noted at the time that he was either too polite to mention, or too engaged to notice, the scars on my breasts from the breast-reduction surgery I'd had ten years prior.

Soon enough it was morning, and Jarda began acting weird. The morning after is often awkward, but when all verbal communication is in a language in which you are only half fluent, it's downright surreal. We breakfasted in a place with sickly fluorescent lighting, heinous espresso and pastries that seemed to have been baked back when the Communists were still in power. We stared over the bitter coffee, and I wondered about the cultural significance of the previous evening. Had I violated any codes? Gone in for any unsanctioned activities? I sorted through all the files in my mind of what I had heard and read of Czech sexuality and social mores, and decided that all was well: In a sophisticated European city where the age of consent is fifteen, established clubs exist for swingers and people are worldly about things like prostitution, a little consensual fooling around between two adults seemed okay. These musings, while comforting to me, did not help the ailing conversation much. After interminable silence he mumbled something I didn't understand, in Czech of course.

"Excuse me?"

"Nothing."

"I just didn't hear you. Say it again."

"Forget it."

And so we went back to staring.

Despite this awkward exchange, we arranged to go out on another date. I suggested we do something active: go for a bike ride or a hike. We settled on rollerblading. When the day came (a hot, sunny summer day) Jarda showed up in what has since become for me a recognizably Eastern European male outfit: a corporate-logo T-shirt tucked into vertically striped cotton-jersey shorts with an elastic waistband, and dark socks. As a traveler sensitive to cultural differences, I resisted the urge to untuck his shirt for him and warn him about dress socks with gym shorts. For my part, I came dressed in a sporty tank top specially chosen to show off my arms. When Jarda saw me in this garment, he looked down to the ground.

"What's up?" I asked. He looked back at me.

"Why are your shoulders so big?"

I was used to this question. I rock climb and windsurf, and in the Czech Republic, where most of the women under thirty-five are frail-looking and tiny, my muscular shoulders and arms were a novelty. I got looks and questions all the time. One notable day I was doing pull-ups in a gym when I heard clapping behind me. I turned around and saw six men gathered in a semicircle, eyes trained on me, watching this most unusual event. At times like that, I was flattered by the attention, and reveled in being so strong in a place where the women made heroin-chic models seem corpulent.

Other times this was harder to do. Try as I might to hold on to my positive sense of my body—my belief that it's better to be strong and healthy than small and bony—there were days when I just felt big. Sometimes being near all the tiny Czech women made me feel like a lumberjack who had haplessly stumbled into a troupe of ballerinas. In any case, though, it seemed strange that this should come up for Jarda now, when he'd already heard my "I'm a jock" explanation. But I repeated the explanation, and we headed to the skate-rental place.

Jarda got his skates without incident, but when I asked for my size (I wear a U.S. women's eight and a half), Jarda gasped as though he had stepped on a slug.

"Why are your feet so big?" he asked.

"They're not." I meant this to sound authoritative, but my voice wavered a little bit: I was surprised by his question and felt criticized, as though he had come right out and said, "Why are you such a sasquatch?" But I went ahead and laced up.

Skating was nice, partly because we didn't have to talk much. There was only one moment when he muttered, "You're very strong." It did not sound like a compliment. I ignored him.

After skating, we packed off to one of Prague's innumerable superb bars. This was fine by me—the situation could stand a little social lubrication. However, things only got worse: In the bar, Jarda broached the topic of gender relations. Sitting there in his ridiculous shorts, he leaned back in his chair, crossed his arms over his belly and looked at me confrontationally.

"In America, you have feminism," he said. "It's strange. Women don't act like women, and men can't be men. They aren't real women, and if a man acts like a man, they call it sexual harassment and he goes to prison. Here, we don't need feminism, because the women like being women."

While I couldn't help being amused by this burlesque characterization, I was nonplused and more than a little chagrined that Jarda, who had never been to the United States, had chosen this moment to air his theories about gender roles in my culture. It felt like another criticism, a thinly veiled suggestion that I was unfeminine, and that this lack of "femininity" was tantamount to wanting to be a man. How does one engage in a conversation like this? How could I defend myself against an accusation that I wasn't a proper woman, an accusation leveled against me just because I had slightly more assertiveness than a soap dish? Did I really have to explain? Should I have told him that his idea of what it means to be a woman was just different from mine? Or, as a traveler in a different culture, was it my job to sit there like a good anthropologist and keep my views to myself? This last possibility was basically moot, since I am who I am: a mouthy broad with a feminist chip on her shoulder. For the moment, however, my stunned silence gave Jarda the chance to elaborate.

"We don't have feminism," he continued, as if by way of explanation, "because we don't need it."

"No, of course not," I thought. His argument depended on the definitions of the key words "we" and "feminism." Especially if the "we" was male, or if the universally agreed-upon intent of "feminism" was to eliminate all gender differences. To be honest, though, I had heard women say things that were surprisingly similar to this when the topic of feminism arose. "I am not a feminist; I *like* being a woman," went the familiar refrain. It's a neverending source of gape-jawed wonderment for me that people *still* confuse feminism with the desire to be male. Ladies and gentlemen of the jury, please let the record show that I like being a woman, too.

I was getting riled up at this point, and I cocked a skeptical eyebrow at him. My somewhat scornful look was backed, I felt, by the full force of the academy I had left back home. "Oh really? You don't need feminism here? How's that?"

Jarda took out his index finger and poked the top of the table with it decisively to emphasize his words: "We don't need feminism because we don't have sexism."

Wow. As anyone who has ever been to the Czech Republic can tell you, this is patently untrue. The symptoms of sexism are everywhere. Just that day I had seen an ad on the subway, featuring an almost completely naked woman giving a full-lipped pout and bedroom eyes to the viewer, her left hand outstretched at waist level to offer the overwrought onlooker a tub of margarine. To drive the point home, underneath the ad sat a painfully skinny woman of maybe twenty-five, in hose, a tiny miniskirt, a low-cut blouse and heavy makeup. In spite of her slightly garish look, however, she kept her eyes nailed timidly to the floor in front of her and her hands folded demurely on her knees, which were tightly pressed together. She had the look of a nice girl who just happened to be aware of her status as a commodity and knew all too well that packaging can increase a product's value. Daily scenes like this convinced me that sexism was certainly no less of a problem in the Czech Republic than in the United States. Still, instead of laughing at Jarda's preposterous statement, I asked, "What on earth could possibly persuade you that sexism doesn't exist here?"

"Because we don't have a word for it. We only have your word, imported from English. There is no Czech word with that meaning, which proves that it doesn't exist here, only over there."

I was momentarily stunned. Then, without even bothering to address his flawed mental algebra, I launched into a lecture about sexism in the Czech Republic. I explained to him that women of marriageable age starved themselves, were always dressed to the nines and were perfectly coiffed and made up, while their male counterparts walked around unshaven and unkempt with their beer bellies hanging over their sweatpants, and that this might have something to do with sexism. I argued that the fact that no women worked at his computer company might be a symptom of sexism, and the fact that married Czech women stayed home and cleaned while their husbands drank beer at the pub might, too, be a sign of sexism.

His eyes narrowed and he gave me a cold look. "Why are you so hardheaded?" he sneered.

That was it.

"What is it with you? My shoulders are too big, my feet are too big, I'm too strong, I'm hardheaded—I've had it," I snapped. "You've been acting strange all day and if you don't tell me why right now, I'm walking out of here. Now."

Jarda blushed. He looked past me, stared at the floor for a minute and said, petulantly, "I think you should have told me."

"Told you what?"

"I thought you were very attractive, and I thought you were just a normal woman. But then I realized that you weren't." There followed something about how I was strong and had big shoulders and was argumentative.

By this point I had my groove on. Nothing could have pleased me more than the things Jarda was saying. "Exactly," I thought. I was not normal from his point of view, precisely because I was a musclebound, strong-minded woman. After feeling like a battle-ax all day, I felt a surge of righteousness and a swelling of pride. He was paying me compliments in the guise of criticisms—like when you're asked in a job interview what your weaknesses are and you mention something that is really an asset: "My biggest weakness? Hmm, I guess I'd say I'm a perfectionist." In this state of mind I came up with a new interpretation of the strange events of the day: Jarda was saying that he had originally been attracted to me, only to be astonished and intimidated by my strength of body and will, emasculated by my fabulousness. Maybe that was why he was saying I wasn't a normal woman. "Maybe you're right," I said. "Maybe I'm not."

"It was wrong of you not to tell me," he said.

"What should I have said to you?" I baited him.

"You should have told me that you were born as a man."

This statement confused me. I decided that he must have been speaking metaphorically, that he was trying to say something about how my spirit didn't jibe with his idea of feminine subservience, but I wasn't sure. I tried to clarify: "What do you mean, I was born as a man?"

"I mean when you were born, you were a man," he hissed bitterly. He looked me straight in the eye, with a look that conveyed his disbelief in my stupidity.

I stared at him blankly.

"I saw your scars the other night," he continued, "and then all these other things about you made sense."

While Jarda sat, pouting and looking bitter, I laughed so loudly that everyone in the bar turned to look and started to let loose stifled giggles along with me.

Needless to say, that was our last date.

TRAVEL WARS

Elizabeth Roper Marcus

To MOST, the sixties "generation gap" was a vague, pop-culture generality. To us—my parents on one side, my husband and I on the other—it was my family's defining motif. We were deeply, truly, madly split on every subject. Police brutality. Dean Martin. Granola versus Special K. It was all equally significant. Where you stood on thank-you notes said as much about you as where you stood on Malcolm X. In fact—and here we actually agreed—it said exactly the same thing. You could deconstruct any difference of opinion and get to core values in a heartbeat.

But no issue drew a line in the sand more definitively than our differing travel styles. My parents preferred to see the world from deep within a prearranged bubble of five-star comfort and security. For my husband, Michael, and me, breaking out of the bubble was the whole point; what we most wanted was a sense of immersion. We sought out the obscure, the sense of going beyond. A tour? To us it was sheep herding.

It wasn't just the forty-year age difference that underlay our divergent preferences; it was divergent self-images. My parents,

Edna and Leo, saw themselves as *discriminating* travelers. They proudly carried their quality standards like a regimental banner making uncompromising judgments about cleanliness, punctuality and the thread count of linens. We, on the other hand, felt obliged to prove we didn't need any of the creature comforts they regarded as the hallmarks of civilization. We wanted to be *good* travelers—open-minded, flexible, tolerant, hardy—and were fervently committed to appreciating everything, no matter what. They were a visiting accreditation team, we a couple of earnest scouts.

Not surprisingly, traveling together wasn't a piece of cake. Yet we refused to be daunted by experience. Optimistic to the bone, we fully expected each journey to demonstrate our family's capacity for fruitful togetherness. Of course, it didn't hurt that there were 355 days between trips—just enough time for hope to triumph over history. And so, year after year, we ventured out—with our two children—from my parents' winter home near Guadalajara, Mexico.

A trip on Mexico's scenic Copper Canyon railroad—my suggestion—when Edna and Leo were in their early eighties set a new benchmark for family hopefulness. The train ride itself had plenty to recommend it; one of the greatest railway engineering feats of all time, it traversed the most rugged and spectacular scenery in northwest Mexico. The departure times seemed vague and the photos a little out-of-date, but our brochure described an elegant train with dining car, "360-degree glass dome and bilingual guides." Perfect for my parents, who were train-travel enthusiasts; they loved to reminisce about eating fresh caviar straight from the tin with a spoon on the Trans-Siberian Railway. Our excursion required an overnight stay at each end of the line in remote, provincial towns, but I was sure my parents were up to it.

Complicating matters slightly, Michael and I argued for getting off the train midway to spend a couple of days visiting the canyon area. In those days, most tourists just rode the train from Los Mochis, on the coast, to

Chihuahua, twelve hours inland, and, to be honest, for Michael and me this was reason enough to get off. But we were also enticed by the fact that until the railroad's completion in 1961, the region's network of interconnecting canyons had been largely inaccessible to visitors, its unassimilated Tarahumara population virtually unknown.

I spoke to the manager of an American-owned inn that called itself a "*1st class* rustic hotel," located at about the halfway point. It sounded perfect: comfort for them, style for us. If they didn't want to come for nature walks, my New York–sophisticate parents could relax on the porch rockers and soak up the ambiance. As an opportunity for isolated togetherness—something we had never previously come close to enjoying—it looked unparalleled. "If there's a hard way to do something, you'll find it," they said. But they let us persuade them.

Our launch was not auspicious. We arrived at night in Los Mochis to find that our motel was not just no-star, it was straight out of '50s film noir—cracked linoleum floors, torn windowshades, mix-matched furniture. What guarantee did we have there weren't bedbugs, Leo wanted to know. Then we learned that our 8:00 a.m. train was actually leaving before dawn, at four, an "unspeakable" hour, according to my mother. The children, Jared and Zoë, were thrilled at the prospect of getting up in the dark, and I pointed out the bright side—less time in our sleazy motel—but Edna and Leo didn't appear to take much comfort from my cheery words. Climbing into a broken-down taxi a few hours later, rumpled and bleary-eyed, they announced they had only survived the night by sleeping on top of the bed in their clothes.

At the station, my mother mustered what good humor she could, but my father, something of a curmudgeon in the best of times, saw no reason to bother. The train and our vision of it were on two completely different tracks. Not only was the real thing not the plush one of the brochure, it was ancient and dilapidated. No glass dome. No guides. As the sun rose, we could see the windows were completely opaque, a serious hindrance to sightseeing.

Initially no one complained. My father, who'd decided his only salvation lay in a book, wasn't picking his head up in any case. Michael and I chose to see the train's decrepitude as atmospheric patina, while Jared and Zoë—ten and eleven and traveling the rails for the first time—were thrilled to discover there were no seat belts; they could walk around as they hurtled through space. And for a few hours my mother's delight in their excitement seemed to distract her. Staying upbeat took effort, and she worked at it heroically.

But at 7:30 a.m. a meal—the only meal of the day-long trip—was served in a styrofoam box. My mother lifted the lid, eyed the buttered rolls with sliced gray meat, the macaroni salad and the oddly foamy custard, and gasped with horror. "They're kidding. They *must* be kidding." It was the straw that broke her attempt at resilience. For the rest of the ride, like my father, she gritted her teeth and gripped her book as though for dear life. The two—who, under normal circumstances, fought like cats and dogs from morning to night—became a united front of disapproval. If there was something spectacular to view, they didn't care. "We've seen scenery," was how they put it, glowering.

Michael and I, meanwhile, were reveling in the sights they were missing. True, we had to lower one of the windows or stand between the cars to see it—but we didn't mind. If anything, the inconvenience added to our pleasure; it made us feel more in sync with the rugged landscape. Except for an occasional power line, this was pure John Wayne country: wide vistas of flat prairie, cactus, an occasional horse-drawn cart. Narrowing our eyes in the gritty wind gave us what felt like a flinty, chiseled look; standing outside on the dusty platform, we rolled with the lurches, only one short step from actually riding the range. After a few hours we entered a deep, semitropical cavern that sprouted air plants from the cracks in its sheer walls. We traversed enormous tunnels, made complex switchbacks up the mountains and crossed suspension bridges so high that hawks soared far below us. We were enthralled—and entirely unperturbed by my parents' negativity.

Where was our guilt? Had we talked some friends into a trip they weren't enjoying, we would have been riddled with anguish. But since it was my parents, we were impervious. Over the years we had inured ourselves to their frequent bouts of outrage and had cultivated a measure of detachment as a prerequisite to traveling with them. It wasn't too difficult. My parents may have been in their eighties, but they had none of the vulnerability of old age. They were a dynamic duo who disdained victimhood. Infinitely resourceful, they habitually turned disappointment into a feeling they could enjoy: indignation. They loved to complain. In fact, I suspect they received as much pleasure from the trips they hated as they did from the ones that worked out.

At El Divisadero the train stopped so everyone could get off to see the natural lookout over the gorge of the Río Urique. The Copper Canyon Rail Tour was misnamed: The canyon could only be seen from this one stop, and even there, it wasn't visible from the train itself. The gorge is touted as four times the size of the Grand Canyon and one and a half times as deep, but such statistics intentionally miss the point: It is infinitely less beautiful. Instead of a vast ravine of pink-to-coral-to-plum striated rock walls dropping vertically as far as the eye could see, we looked out at what seemed to be a large mountain range covered in dry vegetation. Michael and I didn't care— but then, we were committed to not letting anything bother us. We focused on the positive: the pleasure of stretching our legs on terra firma, the charm of the Indian girls selling dolls and baskets by the side of the lookout path. My parents, however, were incensed. "They compare *this* to the Grand Canyon?" We would reach the inn soon, I consoled them. Things were bound to improve.

An hour later, we arrived at our debarkation point in Creel, a dusty outpost, where we were met and driven to our hotel, a long log building with a pitched tin roof and a continuous open veranda. A pig and two roosters ambled in front of the wide central stair leading up to the entrance. Edna and Leo seemed not immediately taken with the hotel's charm. But I was in heaven. The rooms, opening directly onto the porch, had varnished log and wattle walls, tile floors and dark plank ceilings. Each was heated by its own wood stove and was lit by glass kerosene lamps. The whole place had a fabulous Wild West aura. Turning their backs on the rockers and the view, my parents retired to rest until dinner, while we eagerly set out with the kids on a hike to a nearby waterfall.

The evening meal was served in the central dining room, a stucco-walled room framed by a huge stone-studded arch between it and the little bar. Tall mission-style chairs with leather seats and backs had been arranged around three long refectory tables placed in an open C. The flames from heavy wrought-iron kerosene lamps cast the whole room in a deep, atmospheric glow. The flickering light reflected off the enormous hand-blown spherical jugs filled with cold spring water. Every detail showed the great care that had gone into creating this romantic Sierra Madre hideaway. Surely my *madre* was impressed. "It's so beautiful, it takes your breath away, doesn't it?" I whispered to my mother. If it did, I never found out, since it seemed to have taken away her voice. She didn't answer.

Both she and my father were uncharacteristically quiet at dinner. The other guests were an interesting mix of Mexicans and Americans, just the sort of people my ordinarily outgoing parents loved chatting up. The meal was served family-style, and Michael and I and the children enjoyed it. But then, unlike our elders, who managed to spend part of each year in Mexico while avoiding the local cuisine, we liked Mexican food. Cheerily oblivious to the end, I asked my father, hunched over and mumbling to himself, what he thought of the meal. "If I could see it, I might be able to tell you," he shot back.

At breakfast the next morning, over fresh orange juice and *huevos mexicanos,* my parents lowered the boom. They were leaving. They were taking the next train out—that very afternoon. It was so dark at night they couldn't read. They could barely find their way around their room. The icy floors were giving them chilblains. They couldn't stand the smell of kerosene. "We'll wait for you in Chihuahua," they said. "It can't be worse than this place."

We spent the morning together touring the area by car. Even in anticipation of imminent escape, my parents seemed only slightly less glum. They were not enchanted with the surreal moonscape of bizarre, eroded rock formations, jutting up like gigantic mushrooms. They were not intrigued by the cave-dwelling Indians who welcomed us into their surprisingly cozy winter apartment, scooped out of the side of a cliff. Edna and Leo were not taking any chances. They left for the train good and early.

Our first reaction was relief: Now we could get into some serious sightseeing. We arranged to take a horseback excursion that afternoon to a centuries-old Tarahumara church. Our stalwart-traveler image, however, came under attack almost immediately. The horses turned out to be seriously bedraggled animals, bags of bones with worn-out, patched-up saddles. The two guides—horseless themselves—intended to follow on foot. We pointed out that with such an arrangement we could go no faster than the men could walk, but they didn't seem to grasp the problem. Once mounted, we understood: The horses would only move if the men drove them on with a stick. With the kids keeping up a steady wail of empathy for the poor creatures, our resources of positive thinking proved unequal to the situation. I tried to start up one of the old camp songs we resorted to on long car trips, but no one was inclined to join in, and I soon gave up. We rode on silently across a thinly forested, monotonous, rocky terrain that increasingly seemed like the Slough of Despond in *Pilgrim's Progress.* The obvious poverty of the region was suddenly overwhelmingly depressing. The excursion had just begun, but we couldn't wait for it to be over.

When we finally arrived at the church, we found a simple structure. It didn't look like much. Three pigs were rooting in the dirt outside. The interior was plainly painted and had no benches, since the Indians prefer to sit on the floor. My parents would not have been impressed. I could hear their classic response: "They dragged us all the way out here to see this!"

But just imagining their words seemed to increase the church's austere beauty. Seen from the right vantage point, in the quiet of the moment, in its dusty pastel setting, the place had a certain poetic otherworldliness. It began to dawn on me: Our previous enthusiasm may have owed something to my parents' lack of it.

At dinner that night I got another rude awakening. Turning to my new neighbor at the table, I asked how long he was staying at the hotel. He and a companion were leaving the next day, he said, on a hiking trip down four thousand feet to the bottom of the canyon, where there was an old silver mine and the ruins of a hacienda. He hadn't finished his sentence before my notion of having traveled to the "back of beyond" shriveled like a leaky balloon. The Lodge at Creel, which seemed so remote to me, was only the beginning of their journey; my "beyond" was my neighbor's home base.

Coming on the heels of our afternoon equestrian adventure, it was clear that this lesson in relativity applied not just to distance. My family's two supposedly character-defining modes of travel were looking less black and white with each passing minute. We may have been hotshot travelers in relation to my octogenarian parents, but in relation to the hikers we were marshmallows. Not only was the line in the sand less fixed than I'd imagined, but my position on one side seemed to depend on who happened to be on the other.

Most shocking was the realization that if our rosy take owed something to my parents' bleaker view, the reverse was probably true: Our monopoly on virtue may well have made the floors seem colder to my parents, the room darker. Had my relentless good cheer pushed them over the edge? When they took off for Chihuahua, had Edna and Leo been fleeing more than the rusticity of the lodge?

Ironically, when we were reunited in the provincial capital a day later, we found the tables turned. Having familiarized themselves with Chihuahua, my parents acted as though they owned the place and were surprisingly keen about what struck us as a grim, down-at-the-heels town. They were charmed by our seedy hotel—so evocative . . . picturesque—though our dank rooms looked into an airshaft, and the sounds of the marimba player in the lobby wafted up to us at all hours of the day and night.

They'd already made a complete tour of the town but were happy to revisit the sights, especially Pancho Villa's house, where in the courtyard stood the very car in which he was assassinated. They couldn't wait to take us to their favorite restaurant, where we had to try the completely unremarkable caesar salad they insisted was the best they'd had anywhere in the world. We ate without much gusto, picking at our food, but they didn't seem to notice. While we were glad they'd found something on the trip to enjoy, whatever it was they saw in Chihuahua was beyond us. In the end, there was only one thing we *could* see clearly: To feel like a good traveler, it helps to have a couple of grouchy companions in tow.

TROUBLE BEAR

ALICE EVANS

IN THE summer of 1979 I had just completed my master's degree in journalism and needed a little freedom. My husband, too, was ready to take a break from computers, lose the machines, gain the pleasures of the green hills. Our relationship, after all, was founded upon wilderness exploration.

We'd spent our first summer together practically living in the wilderness areas of northern California and southern Oregon, with Jon introducing me to one mountain after another. Mt. Shasta, Mt. Lassen, Mt. McLaughlin, Pilot Rock. He also introduced me to the High House, where he'd been living with a motley group of lost boys prior to my appearance in his life. I, in turn, had reintroduced him to college, and he had agreed to leave Oregon and journey back to Indiana with me.

Now we were heading back into the mountains—this time, the Great Smokies in the southern Appalachians, a place dear to my heart, where my family had taken the one true family vacation of my early childhood that ventured beyond state lines.

Jon and I drove south through the cornfields, crossed the

Ohio River, steered hard through Kentucky and the Cumberland Gap and sang about poor, doomed, about-to-be-hanged Tom Dooley all the way into Tennessee. I always thought about dying when I traveled—be it from a car wreck, drowning, hanging or wild beast—a trait that often prompted me to say inappropriate things, like "We're going to die." It had something to do with growing up in a house where my mother's favorite reading materials were horror novels and grisly detective magazines.

When Jon and I reached the Great Smoky Mountains National Park, we obtained our wilderness travel permit, plotted our course and chatted with the ranger. His advice? "Watch out for bears. We've been having some trouble."

I nodded my head, remembering: 1957, my first visit to the Smokies. Five years old, I sat on a picnic blanket with my family, eating lunch next to a cold mountain creek. I would have been wearing my baseball cap, placed backward on my head, maybe my striped Wyatt Earp pants with the matching button-down shirt, maybe even my sheriff's badge. When my sister screamed, I gazed first at her, then at my mother, who also was hollering fit to kill but not as loudly as my sister. I turned my head in the direction they were staring and spotted an approaching bear.

Earlier we had stopped to take pictures of the bears, and nobody had screamed then. My sister, in fact, had persisted in getting closer and closer, all the while exclaiming loudly above my mother's cautioning statements, "I've got to take a picture of the bear." It's a scene my now-elderly mother still likes to enact at family gatherings: She dances across the floor, pretending to hold a camera in one hand, and talks in a high-pitched squeak.

When the bear approached our picnic and set off my sister's scream, I continued eating my peanut butter and jelly sandwich. I would have sat there calmly witnessing it all had my mother not grabbed my hand and dragged me toward the safety of the car. In our hurry, I dropped what remained of my sandwich, but nonetheless, we weren't fast enough. My sister had long ago reached the car and was inside, screaming hysterically with the doors firmly locked—to keep out the bear. My mother and I stood outside; I soaked in her sense of helplessness and vulnerability while my strong, manly father and my seven-year-old brother bravely chased away the bear. Real frontiersmen, like Wyatt Earp.

Why I remained so calm I do not know, except that in those early years, my emotional makeup more nearly resembled that of the men in my family than the women. My ancestors had come through the Cumberland Gap with Daniel Boone, and I was programmed to be heroic, like Daniel Boone and Davy Crockett, the role models I watched on TV every week from our home in the suburbs of Louisville, Kentucky. Later, following puberty, I gradually achieved a balance between the tendencies toward panic and the reality-defying calm of the frontier hero, a perfect combination of my mother and my father.

But now the ranger was speaking. "You're going deep into the backcountry," he said. "That's where we put all the trouble bears. One offense, we yellow-tag their ears. Two offenses, we airlift them into the backcountry. Three offenses, we take them in deeper. Four offenses—well, then we have to reconsider. There's a little female who lives up the way you're going, about two hundred pounds. Been airlifted twice this year already. She's one of the worst. Very persistent. Don't encourage her."

"Don't encourage her?" I queried. "What do you mean?" I was remembering the remnants of the peanut butter sandwich I'd dropped as a five-year-old, hoping the ranger couldn't see into my memories, hoping he didn't already have me pegged as one of *those* kinds of tourists.

"Don't give her any food," he continued, frowning at me a bit harshly. "Bang pots and pans if you have to. Throw rocks. Hang your food pack out of reach. These animals get into trouble too many times, we have to put them down."

Put them down! As Jon and I started up the steep trail, I ran the conversation back through my head and came up with Glacier National Park in Montana. I'd backpacked through Glacier seven years earlier, two weeks of quaking in my boots every time a hummingbird whizzed by—because I'd chosen as my reading material *Night of the Grizzlies*. The bears that had killed hikers at Glacier became dangerous because of a food dump. Get a grip, I reminded myself. Here in the Southeast we weren't dealing with the grizzly *(Ursus horribilis)*, only the mild black bear *(Ursus americanus)*. No one to be unduly afraid of, I convinced myself, just someone to treat with respect. I could rattle pots and pans with the best of them, if it came to that.

Midafternoon came and I was glad to be out of the car. Glad to be away from books. Glad to be away from the city and among the trees again. But good grief, what a climb! Oh, what a very definite pain in the ass it was to carry a thirty-pound pack up a mountain trail into the wild woods of Tennessee. Somewhere—wasn't it at the top of the ridge?—we would cross into North Carolina. Somewhere—wasn't it at the top of the ridge?—we'd enter the berry meadow the ranger had talked about. The berry meadow: the first place to be on the lookout for a trouble bear.

"Okey dokey, then," I said aloud, startling myself. What I was really looking for at the moment was my husband, who was so far ahead I couldn't see him. "Yoo-hoo," I hollered a little more loudly, hoping he would hear me and let me know I wasn't alone with the bears. Finally, from up ahead—too far ahead, in my opinion—I could hear him singing.

I stopped for a moment, caught my breath and looked around at the thick, dense trees. The not-so-silent forest stared back at me, all eyes, a bear behind every oak and hickory.

Jon, bless his heart, stopped and waited. Waiting is always hard for him when we're climbing mountains. Still feeling a little scared, I caught up with him. I was also feeling bad.

"You know, bears are the ones being punished for the bad behavior of people. What bear wouldn't eat a peanut butter sandwich if some little five-year-old girl dropped it on the ground for him?"

Jon snorted at me. He'd heard the story about the picnic many times, and many times he had simply rolled his eyes at me when I expressed my guilt over the dropped sandwich.

"Let's get going," he said, charging ahead once again.

I was getting myself worked up, climbing the mountain. I had to remind myself to look at the flowers. Let go of research papers. Let go of the rational world of words and human society. What made sense was bears, a whole lot of sense. Who better to clamber around these steep hills but an animal with thick fur and enormous thighs?

Beneath the silence of the trees I began to pick up the language of wind and birds. Time began to disappear. I entered that extraconscious state I go into deep in the wilderness—a place where large mammals have the upper hand and humans are just, well, an easy source of food.

"Helloo," I hollered up the trail to my hubby. "Could we stop for a snack, maybe a drink of water, maybe even a brief rest?" What I really meant was, I want to go stay in a motel for the night. Eat at a nice restaurant.

"Let's wait," he hollered back. "We're almost at the top of the ridge."

My heart sank, and so did my stomach. My big strong husband might feel like he had plenty of steam, but I felt like any second I was going to have to drop down on all fours and crawl the rest of the way to the top.

But Jon was right. We were nearly there. After just a few more minutes of thigh pain, I joined him at the top of the ridge in the open meadow the ranger had described. Blackberries everywhere. To our right, an overnighter's cabin, a place for Appalachian Trail hikers to bunk for the night, a place safe from bears. Jon pointed out where we were on the map, then traced our route. Although the cabin looked like heaven, apparently it was not for us.

Our permit clearly stated we were to go to the next camping spot, on a seldom-used trail that would carry us deep into the wilderness. We had already come five miles, Jon said, and had only eight more to go. This was typical of my husband—hike as far as one possibly can in as short a time as possible until one, if not both, parties drop from complete exhaustion. I'm the one that drops, every time.

"Thirteen miles?" I queried. "You picked a route thirteen miles long? I've been sitting in front of a desk for two years! My gosh, we have to hike out again tomorrow!"

Jon just smiled. He knew I'd always been able to find a second wind, and a third and fourth. He settled on the ground against his pack, smack in the middle of the meadow, and lifted his canteen to his lips. I sat down beside him, removed two granola bars from my pocket and offered him one. "You know," I said. "I'm not sure we should be eating any food here in this meadow. Maybe the bears will smell it, do you think?"

My husband swallowed, waved his arm toward the blackberries. "They've got plenty of food," he said. "Besides, we have to eat. So why worry? A bear could be anywhere."

"That makes me feel a whole lot better," I answered, offering him some peanut M&M's.

We left the meadow behind us, and hiked fast through the woods toward our designated camp spot. "Nobody else will be there," the ranger had said. "Only big enough for one, maybe two tents."

I thought about this as we marched on. Thought about why I continued to trust my husband's judgment when it came to selecting vacation routes, despite previous troubles. Together we'd battled hail, sleet, whitecaps, hypothermia and rattlesnakes. We'd lived through ice storms in Texas, snowstorms in the Grand Canyon and massive bouts of diarrhea in Mexico. "I must just like trouble," I muttered to myself. "I married the man, didn't I?"

"For better or for worse," he answered.

I looked up, startled. "I thought you were a little farther ahead," I said.

"I was just waiting for you," he said. "I wanted to give you a kiss."

We kissed, a sweet little smooch on the lips, and off he went, looking every bit like he was completely at home, like he always looks in the wilderness. Completely at home.

Walking along, I replayed the earlier conversation. "A remote spot," the ranger had said. "No other people. Trouble-bear territory." Oh boy. This was about as far from graduate school as I could get on a two-day journey.

The trail seemed endless, the old-growth trees whole worlds in and of themselves. Big-tree stories started running through my head. Suddenly I was Frodo Baggins, small and heroic, talking to one large tree after another. Pretty soon I was singing tree songs. I wished I had my guitar with me, wondering if anyone had ever thought to design a backpacking model.

Stumbling over a root, I cautioned myself to pay attention. Hard to see, and getting harder by the moment. Canopy so thickly woven the late-day light was barely filtering through. It could be dark before we reached our campsite. We might have to stop, anywhere, and roll out our bags. Not even a tent between us and a bear.

And then finally, with the sun going down, we arrived at our destination. "This is it," said Jon.

"Oh no," I responded, my heart sinking as I looked at the tiny clearing in the middle of the thick woods somewhere in the mountains of North Carolina. As dark thoughts began to take shape in my mind, something nasty bit me right in the middle of my forehead. Automatically, I squashed it flat. It was, of course, a large mosquito, already fat with my blood. I took off my pack, sprang into action. Had to set up the tent and get behind the mosquito net fast before all the blood was gone from my body.

But something stopped me. I was looking at a fire ring, and my eyes had settled on something there—something incongruous. It was just a can, an empty can, one that might have once held beans, or beef hash. "Jon," I said, very quietly, very calmly. *"Jon!"*

The can still had both its top and its bottom lids in place. And yet it was empty of any contents—a twisted can, a can with a peculiarly distorted shape made by heavy gash marks ripped through a crumpled middle. "Jon," I said. "What have you gotten us into this time?"

I leaned over, picked up the can, held it out to him. He was absolutely delighted, as if I had just handed him a treasure. As he examined the can, the grin on his face grew bigger and bigger and bigger. "Oh," he said, breaking into laughter while he continued to stare in awe at the mangled, crumpled, once-upon-a-time can of beans. "Oh."

I was really hoping Jon would take charge of the situation—perhaps suggest a return to the cabin in the meadow, with him carrying both our packs. Or maybe just say something reassuring: "I'm sure that bear is far, far away from here by now."

But he just stood there, marveling at the can. Finally, realizing I was itching all over and our campsite was growing darker by the second, I decided to take action, and this time to enlist Jon in my plans.

"You know what this means," I said.

He looked at me suspiciously, and for a moment, I let it drop. I often let things drop—for a moment.

Scanning quickly in the fading light for a place to put up our tent, I spotted a dark pile of—excrement! A large pile, very fresh and very odiferous.

"See this?"

"Yes. What do you want me to do about it?" he asked. Somewhat defensively.

"Well, you're going to have to climb a tree," I said. "After we eat, of course. I'll put up the tent while you climb the tree and suspend our food bag."

"Oh, thanks loads," he said.

"Well, you can't expect me to do it," I said. "You're so much better at tying knots."

"Does it really have to be done?" he asked.

"Yes. Yes, it does. Even the ranger said so."

To say I slept fitfully would be a lie. I slept soundly, too exhausted to worry about bears. Which was just as well, as it would have been a waste of my energy. Nary a bear passed through our camp that night, so far as we knew.

In the morning Jon recaptured our food bag and flamed up our stove. I cooked rice, and when it was done I opened a can of Salisbury steak and mixed in the contents. I thought about the gashed, misshapen can we had found yesterday, very nearly at this same spot, and it occurred to me that we were being stupid. And yet we had to eat, and this was the food we'd brought with us. So far nothing bad had happened. Had I worried too much yet again?

I looked at Jon, and he held out his Sierra cup. I filled it, then filled mine. I watched the steam float across the tops of flowers, barely clearing the logs, then rising, lifting, moving on. The smell wafted across the slope, slipping through the trees in little wisps of delectable aromas. We sat eating our hearty breakfast and singing. *"Nothing could be finer than to be in Carolina in the . . .* What in the world is that noise?"

A big sound. A crashing. A thundering. A snapping of branches. Lord have mercy, could it be? Was it? Oh no! Yes it was! A trouble bear!! Yellow tag sticking from its ear, snout held high in the air as it let its nostrils lead, head wagging left, then right, nostrils quivering. Lord, that bear could hardly see a thing, but it sure could follow a smell.

"What should we do?" I demanded, standing at full attention. I was wavering in my emotions—part my father's daughter, part my mother's. Ready to take heroic action but equally ready to start screaming. A third part of me hung out somewhere in the middle, waiting.

My husband simply continued to sit there, calmly eating his breakfast, watching the trouble bear come on. I had once sat there just as calmly—when I was five. But now, I really thought something else was called for: acknowledgment that we were in trouble. I didn't need Jon to sprout a coon-skin cap, but I hoped for some kind of response. "Jon?" I queried. *"Jon?!"*

The bear kept approaching, a relentless natural force, great-great-granddaughter of the bear at that long-ago picnic. I was wishing for a car to flee to, for my mother to take my hand, for my father to take charge. For Jon to *do* something. But the only one doing something was the bear, who kept on coming toward the food with no recognition to the people who thought the food belonged to them. Kept on coming right to the edge of camp, nose held high in the air. Sniffing. Snuffing. Weaving its snout back and forth, up and down. Taking it all in, as if smelling our food was the next best thing to eating it.

Remembering what the ranger had told me, remembering the heroics of my father and brother, I picked up the pot, removed the spoon and began banging metal against metal, making as much noise as I could to scare off that trouble bear. It circled the camp, snout held high. Kept on sniffing, then feigned a lunge. Feint. Lunge. Feint. Lunge. With a little bit of growl tossed in for good measure.

Jon continued to eat the rice and Salisbury steak. He took a second helping. I continued to stand at full alert. I didn't scream. Just like Daniel Boone would have done, I set down the pot. Picked up a rock. Threw it at the bear's head. Missed. Okay, Daniel wouldn't have missed. But then, like Daniel, I calmly picked up another. Took aim, launched it, missed again.

Confidence waning, panic running higher and higher, I picked up a stick, threw it, hit the bear smack on the nose. The bear shook its head but kept on coming. First left, then right. Feint. Lunge.

Incredulous, I stared at my calm husband, unnerved by the realization that he was not going to do anything. "Let's get moving!" I hollered. "Now!" I commanded. "Up!" I screamed, full panic finally taking hold. "Get up!"

Reluctantly, even somewhat sluggishly, my husband dumped what little remained of our rice mixture into the dead fire pit. Oh no, I silently gasped. But I didn't say a word. It was too late to take back the food, and Jon was finally doing something. Something was certainly better than nothing, even if it was wrong. As the bear circled in closer, Jon picked up the pace.

I moved as quickly as I could. Not as fast as I wanted to, but as fast as one could expect from a grub worm, which was what I felt like at the moment: soft and fleshy and pale, a good hors d'oeuvre for a bear. I kept that bear in sight as I balled up the rain fly, ripped down the tent and snatched the tarp from the ground. We stuffed the gear into our packs with no concern for who carried what, and got the hell out of there. I hardly noticed the throbbing pain in my thighs as I practically ran the eight miles of trail between our campsite and the top of the ridge.

Mile after mile after mile, a dark shape lurked in my mind. Something troublesome, something that I could not see but whose presence I felt. Something I worried about. Following us. I thought I heard, somewhere in the not-so-distant distance, a troubling sound. Just that occasional snapping of a branch, close, yet far enough away to make me think I might, just might, be imagining it.

Meanwhile, I was showing Jon nothing but my back. No way was he going to get ahead of me on the way out. Only once did I dare to mention my fears to my husband. "Jon," I queried. "I thought I heard something. Do you think that bear might be following us?"

"You're a worrywart," he answered from just behind me. "That bear would never follow us," he said. "That bear has no reason to follow us."

"Peanut M&M's," I shrieked.

Jon looked at me like I had just given way to full insanity. We were the perfect mirror for each other; I was convinced that he was totally out of his tree. We would have to address our differences later, though. Right now we were on the run, and after what seemed like a stretch of fifteen minutes or so, give or take a few days, we reentered the bear meadow. A short hop, skip and jump along the Appalachian Trail and we reached our place of descent. I finally felt confident enough to take a break. We'd left that trouble bear behind.

I sat down but did not remove my pack. I did, however, lean my back up against an oak. Eight miles between us and the campsite, and Jon was probably right. The bear was still back there, digging up grub worms.

Taking out the only food we had left, the bag of peanut M&M's, I gathered a handful and commenced munching. Jon settled in beside me, and I handed over the bag. First the oak swayed, then a branch snapped behind my head. I shot forward down the trail in one smooth motion, a cannonball of human fear. By the time I paused to turn around, thirty yards down the mountain, I could hardly see back to where I'd been sitting only seconds before. What I did see provided a mixture of amusement and worry.

There stood my husband, practically nose to nose with a trouble bear, yellow tag sticking from her black ear. Jon had been talking about having one of his ears pierced for a long time, and suddenly I envisioned him with just such a yellow tag. But this wasn't funny. And yet it was, not only because I'd been right, the bear *had* been following us and my paranoia *had* actually proven to be acute sensitivity, but also because it looked like a fair standoff, the two of them facing one another, almost equal in size, vying for a bag of peanut M&M's.

Jon leaned back and the bear leaned forward. Jon took a step forward and the bear stepped back. They looked as if they were doing a little dance together. And then the bear hissed.

"Throw a stick," I hollered loudly at my husband. "Drop the M&M's!"

Jon ignored me entirely and continued dancing with the bear, the three of us locked in a stalemate. Finally the bear hissed again, extending her paw. And Jon—Jon backed away. Not only that, he picked up a stick, threw it at the bear and began moving rapidly toward me—trotting, in fact, at a rather fast clip, the peanut M&M's still in his possession.

And we were off, headed down the mountain, beating our hasty retreat while the bear, so far as we knew, wisely remained at the top of the ridge. Vague in the back of my mind a troubling memory rattled: Mea culpa. I could almost see that last dollop of breakfast stew, spooned into the fire pit, given up to the bear, sure reinforcement for future bad behavior like that itty-bitty piece of peanut butter sandwich I'd dropped long ago. Jon had held on to the M&M's, but I'd been ready to let the bear have them in order to save my husband. I made a decision not to talk to the ranger on the way out. I wasn't about to get that bear into trouble again.

Usually, I reach the bottom of a mountain much faster than Jon. But this time, he arrived ahead of me. Not by much, but still worth remarking upon. There he stood, proudly holding in his hand a trophy of our encounter—an empty can. Twisted, gashed and rusty, it is the treasure that even to this day he keeps on his desk at the office to hold out to coworkers, and from which the story of the trouble bear comes dancing forth.

LYING LIKE A RUG

SUSAN DANBERG

WHEN I first told friends about my plans to spend a month in Turkey, many of them reacted with furrowed brows and the same disconcerted response: "Why?" And I guess their reactions were appropriate, since Turkey isn't exactly a frequent travel destination for most Americans.

I wanted to say I was drawn to Turkish culture, to the country's history, music and food. But the truth is, I didn't know much about Turkey at all. Except that, like many Middle Eastern countries, they were famous for their exquisite handwoven rugs. My friends shared the same impression because, while most had never been to Turkey, the next question usually asked was, "Are you going to buy a carpet?"

I'd had a dose of carpet salesmanship on a previous trip to Morocco. Despite traveling on a backpacker's budget, I'd been easily enticed by the carpets' beautiful colors and patterns. Several salesmen had tried to convince me I simply could not leave Morocco without purchasing a rug. And, of course, I hadn't.

I still love my Moroccan rug and the way it brightens my studio floor. But I hate the hard sell I succumbed to in purchasing it.

In America, I purposefully avoid used car lots and door-to-door solicitors because I loathe being pressured into buying anything. I vowed that, no matter what, I wouldn't let Turkey's rug salesmen get to me.

I would focus on enjoying the real reasons I ached to leave Seattle for Turkey: to surround myself with an exotic culture and language; to savor spices foreign to my American tongue; to immerse myself in a world of spectacular ancient architecture; and to hang out with my friend Caz.

Caz and I first met in college, slugging beers in a Wisconsin bar. After graduation she moved to Australia, and the last time we'd seen each other was nine years ago, during my visit down under.

Every year or so we'd send letters across the Pacific. Eventually email brought us closer, and one day Caz wrote that she'd been drooling over her Lonely Planet guidebook for Turkey for the last four years. She caught wind that I was scouting for an adventure, and our reunion began to take shape. Before I knew it, we had roped two others into our Middle East escapade: Anne, a colleague of Caz's who traveled to satiate her appetite for new foods, and Lisa, a former high-school friend of mine who traded her Minnesota café for a backpack.

A few months later, our worlds joined as we stepped from the orderly, Westernized capsules of our respective airplanes and were swept into the dazzling city of Istanbul.

Our long-mustached taxi driver left the airport and zipped through traffic like a madman. Only the sensory feast around me balanced my fear of death by auto accident. Blue-and-white evil eyes encased in gaudy gold-colored plastic decorated the rearview mirror. Turkish pop emerged from scratchy radio speakers. Outside, minarets pierced the sky, gold-domed mosques glittered on the horizon and people packed the streets, sporting everything from head scarves to blue jeans.

Before we could sideswipe another vehicle, the driver pulled up to our hotel. We fumbled through wads of cash, trying to discern rumpled one-million-lira bills (equivalent to $1.50) from one-hundred-thousand- and ten-million-lira notes. We knew that if we didn't get our bearings quickly, the storekeepers' enticing wares would help us deplete our month-long travel budgets before we even left the city.

Our plan was to stay in Istanbul a week before exploring the rest of the country. We envisioned ourselves meandering along cobblestoned streets, basking in the glory of ancient mosques and swapping smiles with the Turkish people. Instead, we found ourselves following a somewhat disturbing routine. Each morning before we left the hotel, we'd inhale deeply, duck past the hotel desk clerk who always hounded me for a disco date, then race like hell to our destination as the carpet salesmen descended upon us.

"Miss, can I help you please?"

"Miss, are you American?"

"Holda your horsies, miss!"

"I know you, miss. We've met before!"

"Miss, you promised me yesterday you'd buy a carpet today!"

"Are you married, miss? Can I be your boyfriend while your husband is away?"

"Miss, I remember you. I cannot believe you don't remember me. I am number one man!"

At first the attention was almost flattering. It's not often a woman has so many men falling at her feet. Within a few days, however, it became embarrassingly obvious that the compliments were not created specially for us. None of the salesmen recognized us from the day before or distinguished us from the myriad other tourists; they used the same lines every time.

By week's end we felt, in a way, misled by the brochures and travel guides boasting of Turkey's generous spirit, and surprised to find ourselves constantly targeted for our monetary potential. But much later in our travels, we discovered that in our efforts to avoid the rug salesmen, we actually missed Turkey's truly outstanding hospitality and the soul that emanated from their amazing carpets.

It wasn't until we left Istanbul and befriended a woman with a family carpet-export business that I learned how months, even years, went into each unique creation. Nesrin told me most pieces were crafted by hand, using natural wool dyed with indigo, acorn and the juice of berries. Geometric shapes in red, gold and blue hues represented prayers for fertility, strength and enlightenment. Women wove their most personal hopes and dreams into the symbols and patterns of carpets.

Nesrin also warned us about what she referred to as a sort of rug mafia. She confirmed our belief that most of Istanbul's hotels were connected to carpet businesses. Hotel proprietors would find ways to deliver visitors to carpet shops en route to or from popular tourist sites. Shop owners were less than happy when a hotel's patrons decided to purchase their carpets elsewhere.

Unfortunately, we had to learn these lessons for ourselves before leaving Istanbul. By our fifth day in the city, we'd heard all the sales pitches we could take. Carpet salesmen would follow us down the *caddesi,* interrupt our conversations and block our way into tiny shops and bustling restaurants, relentless in their pursuit of a rug sale.

Saying "no" was never a deterrent. It simply acknowledged the fact that we knew English, and when we turned them down in Turkish, saying *"Hayır,"* their reaction was no different.

Sometimes, if I jerked my head upward quickly and defiantly enough, the Turkish gesture for "no" would work. Other times, my friends and I would feign Swedish. Seldom did a disgruntled face and distant focus work. However, I once heard a man say, "Don't bother. The look on her faces."

On my last evening in Istanbul, I sought relief in my work: photographing the sunset and the Turkish people enjoying the beautiful light. I chose a park between the famed Blue Mosque and the rose-colored walls of the Haya Sofya. Families strolled. Couples embraced. Carpets were nowhere to be seen. At last, I thought, peace.

But if I imagined I'd found refuge, I soon learned I was wrong. It wasn't long before I heard a man yelling at me from across the grounds, demanding my attention. The urgency of his cries could mean only one thing: rugs.

"Hello! Where are you from? Excuse me! Miss! Are you from America?"

Desperately wanting to capture the evening light, I was determined not to let this man interrupt me. As he approached, I continued to ignore him for at least five more minutes before realizing he would not give up without an answer. Lowering my camera, I growled, "I'm from Seattle."

"Seattle, is that in America? I am from America, too!"

The phrase "You lie like a rug" crossed my mind.

"I am from Ball-tee-more. Ball-tee-more, Mar-ee-land. Have you ever been to Ball-tee-more?"

"No," I replied. Although anxious to finish my work, I was also curious how this question might weave itself into a sales pitch. "I've never been to Baltimore."

Placing a finger on his chin in a thoughtful pose, the man crooned, "I think we have met before. Are you sure you've never been to Ball-tee-more?"

"Yes, I'm sure I've never been to Baltimore," I responded.

The man struck his contemplative stance again, "Hmmm. I am sure we have met before. Have you ever been in the Peace Corps?"

"No, I've never been in the Peace Corps."

"Are you sure?" he prodded.

I played along. "Yes, I'm sure I've never been in the Peace Corps. But you know," I teased, assuming my own thoughtful pose, "I have a friend who lives in Baltimore and *she's* been in the Peace Corps."

"Ah! Your friend!" he exclaimed. "I have met your friend!" He looked pleased with himself, then changed his expression. Shaking his head, he scrunched his brow and shot a finger back to his chin. "Ahhhh. Now what was her name?" he mumbled, only half to himself.

"Jill. Her name's Jill," I said, which is quite true. I do have a friend named Jill, a six-foot-tall blond who once lived in Baltimore and was, indeed, in the Peace Corps.

"Ahhhh, Jill. Jill. She is a very nice lady, your Jill."

"I'm sorry," I pressed, "I'm curious if Jill's actually the one you met. Can you please tell me what color her hair is?"

Fear flickered in the man's eyes. His gaze shifted to the sidewalk. "Jill," he frowned, "Jill . . . she has . . . " he turned and looked at my own light locks, "she has blond hair."

"That's right!" I exclaimed. "Jill does have blond hair. Perhaps you can tell me, how tall is Jill?"

Again, the man looked like a deer caught in headlights. "Um . . . " he carefully chose his words, "Jill. She's not very tall. She's only about this tall," he motioned, waving his hand at chest level.

I noticed the sun quickly slipping beneath the horizon and decided I'd had enough.

"You know what? My friend Jill is actually six feet tall. Goodbye!" I turned on my heels and bolted.

As I sped past the Haya Sofya, dodged strolling Turkish families and slipped around Istanbul's famous fountain, the man did not stop his incessant cries: "Wait! Wait! I really do know Jill! We met before! I know we met before! She is very tall. She was in the Peace Corps. We met in Ball-tee-more. I *am* from Ball-tee-more. Ball-tee-more, Mar-ee-land. Wait! Wait!"

Just before I was out of hearing range, I heard him unravel in one loud, last-ditch attempt.

"Do you wanna buy a carpet?!"

FIRST NIGHT IN TOKYO

MICHELLE KEHM

THE FIRST time I saw Tokyo, I was on a Korean Air 757 nonstop from Seoul to Seattle. I looked out my window at the night sky, and damned if I couldn't see that pulsing mecca of neon thirty thousand feet beneath me. If this was what it looked like from the air, what would it be like to stand on one of Tokyo's buzzing sidewalks?

Oh, how exciting! What an electric metropolis! I wanted to stand atop a huge Tokyo skyscraper and gaze at the infinitely glowing horizon. I wanted to shop 'til I dropped for Hello Kitty tidbits, hip Japanese threads and Godzilla paraphernalia. I wanted to stuff myself with sushi and Sapporo. I wanted to play video games and ride the maze of a subway system Tokyo carries in her bowels. I wanted to be right smack in the middle of it all.

Three years later, I stood in Tokyo's Shinjuku subway station in the heart of weekday rush hour. I had arrived, but at this particular moment, I was wishing I'd never left home.

Shinjuku, the largest and most confusing subway station in all of Tokyo, was my first stop after the airport. Two million people pass through its tunnels every day, making Shinjuku one of the busiest stations in the world. It's a neverending maze of giant department stores, noodle shops, bookstores and magazine stands, bakeries, sushi bars and sundries stores for on-your-way-to-work toothpaste, legwarmers, nylons and ties. The walls are lined with vending machines selling everything from sandwiches to new jeans to a juicy array of *manga,* your basic Japanese porn cartoons. Shinjuku station is only one of Tokyo's many "underground cities," a shopping haven for hordes of overworked commuters who don't have time for such frivolities as lunch hours and fresh air.

And then there was me. While I wasn't one of the overworked, I sure as hell was overwhelmed. Hundreds of the fastest-moving people I have ever seen flowed like rivers down stairs, through lobbies, around corners. They hurried into lines to feed coins into ticket machines, vending machines, pass machines, machines, machines, machines . . .

I stood there, dumb and dumfounded by the chaotic yet somehow organized scene unfolding before me. People moved quickly, efficiently, eloquently. Cell phones rang; people ran, talked, shopped. Tension filled the air, but not the kind of tension I was used to in the States. There was no pushing, no yelling, no aggro energy at all. Each individual just went where they needed to be. I tried to imagine the same situation in the States. In New York's subways, people would prod strangers with elbows, pass dirty looks like a cold virus and call each other words excluded from even the more liberal dictionaries. But not in Shinjuku. Here everybody worked peacefully together, sharing space—the one thing there wasn't much of.

And there I was, this tall, light-haired foreigner, so new to it all I'm sure I smelled different than everyone else. Not only was I not a working part of this well-oiled machine, I was an obstruction lodged in it. But I didn't receive a single dirty look. People just walked around me and continued on their way. Logged down with a huge pack, I felt like a snail in a rabbit race; considering I didn't even know where the finish line was, I was losing terribly.

I set out for the train line that would take me to the youth hostel where I would be staying. I attempted to follow the English-subtitled signs, but became lost almost immediately and ended up in a huge food court in the basement of one of the department stores. Noodle vendors yelled out their specials of the day. Fruit vendors displayed all sorts of mysterious fruits. Sushi chefs chopped, arranged and rolled; the air was a delicious mix of sweet, salt and fish. People lined the counters, picking up dinner, moving on to the cosmetic counters to check out the latest fragrances and skin creams. It was exciting, but I was lost, and my pack was getting heavier by the minute. I decided to play sheep and follow the herd. I trailed a massive crowd up an escalator, but when they all wandered off in their specific directions, I was left simply wandering. I wanted to buy a cold soda, sit down and rediscover my whereabouts, but nobody sat in Shinjuku—there wasn't a single bench anywhere. I bought a soda, backed up against a wall and tried to stay out of everybody's way. I glanced at my watch, trying to look as if I were waiting for a friend who was rudely late. Right. "Hi, Suzie? Meet me in Shinjuku station at rush hour in the hallway by the soda stand, where I'll be backed up against the wall trying not to trip anybody with my enormous American feet." I wasn't convincing anybody; it was painfully obvious I was lost.

Determined to beat this underground beast, I set out again, only to get lost again. After an hour, my pack might as well have been filled with lead. I was tired and needing nourishment, my stomach growling from the smell of hot udon and cold sushi. But all the restaurants had machines out front, and people would put money in the machines and get a ticket and take the ticket to the cook, and everything was in Japanese so I had no idea what it was all about, and I just kept walking and everybody was moving so quickly that I couldn't approach anybody to ask for help, and nobody seemed to notice me anyway and—somebody stop this crazy machine!

One could conceivably get lost in Shinjuku for days. I was lucky; I only got lost for one day, but with a heavy pack and a booty-kicking case of jet lag, it seemed more like a week.

Eventually I found the correct subway, the Odakyū line, and it felt like land after years on the open sea. I squeezed onto the train, peeled off my pack and grabbed an overhead handle. The train was packed with schoolgirls in pleated miniskirts, starched white shirts and clean bobby socks, businessmen nursing cans of cold Sapporo, hip twentysomethings in dark blue denim and platform shoes and businesswomen in nude hosiery. I was disheveled and had a lot of baggage, but again, nobody stared. And then it hit me: In my struggle to find the train, I hadn't devised a plan for getting off. Amid the tight crowd, I managed to bend down, open my pack and retrieve my subway map. I didn't have much room to work with, and every time the train stopped, everyone would push for the door and I'd lose my balance. Keeping my arms tight at my sides, I opened the map and found the name of my stop. Finally, the doors opened on my destination, beckoning me to fresh air and cherry blossoms, but there was a sweaty wall of people between us. I started yelling "Excuse me" at the top of my lungs and pushing for the door, but I was swimming upstream in rough waters. People moved aside as much as they could; there just wasn't space. I pushed my pack above my head, and using my best mosh-pit maneuvers, I squeezed my way through just in time. The doors closed behind me. I was, for the first time, standing on a Tokyo sidewalk. I took my first deep breath of Tokyo's sweet springtime air. It was dark out.

Time to find my hostel. Tired and disorientated, I didn't know up from down, north from south. Standing there on the platform, my face buried in my guidebook, I must have looked as forlorn as I was because a nice, older Japanese woman walked up behind me and gently asked where I was going.

I said "hostel," and she nodded and led me to a street corner where ta sign reading "youth hostel" was posted on a telephone pole. She motioned that it was just down the street. I thanked her, and she continued on her way. I walked down the road, amazed at all the people out after dark. Unlike the States, where everybody goes home once it gets dark, locks their doors and turns on the TV, Tokyo was alive after five. The streets bustled with energy. Old people, young people, families, singles—everybody was out, walking, shopping, going out to eat, getting coffee. I drank it in, feeling safe among the crowds, searching for any building that might be the correct one. I asked people for directions, but nobody understood what I was asking. Finally, a girl took pity on me. Her English was broken, my Japanese nonexistent, but she eventually gathered that I needed a place to rest. I wasn't sure if she understood I was looking for the hostel, but she started heading somewhere specific, which was more than I could say, so I followed her.

She led me to the hostel, which I never would have found without help—a good half-mile away, it was tucked into a campus on a maze of streets. I tried to note where she was leading me so I could find my way out in the morning, but every bush, tree, park, sidewalk and building looked exactly the same. I gave up and trailed behind her. I'd had enough for the day. My friend led me straight to the reception desk, and although they refused to give me a room at first because I had no reservation, she persuaded them to let me stay for one night.

The hostel was in a dorm, with long, sterile hallways and a communal bathroom. My room was small, and my sheets and down comforter were crisp and clean, smelling of dry wood. There were slippers for me and a cup for water. Peace, comfort and quiet enveloped me for the first time in hours as I took off my pack, cursed it and then got deliciously horizontal.

I had survived my first day of Tokyo—more than I ever could have bargained for. Sure, I had craved the neon lights, cell phones, crowds, video games, even the subway tunnels, but at that moment I didn't want to be anywhere but exactly where I was. My sanity needed rest. After all, they were going to kick me out in eight hours, I would need to find a new place to stay and I didn't even know where I would be starting from. Tomorrow I would have to find my way to the subways and fight the mystery machines to get tickets for trains, buses and food, which I desperately needed. It would start all over again. Welcome to the electric metropolis of Tokyo, I laughed to myself, and passed out.

VIP TREATMENT

CARYN BARK

"NOW THAT you're a travel reporter, I'm sure you'll get special treatment," my husband, Fred, mused as we packed for our family vacation. I had planned a cruise because I thought it would be good to go someplace where the children would be held captive. Since I had recently become a contributor to "The Savvy Traveler," I emailed the cruise line to inform them that I would be covering this trip for Public Radio International. And then I began to envision the perks: maybe an upgrade on our stateroom, some free massages, dining with the captain.

I got my family to O'Hare Airport by 7 a.m. on the December morning of the cruise. The terminal was mobbed with excited holiday travelers, people sitting on their luggage sipping lukewarm cups of coffee as we made our way through the maze. When we arrived at the ticket counter, United didn't have a seat for my husband. The cruise line had made our flight arrangements, but the airline claimed that they had never booked my husband's seat. It seemed our VIP experience was off to a slow start.

The flight was full, and though most of the passengers were heading to the same cruise, strangely there was no cruise line representative at O'Hare. I was told there might be a seat on a later flight, but it would not arrive in Miami in time. Fred would literally "miss the boat," have to wait in Miami and be flown to an island to meet us two days later. This was not my idea of a relaxing vacation; rather, it was my idea of escaping the Nazis. Besides, I always handled our travel plans—what if Fred got lost? Knowing him, he wouldn't even ask for directions. I imagined him wandering aimlessly from island to island in a broken-down fishing boat.

The ticket agent felt my frustration, though; eyeing my big belly, perhaps she became concerned I'd go into early labor. She began typing away on her keyboard, fingers flying furiously. It must have been a holiday miracle, because she eventually located one remaining empty seat. She suggested I check with the cruise line rep in Miami to confirm that Fred really had a return seat.

"I'm sure things will get better from now on. After all, the cruise line knows you're a member of the media," my husband told me, holding tightly to the idea that my new status would bring us special treatment.

When we arrived at Miami International, I was pleased to feel the Florida humidity hit my dry, chapped Midwestern skin even though I knew that hair frizzing would follow immediately. And it did—just as we met Carmen, the cruise line representative. I politely asked her to confirm my husband's ticket home, but she refused. Wasn't she a member of the hospitality industry? Isn't "hospitable" the root word? I figured Carmen never studied Latin.

I told her that *her* company had booked the flight but she insisted I follow up with United myself—it was my problem. Those were her exact words: "It's your problem." Ironically, the very reason I didn't make the flight arrangements myself was to avoid this very scenario: When the cruise line makes the arrangements, they are responsible for getting me where I have to go. Mentioning that I was a travel writer made no impression whatsoever on Carmen. Not only was I not getting VIP treatment, I was getting "the treatment." I finally found a sympathetic representative from the cruise line who rebooked our reservations for the flight home.

Our worries behind us, we joined the line of cruise guests loading onto the bus headed for the dock. With Fred's return flight taken care of, I could relax and take in the enormity of the ship as we approached it. Looking around, I noticed many people had brought along their cellular phones. Although I wasn't sure how far out of port they worked, they seemed like an economical idea, as calls on the ship were quite expensive: The notice displayed in the cabins stated that calls were "only $15.50 a minute." Were those prices for ship to shore or ship to Jupiter? At that rate it would be easy to procrastinate checking my voice mail, leaving me sure to relax. I resolved not to think about business until I was forced to return, relaxed and tanned.

Even though I wouldn't be in touch with things at home, I definitely wanted to stay in touch with my kids on board. That's why I came equipped with walkie-talkies. I thought this was such a great idea but soon realized everyone else must have had the same brilliant flash. It seemed every family had brought a set; frequencies were so confused I kept making plans to meet up with the wrong children.

When I finally did locate the right kids, they were in the beeping, buzzing arcade room. The games ate up more change in a half hour than what I'd lose in a week at a slot machine, but luckily I had plenty of change.

What I didn't have was a change of clothes. My luggage never arrived, VIP or not. I don't know why, since the cruise line had an elaborate system for delivering suitcases, which consisted of dumping the guest's luggage in the hall outside of each room. Actually, to be honest, some of my baggage did show up, but not the most important bag of all—my big bag containing all my maternity clothes, my husband's sport clothes, all the kids' shoes and a valuable prayer book Fred had packed because we would be traveling during Chanukah.

I made my way to the purser's desk to report my missing bags, and met a distraught woman in the same boat as I (no pun intended). Not only was she missing clothes, she had packed her medication and was terribly agitated that it was inaccessible. Trying to be helpful, the purser asked what kind of medication it was, and the woman exclaimed hysterically, "My antidepressants!" The whole time I was thinking that if anyone ever needed antidepressants, it's a pregnant woman on a cruise with three formal dinners ahead of her and no clothes. I told the woman if she ever recovered her medication, I would love a pill or two.

I spent the next few days trying to hunt down something suitable to wear. As luck would have it, though, the shops on the ship didn't carry maternity clothes, or children's shoes, for that matter. The roster of activities on the ship mentioned nightly meetings for Friends of Bob, which is code for Alcoholics Anonymous meetings. After running into several more people distraught about not getting their luggage, I considered forming a Friends of Samsonite group to commiserate. Unable to find sandals and water shoes for the children, I began trying to make friends with other parents whose kids' feet might be the right size. I have never been so outgoing and friendly in my life. I could've been running for political office.

I approached one woman by the poolside, and in between sips of her exotic coconut drink she told me she had a nine-year-old. I perked up until she informed me that he was rather big for his age. "Really. Isn't that interesting," I shouted over the rhythmic sounds of the Calypso band. "For instance, what size shoe would you say he wears?" When she told me he wore a size six, I decided it was time to make new friends. Soon though, I met a handsome Englishman, who smelled faintly of tropical suntan oil and had a petite teenager. I checked her feet and realized she wasn't quite petite enough. Sadly, I left the handsome Englishman in search of further footwear.

Meanwhile, I had no change of clothes. Had I spotted another expectant mother, I might have told her of my predicament, hoping she would loan me something to wear. But I must've been the only pregnant woman on board, or at least the only one who was showing. And I just couldn't bring myself to approach plus-sized women and say, "Hi, I'm seven months pregnant—can I borrow something of yours to wear?"

For formal evenings I rented the top part of a tuxedo and wore my maternity leggings, the ones I had worn the day I arrived. Though dressed appropriately, I looked like Sydney Greenstreet from *Casablanca*. I was tempted to wander around the ship discussing the "letters of transit" in an English accent. On one island I was able to pick up some pareos, the large wraps you tie around your body to make a dress. Where most women needed one, I had to tie three, and looked like a sale display at Linens-N-Things.

I also had no underwear and was forced to wear my husband's boxer shorts, which was no picnic: Men definitely have crazy ideas about underwear. At least women's underwear touches their body. Boxer shorts only touch at the waist, and these didn't even fit my waist. I couldn't decide if I should wear the shorts low under my belly (this was like wearing knee-length culottes) or high over my belly like Fred Mertz from *I Love Lucy*. To add to my already ridiculous situation, the boxers were so loose it hardly made sense to wear them under my leggings at all. It would have been more comfortable to wear them *over* my leggings.

Once in Jamaica, I still hadn't found water shoes for the kids, who were psyched to climb the Dunn's River Falls. The falls were very slippery, and the kids had no choice but to climb around in their only pair of canvas shoes. I turned back halfway up the falls because my pareo began unraveling and I really couldn't trust the boxers to stay in place. As the kids' shoes began to fall apart from the moisture, I became afraid we would arrive at the fancy dining room later, literally barefoot and pregnant. To add to things, poor Fred dislocated his shoulder during the climb. I was down to only two pareos after we fashioned a makeshift sling.

Things began to seem brighter, though, when on Christmas Eve the cruise director announced that Santa would be in the lounge the next morning distributing gifts to the kids. So Christmas morning the kids and I ventured up to the lounge at 9 a.m. to see Santa. But when we reached the lounge, no one was there except one straggling elf, a young employee with a felt hat and an Italian accent. She informed us that we were too late: Santa and his helpers had left by 8:30 a.m. We couldn't believe that the guy worked one day a year and then knocked off before 9 a.m. The kids were disappointed: They were the only children who didn't get to visit Santa. I fumbled to explain that Santa was not an anti-Semite, he just had a strong union and short hours.

Being pregnant, I had to take twelve hundred milligrams of calcium a day. Before the trip I told Fred I was running low and asked him to please pick up some extra pills for me. On the cruise I asked him for the new bottle of pills, and instead of the usual five-hundred-milligram pills I usually take, he had bought me ones that were eighty-two milligrams per pill! Fred proudly told me they were the purest ones at the drugstore. It took me all day to take enough pills to get to twelve hundred milligrams, and I had to figure out the math without a calculator. I was supposed to be here to relax, not study accounting. Now I was lying around the pool dressed only in scarves, constantly popping pills (which caught in my throat with every swallow).

Because I wasn't in maternity clothes per se, I didn't exactly look pregnant. I looked more like a fat woman with skinny legs who happened to have strange fashion sense. People stared at me constantly, chuckling and amused. I finally pinned a sign on the front of my pareo stating that I was pregnant and that the cruise line had lost my luggage. Better the cruise line take the blame than people think I'm a fashion "don't." I didn't want my picture to appear in the back of a future issue of *Glamour* magazine with that black bar across my eyes.

On our last day, Helmut, the ship's manager, expressed his sincerest sympathy for all of the problems we'd encountered. He told me he had personally made arrangements for the company's ground services manager to escort us from the ship to our flight. Just for emphasis and to hang on to any semblance of VIP treatment that may have been lurking, I reminded him that I was not just any unclothed pregnant passenger, but was also a *travel writer.* As he seemed sincere, I almost believed the rest of the day would go smoothly.

But, alas, and not too much of a surprise at this point: The ground services manager never showed up. Instead the company ground-crew workers directed us onto the wrong bus. I subsequently had to schlep our remaining bags, my two small children (wearing crumbling shoes) and my injured husband—not to mention my huge belly—three blocks in the pouring rain to the United terminal.

Incidentally, the bag with my good maternity clothes was never located. It disappeared into the depths of some luggage void. Perhaps it was left behind with my VIP treatment. Resigned, I just wore pareos for the remainder of my pregnancy, disregarding the fact that they were a little cold for a Chicago winter. But I did eventually get used to wearing the boxer shorts. Lounging around the house for the remainder of my pregnancy in this state functioned as a sort of vacation from my vacation. And Fred, although he never did get the special treatment he had wanted so badly, managed to compensate me for my miserable cruise experience quite well. It was pretty refreshing sitting in Chicago in a sarong and boxers sipping virgin margaritas, planning our next family vacation. Sometimes I nostalgically think about the missing bag with my maternity clothes, my kids' shoes and that leather-bound prayer book. I figure that if the suitcase was stolen, we should be looking for a short, fat Torah scholar.

CONTRIBUTORS

A. C. HALL has written for the *Seattle Times*'s *Pacific Northwest* magazine, the *Seattle Weekly* and the *Stranger*. Her work has been anthologized in *Yentl's Revenge: The Next Wave of Jewish Feminism* (Seal, 2001). She dedicates her essay to Cliff, her Buddha of Compassion in his current incarnation.

ALICE EVANS works as an editor for *Midwifery Today* magazine. She is a freelance writer and editor, and her work has appeared in three previous Seal Press anthologies as well as various other publications. She has been married for twenty-four years and is the proud mother of a seventeen-year-old daughter. She continues to enjoy travel adventures with her family.

AYUN HALLIDAY is the evil lactating genius behind *East Village Inky*, a quarterly zine about life with small children in New York City (www.hipmama.com/evinky.html). Her work has been published in *Hip Mama*, *BUST*, Oxygen's Moms Online site and other parenting and humor publications. Ayun is struggling to follow up her essay in *Breeder: Real-Life Stories from the New Generation of Mothers* (Seal, 2001) with a whole damn book about keeping cool as a stay-at-home mother.

CARYN BARK is a contributor to National Public Radio. She writes a syndicated humor column on Jewish life. As a comic, she performs for fundraising organizations all over the United States and Canada. She resides in Chicago with her husband and their three children.

CHRISTINE SCHICK is a former academic and current freelance writer. She lives in the Bay Area.

ELIZABETH ROPER MARCUS is a former architect and a freelance writer. Her stories have been published in the *New York Times* Travel section and various Travelers' Tales volumes.

Bombay-born writer, filmmaker and world traveler GINU KAMANI authored *Junglee Girl* (Aunt Lute, 1995), a collection of stories exploring sexuality, sensuality and power. She is a visiting writer at Mills College, writes features for U.S. and Indian publications, has a play in production and is working on various video projects. She is also a Sundance Institute fellow in creative nonfiction.

INGRID WENDT's books of poems include *Moving the House* (Boa Editions, 1980) and *Singing the Mozart Requiem* (Breitenbush, 1987). She coedited *In Her Own Image: Women Working in the Arts* (Feminist Press, 1980) and *From Here We Speak: An Anthology of Oregon Poetry* (Oregon State University, 1993). Her work has appeared in *No More Masks! An Anthology of Twentieth-Century American Women Poets* (HarperPerennial, 1993) and in numerous literary journals. Winner of the Carolyn Kizer Award and the D. H. Lawrence Fellowship, she was nominated for the Pushcart Prize. Ingrid has also been a Fulbright professor and guest lecturer at several international universities.

JULIE GERK works for the Hesperian Foundation as the coordinating editor of an international women's health newsletter for trainers and groups involved in community-based health care. Julie has lived in rural El Salvador, coordinating grassroots development projects in collaboration with community leaders.

KARI BODNARCHUK is a Boston-based freelance writer, who spends her spare time hiking in the New England wilderness—but never without an emergency blanket, a barometer and a spare pair of shoes. Author of *Rwanda: Country Torn Apart* (Lerner, 1999) and *Kurdistan: Region Under Siege* (Lerner, 2000), she is currently writing a book about her eighteen-month solo trip around the world. She also teaches women's solo travel classes in the Boston area and has contributed to *Islands, Backpacker,* the *Denver Post* and the *Christian Science Monitor.* Her work also appears in *The Greatest Adventures of All Time* (Time, Inc., 2001) and Travelers' Tales' *Australia* and *Gutsy Women: Travel Tips and Wisdom for the Road* (Travelers' Tales, 1996).

KRISTIN BECK, a freelance writer, spent many years as the acquisitions editor at New Harbinger Publications in Oakland, California. She coauthored *Facing 30: Women Talk About Constructing a Real Life and Other Scary Rites of Passage* (New Harbinger, 1998) and is currently editing *The Moment of Truth: Women's Funniest Romantic Failures* (forthcoming).

L. A. MILLER's work has been published in *Sex and Single Girls: Straight and Queer Women on Sexuality* (Seal, 2000) and *Young Wives' Tales: New Adventures in Love and Partnership* (Seal, 2001). She is a freelance writer and cofounder/editor of *de/scribe* magazine, which strives to be a *Harper's* for the non-careered masses. She is currently editing an anthology on young women and food, called "Women Who Eat."

LAURA CARLSMITH is the acquisitions and development editor for a Portland, Oregon, book publisher. She recently coauthored a book in a series of biographies for young adults, and has written for corporate and government clients. She volunteers as a grant writer for her local public schools.

LEA ASCHKENAS has written about her travels for the *San Francisco Bay Guardian, Women Outside, Big World* and *Passionfruit.* One of her Costa Rica travel stories appears in *Two in the Wild: Tales of Adventure from Friends, Mothers, and Daughters* (Vintage, 1999), and a story about her recent travels in Cuba appears in Travelers' Tales' *Cuba*. Lea is currently working on a book about Cuba.

LUCY JANE BLEDSOE has recently returned from a trip to Antarctica as a recipient of a National Science Foundation Artists and Writers grant. She is the author of the novel *Working Parts* (Seal, 1997), winner of a 1998 American Library Association Award for Literature, and of *Sweat: Stories and a Novella* (Seal, 1995). She is also the author of four novels for young people. Her work has appeared in *Fiction International, New York Newsday, Ms., Northwest Literary Forum* and *Pacific Discovery,* and she has written CD-ROM scripts for National Geographic. Bledsoe teaches in the creative writing graduate program at the University of San Francisco.

MARILYN ABILDSKOV's work has been published in *Black Warrior Review, Sonora Review* and *Georgetown Review;* her essays and poetry will appear in forthcoming issues of *Fourth Genre, Puerto del Sol, Quarterly West* and *Alaska Quarterly Review.* She has been nominated for the Pushcart Prize, held residencies at Ragdale and Yaddo artists' colonies and received the Rona Jaffe Award (1998) for her memoir, *Wide Love in a Narrow Place.*

MICHELLE KEHM is a freelance writer in Seattle and writes for girlzines such as *BUST, W.I.G., Girly Head* and chickclick.com. She is currently working on her first travel book.

MIELIKKI ORG is a multilingual, Sino-Finnish travel writer and journalist with a black belt in karate. She has traveled extensively through Europe, Asia and the United States (alone and with her guitar). Her work has appeared in Lonely Planet's *China*, Fodor's *China,* The Berkeley Guides' *Paris and France,* the *San Francisco Bay Guardian* and *Alice* magazine.

NANCY COOPER FRANK is a recovering academic with a specialty in Russian language and literature whose essays and travel articles have appeared in the *New York Times, Islands,* the *St. Petersburg Times* Travel section, *Moxie* magazine's website, GoNomad.com and other publications. She has survived being locked in a Moscow dorm room, falling off a pony in Mongolia and having her long underwear burnt in a microwave in a hotel room in Fresno (her helpful husband's attempt to dry them). She now lives with her husband and without long underwear in San Francisco.

NOVELLA CARPENTER coauthored (with Traci Vogel) *Don't Jump! The Northwest Winter Blues Survival Guide* (Sasquatch, 2000). She writes and raises chickens and bees in Seattle's Beacon Hill neighborhood.

PAM HOUSTON is the author of *A Little More About Me, Cowboys Are My Weakness* (the 1993 winner of the Western States Book Award) and *Waltzing the Cat.* Her stories have been selected for *Best American Short Stories* (1990, 1999) and *Prize Stories: The O. Henry Awards* (1999), as well as a Pushcart Prize. Houston edited the anthology *Women on Hunting* and has been a contributing editor to *Elle* and *Ski.* She lives in Colorado.

PATRICE MELNICK's essays and poems have appeared in the journals *Grain, Buffalo Bones* and *Prism International* and in the anthology *The Naked Anthropologist* (Wadsworth, 1992). She was a runner-up for *Prism International*'s 2000 Maclean-Hunter Endowment Award for Literary Non-fiction. Melnick served as a Peace Corps volunteer in the Central African

Republic from 1985–1987. She received her MFA in creative writing from the University of Alaska, Fairbanks, and currently directs the creative writing program at Xavier University in New Orleans.

RACHEL BERKOFF took up the study of religion after being totally confused by the movie *The Last Temptation of Christ*. She's now an observant Jew living and writing in Northern California.

SARAH WEPPNER has tried fried grasshoppers in Thailand, yak butter tea in Tibet, gallo pinto in Nicaragua and cow tongue in Idaho. She is currently sampling Persian food in Seattle, dreaming of immigrating to Canada, where the money has women and animals on it, and wondering why she ever thought grad school would be fun. She plans to travel again after completing her master's degree in environmental health at the University of Washington.

SHARON GRIMBERG is currently the series editor of the PBS history program *American Experience*. She coproduced *Secrets of the Master Builder*, which aired nationally on PBS in October 2000, and *Miss India Georgia*, which aired on PBS in 1997. From 1992–95 Grimberg worked as a writer and associate producer for *CNN Headline News;* her work has also been broadcast on the Discovery Channel and National Public Radio. Grimberg has a bachelor's degree from the London School of Economics and a master's degree in communications from the University of Michigan. She grew up in Singapore and England.

SUSAN DANBERG is a freelance writer, photographer and producer who left Minnesota to be closer to the ocean and mountains. Her work ranges from film and video to print and has appeared in commercial publications, magazines, newspapers and webzines throughout America and Europe. She lives in Seattle.

TANMEET SETHI divides her time between her writing, activism and career as a family physician. Her activism focuses on the issue of domestic violence in the South Asian community. Her main interests in medicine are integrative health care, preventive medicine and maternal-child health in underserved populations. She would like to combine these one day in a wellness center of her own. She lives in Seattle, Washington, with her husband.

TONI LANDIS has lived and worked in Australia, New Zealand, the South Pacific, Spain, France and India. A writer of nonfiction, she draws upon her experiences as mother, wife, daughter, rancher and traveler for inspiration, laughter and sustenance. She is currently working on a book about her travels in the South Pacific.

TRINA TRUTHTELLA is a writer and activist in New York City. Although you'd never believe it, she holds two degrees from an Ivy League university and has many loving friends who encourage her tirades. Trina really does have a good heart underneath that scandalous tongue and is working on her anger to become a more accepting and forgiving person. Just don't hold your breath.

Resources for Travelers

Adventure Divas
www.adventuredivas.com
A site featuring stories, dispatches and advice from and for women travelers.

Atlapedia
www.atlapedia.com
Atlapedia's site contains full-color physical and political maps for regions of the world, providing cultural facts and statistical data.

CDC Travel Information
www.cdc.gov/travel
Visit the CDC's travel site for advice on immunizations, travel preparations and general health conditions.

Foreign Languages for Travelers
www.travlang.com/languages
Contains language primers for more than seventy languages.

Global Exchange Reality Tours
www.globalexchange.org/tours
An increasingly popular way to learn about the history and current situation of a country from the people themselves.

The Savvy Traveler
www.savvytraveler.org
Public Radio's entertaining, informative travel program and website, produced by Minnesota Public Radio and hosted by Diana Nyad, with Rudy Maxa and Tony Kahn.

Journeywoman
www.journeywoman.com
A fabulous online quarterly and travel resource for women.

Lonely Planet

www.lonelyplanet.com

At this extensive site, you can access dispatches covering dozens of countries, search for information on politics, health advisories and upcoming festivals or find useful tips from other travelers.

Travel Document Systems

www.traveldocs.com

A site devoted to informing travelers about visa requirements and procuring them (quickly, if necessary); also has information on countries' history, culture, weather and recent news.

Travel Health Online

www.tripprep.com

Offers updates and advice on international health conditions.

Universal Currency Converter

www.xe.net/ucc

U.S. Department of State

www.state.gov

Offers thorough advice to U.S. citizens abroad, from links to U.S. embassies and consulates to embassy services and travel warnings.

Weather.com

www.weather.com

Allows visitors to check the five-day forecast for hundreds of major cities.

World Travel Watch

www.travelerstales.com/wtw

A wonderful site for weekly news updates by country.

ACKNOWLEDGMENTS

The editors thank the staff and interns of Seal Press for their support during the editing of this anthology: Adele Johnsen, Anitra Sumaya Grisales, Cassandra Greenwald, Chris Wallish, Christina Henry de Tessan, Dana Youlin, Ellen Carlin, Faith Conlon, Ingrid Emerick, Lynn Siniscalchi, Melissa Walker, Sara Ruiz, Sarah McCarry and Tanessa Dillard.

Thanks are due our in-house editor, Leslie Miller, and our copyeditor, Jennie Goode. Also, heartfelt thanks to the folks at "The Savvy Traveler" broadcast series for their kind cooperation on behalf of this book. Listen to their terrific show on your local NPR station, and visit them online at www.savvytraveler.org.

Rosemary sends special thanks to her parents, Dawna and Sandy Floe, for their unfailing encouragement to travel, and to her most spontaneous travel partner and best friend, Amy Louton. Anne sends love and gratitude to Steve Arntson and the Mathews family: Sandy, Kenneth, Heather, Elizabeth and Diana. Lucie sends her warmest thanks to James Roche for his eternal patience and support; to little Max, for staying up late; and to her East Coast clan: Ondra, Julda, Dada, Kuba, Anda and Barik.

About the Editors

ROSEMARY CAPERTON is the publicity and marketing director at Seal Press; ANNE MATHEWS is the managing editor at Seal Press; LUCIE OCENAS is Seal Press's publicist.

SELECTED TITLES
FROM SEAL PRESS

A Woman Alone: Travel Tales from Around the Globe edited by Faith Conlon, Ingrid Emerick and Christina Henry de Tessan. $15.95, ISBN 1-58005-059-X.

Dream of a Thousand Lives: A Sojourn in Thailand by Karen Connelly. $14.95, ISBN 1-58005-062-X.

Hot Flashes from Abroad: Women's Travel Tales and Adventures edited by Jean Gould. $16.95, ISBN 1-58005-055-7.

No Hurry to Get Home: The Memoir of the New Yorker *Writer Whose Unconventional Life and Adventures Spanned the Twentieth Century* by Emily Hahn. $14.95, ISBN 1-58005-045-X.

Girl in the Curl: A Century of Women in Surfing by Andrea Gabbard. $29.95, ISBN 1-58005-048-4.

Pilgrimage to India: A Woman Revisits Her Homeland by Pramila Jayapal. $14.95, ISBN 1-58005-052-2.

Solo: On Her Own Adventure edited by Susan Fox Rogers. $12.95, ISBN 1-878067-74-5.

Journey Across Tibet: A Young Woman's Trek Across the Rooftop of the World by Sorrel Wilby. $16.95, ISBN 1-58005-053-0.

Seal Press publishes many books of fiction and nonfiction by women writers. If you are unable to obtain a Seal Press title from a bookstore, please order from us directly by calling 800-754-0271. Visit our website at www.sealpress.com.